For family memories and my parents:
Elizabeth Marjorie Ellis McLeod (1916–1985) and
John Clinton McLeod (1920–2006).

For the parents, families, and scholars who continue
to critically engage with the complex convergence of technology
and family.

Acknowledgments

Publishing a book takes the effort, energy, and labour of many minds and hands. We are grateful to many. We thank exceptional researcher Christopher Campbell for assisting us in developing, conducting and analyzing an online survey with one thousand University of Winnipeg undergraduate students exploring millennial attitudes and practices related to online privacy and disclosure values. This research endeavour contributed to our understanding of privacy and provided a steppingstone to this book project.

We offer special thanks to superb researcher/writer Dallas Cant for their transformative work on our blog site, *Family Blog Lines: Ta[l]king Care.* Dallas developed the website architecture and design and opened the *Parenting/Internet/Kids* blog thread (familybloglines.com/p-i-k/), where some of the book's authors have posted to help launch this current volume. Dallas has also contributed to and managed blog dialogues.

We are grateful for the Research Office at the University of Winnipeg for providing grants that have assisted our research over the years and the publication of this collection. We particularly appreciate funding from the Marsha Hanen Global Dialogue and Ethics Award, which sustained earlier research related to family online privacy practices.

Thank you also to the fine team at Demeter Press—especially to its founder Andrea O'Reilly, copy editor Jesse O'Reilly-Conlin, and designer Michelle Pirovich—for their labour ensuring the publication of this collection. Thank you also to the reviewers of the manuscript for their close reading and insightful suggestions.

We greatly appreciate all of the contributors, who have been diligent and timely with their manuscript contributions and revisions. We would especially like to thank Lilia Kamata for her colourful cover illustration that gives visual representation to the theme of the collection.

Contents

Introduction

Domesticating Media: Safe to Curl Up With?

Fiona Joy Green and Jaqueline McLeod Rogers

T he title of our collection, *Parenting/Internet/Kids,* with three key terms slashed together, conveys the idea that the practice of parenting may extend both to the internet and to our children— to the extent that both require attention, care, and forms of regulation and, in turn, provide support and enjoyment. Although the triadic title is somewhat playful, it also strikes a serious note and introduces layered possibilities: We are not simply raising children who have grown up in the internet age but also managing the computer (which is relatively young in age, too, having established itself in homes in the 1980s)—a machine whose intelligence-cum-sentience is receiving increasing recognition as we have learned to lean as a matter of course on connectivity through the coronavirus pandemic and as theorists have continued pondering how we define being human in a posthuman age.

Our subtitle, *Domesticating Technologies,* is an homage to the 1993 Eric Hirsch and Roger Silverstone collection *Consuming Technologies: Media and Information in Domestic Spaces.* Unlike the earlier volume, ours adopts a feminist perspective so that questions of equity associated with domestic labour and caring within the home are foregrounded. And, of course, our volume takes up the multiple issues that have unfolded in the years between their publication and ours. We are using the term "domesticating" to convey that we are examining home spaces as well as taking up questions related to parenting, control, and authority. As feminists and maternal scholars, we have discouraged readings that view mothers or parents as arbiters of technology in the home and encouraged broader exploration of the relationships among family and technology and identification of places calling for systemic interventions. As feminist thinkers, we are also positioned to come to the issue with acceptance of fluidity and open-endedness so that we are not seeking to share solutions or a shared approach as much as we want to frame useful questions and consideration for self-reflective and informed practices while media and technologies continue to manifest and shapeshift in our homes.

Including perspectives from scholars and parents living in Australia, Canada, India, Japan, the UK and the US, the collection examines how the intimate presence of computer technology in our homes and on our bodies affects not only mothers and parenting but also family life more broadly. Some chapters are dedicated to considering how children use and are influenced by the internet and social media; others pick up the question of how much to monitor children and whether and how regulations come into play. An equally pressing question is how such regulation might be responsive to a global world wherein differing contexts affect both perception and actual changes.

When we initially conceptualized the volume and put out the call for contributions in a pre-pandemic world, criticism of invasive communication technologies and the internet was dominant. However, over the time between the initial and final submissions, COVID-19 hit, and people shifted to increased levels of dependence on, as well as acceptance of, the role of digital and communications technology to connect to the world, both within and outside of family life. As we move into and beyond post-pandemic times, attitudes and practices are bound to shift again, and we may well resume skepticism and critique. These shifts demonstrate that our relationship to technology is fluid and responsive to current global and local living conditions. Definitions will not hold, and the regulations a society may choose to circulate and adopt in the years to come will need to be soft and flexible.

Social Media Makes Itself at Home: Revolution in the Domestic Sphere

Observing mid-century cultural patterns, Raymond Williams claimed that advancing public technologies—such as lighting and railways and highways—created a stronger sense of division between home and work and by extension between public and private domains; advances and improvements to communication and transportation enabled folks en masse to easily travel from home to work and, in turn, to return to homes made warm, bright, and welcoming by a host of electronic media (*Television* 26). With the onset of digital technologies, this division was still thought to be in place. In a germinal collection studying the effects of media in the home—*Consuming Technologies: Media and Information in Domestic Spaces*—Eric Hirsch claims that "Most of our information and communication technologies, and broadcasting in particular, are a product of this tendency towards a separation between public/private and home/work" (196). Our collection studying technology in the home argues for an opposite trend, noting that there has been creep—and recently with COVID-19 a leap—that is blurring boundaries so that home literally serves as office for many. Home is not a separate space with a suite of platforms and programs devoted to it as an area of life cut off from others, but instead platforms and programs used at work often are those furnishing home management, entertainment, and personal communications. Moreover, homes receive online visitors or company, welcome or not: The internet secures welcome and sought-after connections, but there are also incursions as well as unasked for online contacts and violations.

Focused on the effects of media in home spaces, the chapters in this book explore how technology—social media in particular—penetrates the home and engages family members in individualized ways so that the family at home can no longer be imagined as functioning like an integrated unit, isolated from others. When the pandemic set in, and so many of us stayed home and spent more hours housed with family members, it did not so much reverse as exacerbate and make obvious the trend of each family member being tied to their own technological device and pursuing interests and friendships outside the bounds of the physical home. As Sherry Turkle sets out in coining the phrase "alone together" to describe how social media creates a disconnect between self and proximate others, individual family members are often indirectly connected to those around them in the same physical space as they direct their attention to others online. Yet virtual is not the same as real, and some chapters in this book probe what our reliance upon online worlds is doing to our capacity to relate to others in flesh-

and-blood friendships and family relations.

Social media and smart technologies connect home bodies to multiple outside nodes. These technologies not only change our sense of home and family as a discrete social unit but also break down or moderate our expectations of what the family looks like—the idealized (if formulaic) conception of the nuclear family no longer prevails. Connection to the world beyond the family unit can allow for the development of community support and creative networks as well as the exchange of vital information among multiple family members. Some of the chapters explore the role of social media and technological developments in making revolutionary change in familial behaviours and boundaries as well as in the physical spaces of domesticity.

In looking at the influences of technology on families and homes, *Parenting/Internet/Kids: Domesticating Technologies* studies an underexamined area. In 1993, the editors of *Domestic Spaces* observed that studying the family and technology was "crucial but barely examined" territory (1); in the years following, there has been minimal uptake. We want to consider how domestic technologies have changed—in particular, the consumption and production of social media by family members. In a chapter in that earlier volume, Jonathan Gershuny argues that the revolutionary character of media can be assessed by considering whether they had "revolutionary consequence" (216). To make such an assessment requires asking questions in retrospect and (in this case of social media) to evaluate the scale of its influence on social "styles and patterns" (Gershuny 216). One of his questions asks how choices are made, and we update this by asking whether "choice" is always available in relation to social media or whether part of its revolutionary impact lies in its firm insertion and installation in our lives and homes, demonstrated with particular vehemence during COVID-19 when most of us migrated to online places. The phrase "you can't go home again" resounds in our collection—not in celebration of personal growth and change but in capturing a change so broad that it is almost impossible to be (or imagine being) home alone, as we were in the 1980s and 1990s.

Questions of Privacy: Self and Others

When thinking about the question of privacy, researchers have found that privacy is not a recent idea in human history, yet it has undergone multiple definitions and conceptualizations over time (Solove; Vincent; Webb). Privacy may include "the right to be left alone, the ability to limit access to the self, secrecy and the concealment of matters from others, control over one's personal information, the protection of one's individuality and the ability to limit access to the intimate aspects of one's life" (Solove 1087). The Latin term "privatus" articulates the distinction between "matters which belonged to the collective arena and were subject to public authority, and those which pertained to an enclosed community governed by the head of the household" (Vincent 2). The modern era's conception of individual privacy—the right to be let alone—became prominent in the last decade of the 1800s (Vincent). By the end of the nineteenth century, the right to privacy appears to have emerged as a significant legal concept across several jurisdictions and has become a foundation for universal human rights (Richardson). Colonial understandings of privacy have spread through Western culture, with the idea of "personal space" in the physical world developing in the past two hundred years or so (Killick in Vincent).

Regarding the internet, concerns about privacy have been expressed since its inception, particularly because users are often trading "information about themselves for access to the services that the Internet may provide" without knowing "how that information will be used or where it will end up" (Goad et al. 1). For instance, 74 per cent of respondents in one US study indicated that "it was 'very important' for them to be in control of who can get information about them" (Goad et al. 1). Research into the Internet of Things (IoT)—a term used to describe the continually growing network of internet connected electronic devices operating around the world today—determines that tens of millions of these IoT devices exist globally and that the numbers will continue to grow as internet connectivity becomes a standard feature for a great number of electronics devices (Statista "Number of Digital"). The existence of IoT devices varies by region. For instance, "more than 70% of homes in North America have an IoT device," whereas "less than 10% of homes in South Asia do" (Kumar et al.). The capacity of IoT to share data and information can certainly provide added convenience for consumers, yet generating data about consumers increases the potential for their control and a reduction in personal privacy (Goad et al.). In 2017, the global market for IoT end-user technology reached $100 billion (USD) in market revenue for the first time, and projections suggest that "this figure will grow to around 1.6 trillion [USD] by 2025" (Statista, "Global IoT").

Additionally, forecasts suggest that the number of digital virtual assistants—such as Amazon's Alexa and Google Assistant that serve as the bridge between this network of interconnected devices and their human users—will reach 8.4 billion units by 2024, "a number higher than the world's population" (Statista "Number of Digital"). Other research indicates that as of 2018, 53 per cent of US adults aged eighteen years and older said they were willing to wear technology that tracks select health aspects, including both vital signs and fitness/lifestyle, whereas 20 per cent were not (Stewart). Another 2018 survey demonstrated that "geospatial data collected from people's movement, which is often derived from IoT devices, was the third largest category of Big Data being collected" (Goad et al. 2).

Of recent concern is the ability of law enforcement to surveil citizens without their knowledge or consent. According to Lauren Bridges, a PhD candidate at the Annenberg School of Communication at the University of Pennsylvania, "one in 10 US police departments currently access videos from millions of privately owned home security cameras without a warrant" (Bridges). Amazon's signature home security product, Ring video doorbells, "is effectively building the largest corporate-owned, civilian-installed surveillance network that the US has ever seen" (Bridges). Smart security devices are some of the fastest-growing smart home products, with an "estimated 400,000 Ring devices sold in December 2019 alone" before the boom of online sales during the COVID-19 pandemic (Bridges).

Research related to understanding the impact that IoT has on "privacy preference" has concluded that privacy preferences "are diverse, context–dependent, and highly personal" (Goad et al. 2). Other research models demonstrate that "tolerance or requirements with respect to privacy/security issues may not necessarily be the same across individuals and their associated IoT devices across different points in time" (Zhou and Piramuthu in Goad et al. 2). This finding may support the view that "more privacy is not always better" and that there is an appropriate level of privacy based on the value attached to the benefits of sharing the data by the individual using a particular IoT in a specific context, such as in smart phone use or in healthcare (Goad et al. 2). This last point—the benefits of technology and sharing data in healthcare spaces—is borne out by the chapters in Section III of this volume, "Enabling: Digital/Physical Nexus," which study the benefits of technology to mitigate the effects of disease and malady and contextualize them in relation to the relief they can bring to parents and sick children.

Chapters in the Volume

Parenting/Internet/Kids: Domesticating Technologies is organized into four sections; each addresses a theme related to the influence of digital technologies and online communication tools and platforms in relation to parents' experiences of childrearing.

The first section of the collection, "Moms on Media: Stage and Screen," explores how mothers in particular take up and rely on communication technology for self-exposure, relationship building, and research. The four chapters in this section tackle the question of use and abuse of internet media, keeping in sight the degree to which mothers should be aware of self-regulating as media users and visible role models. Yet three of the four emphasize how social media proffers new opportunities for mothers to explore identity and relationship; the fourth makes the case that social media is a powerful tool for good for those with neurodivergent conditions that might otherwise lead to isolation (a resonant and unassailable point for readers who have in the recent COVID-19 pandemic relied on the internet as a lifeline to access outside communities, allowing us both to listen and to talk back).

Shelley Buerger and Astrid Joutseno take up the issue of whether mommy blogging and life writing online provide legitimate and even liberatory spaces for expressing and exploring identity. In Chapter 1, "Impossible Subjects: Mothers and Maternal Ethics in the Digital Space," Buerger explores the complex and contradictory implications of the transformation of the mother into digital subject via mommy blogging, focusing particularly on issues of privacy, consent, and the intricacies of the mother-child relationship. She examines the tension between the idea of the internet as a textual space in which the maternal subject might explore their identity in ways which challenge the identity crisis of maternity and maternal abjection and the ethical questions this raises regarding the potential overwriting of children's subjectivity. This chapter questions whether maternal writing on the internet can be seen as a reflective or reactive textual space; it considers the implications attendant upon the public performance of the intimacies of the mother-child relationship in an open-ended, interactive medium.

Joutseno takes a different position in "Making Time and Space: Digital/Material Divisions and Maternal Life Writing." Drawing on Karen Barad's concept of "agential realism," she suggests that we can view the digital and material as inseparable realms rather than accepting the standard observation that imagines a divide between these spheres and between what is private and public. She also cites well-known entanglement theory to make the case that the self that one writes is intimately attached to the life one lives. It is outmoded, Joutseno argues, to think about the embodied mother as being separated from the mother in writing, for these two are entangled. Writing often contributes to the generative work of self-assembly.

Turning from written text to camera images, Carolin Aronis in "The Smartphone Camera as a Maternal Technology: Reconstructing Mothers' Relationships with Their Children in the Digital Age," examines how many mothers have developed practices of using smart phones to photograph their children—especially to capture moments of accomplishment in order to celebrate achievements and share them through online posting, in what she characterizes as a healthy source of family pride. She further celebrates mothers in the role of photographer and curator by charting how, by adopting these roles, they have appropriated the erstwhile male terrain of photographic technology— not only becoming comfortable with the device but also using it to document their child's life and, thus, finding a mother-driven form of use. Against those who might criticize moms for engaging in an act of commodification by photographing children as part of their parenting repertoire, Aronis says this is a new mode of recordkeeping and letter writing, and, as such, it expresses a new kind of bond and care.

Daena J. Goldsmith and Amalia Ackerman also locate a positive space for social media. In "Whose Story Is It? Sharenting in Blogs by Some Mothers of Autistic Children," they point out that online forums provide gathering places for autistic children who may otherwise face isolation and for their parents seeking support and information. Whereas Section III, "Enabling: Digital/Physical Nexus," amplifies the idea that the internet and social media provide helpful resources for parents and children who have medical issues or concerns, this chapter relates to parents' choice and use and considers whether there is still a need to set limits on unbridled "sharenting." Even in the name of circulating helpful stories to advise others, should parents nonetheless exercise a measure of circumspection when sharing stories about events and episodes in their children's lives?

The second section of the collection, "Kids on Media: Windows and Doors," shifts the emphasis from parental to children's media use. It contains three pieces—a poem and two chapters—composed by parents who reflect on their relationship with technology and with their children. The first two pieces are written from the perspective of mothers who are parenting their children into or through their tweens to adulthood. The final chapter in this section is written by the parents of a preschool-aged child, who reflect upon their approach to using online tools and screens during early parenthood. Their young family deliberately engages with multiple online communication tools and platforms to help their son learn about himself and stay connected with family.

Fictions often explore how parents imagine their children's safety and vulnerability within home confines and the expectation that the intimate space of a child's bedroom should be a protected zone. Even before digital technology, parents were invested in real world threats to their children's innocence. In the opening section of *To the Lighthouse*, called "Window" (which our section verbally echoes in its subtitle reference to doors and windows), Virginia Woolf explores the hopes and fears of ubermother Mrs. Ramsay, who often worries that she cannot protect her children from dangerous outside influences and inevitable loss of innocence. In a more recent example that brings us into the digital age, in *Fault Lines* (2008), Nancy Huston portrays a mother who falsely imagines herself able to protect her son from exposure to painful reality, completely unaware that at age six he had already found the dark web with images of military murder and graphic sexuality.

The section opens with a poem, "The Kids' Bedrooms," by Victoria Bailey, a mother who raises issues connected to those sounded by Woolf and Huston. The bedroom is not a safe enclave but a portal to outside communications and contact so that children do not cultivate privacy but instead willingly expose themselves to others outside the home space. Although protecting children is something of a universal parental commitment, the internet and social media connection insinuate more avenues of transfer and introduce more possibilities of two-way exposure.

In "Mothering, Digital Media, and the Privatization of Risk: Negotiating Boundaries of Use with Academic Expertise, Tweens, and a Global Pandemic," Janis L. Goldie examines the dialectical tensions of mothering two tweens while holding academic expertise in digital media and privacy. Goldie ultimately argues that the neoliberal demand to privatize family happiness and risk places an impossible burden on mothers, notably heightened with the stress of a global pandemic. Although her chapter does not offer a prescriptive one-size-fits-all solution for parents struggling to manage how their children use digital media, Goldie offers autoethnographic insight into one academic mother's struggles to negotiate practical use of digital technology amid an (over)awareness of its pitfalls. Her shared insights about the pressures to curve interventions may resonate with others.

"Parents, Technicians, Curators: Shrinking Space and Time in Early Parenthood," written by Andrew McGillivray and Angela McGillivray, is the final chapter in this section. These parent authors evaluate the effects of space- and time-binding technologies on their young son's development, identity, and experience of the world as well as how these technologies influence them as parents. They reflect upon their purposeful choice to send photographs and videos through SMS and a private Instagram account in order to be connected with others and to provide an archive of their son and of their lives. They ponder the ways in which video-calling technology has changed the space of their home and how the boundary between home and the outside world has been both altered and eroded by digital technologies. They demonstrate how changes in the new media landscape are placing more demands on parents today in relation to growing up digital. As they participate in the first phase of "transcendent parenting," whereby their son becomes familiar with mobile media, they recognize that they will continue to use it extensively in their parenting to communicate with their son as he moves through the city, to communicate with his teachers, and to communicate with the parents of his friends. They conclude that they must not only monitor and direct their son's media consumption and exposure but also engage with media as part of their parenting role.

Section III, "Enabling: Digital/Physical Nexus," consisting of four chapters, explores the ways in which parents have found connection, help, and resources within digital and communications technologies when dealing with challenges within their families. If we recognize that it can take a village to raise a child, voices on the internet can help fulfill this role. The loss of spouses and parents due to illness and death, the challenges of dealing with ongoing illnesses and disabilities of children, and the search for and access to support for wellness are themes in these chapters.

Chapter 8, "Crossed Wires: Mothering/Death/Adult Children," opens the section. In this moving and deeply honest piece, recently widowed Elaine Kahn uses a slice of technobiography to examine how the use of communication technologies across generations within her family helped them during the end of her husband's life and after his death. She reveals how communication technologies became a source of support to her and her adult children and helped them to communicate and to rebalance their relationships during this time of grief and loss. Through her reflection, Kahn exposes how the uses and speeds of differing digital media are complicated—sometimes a help and other times a hindrance. She discovers that while communication technologies may make for efficiency and even offer comfort, they can also potentially lead to hurtful misunderstandings.

Chapter 9, "Bionic Parenting: On the Enabling Possibilities and Practices for Parenting with Digital New Media," is authored by the parents of a young child with type 1 diabetes (T1D). Robyn Flisfeder and Matthew Flisfeder have seen firsthand some of the more advantageous aspects of new digital technologies and social media for families. In this chapter, they draw from their own personal narrative to examine some of the enabling aspects of digital media, communications technologies, and biotechnologies in raising a child with T1D. They present their narrative against proliferating scholarly discourses about new, posthumanist, and biopolitical ethics to rethink the future of human and societal possibilities, including parenting practices for those managing chronic illness. They demonstrate how various pages, groups, and organizations on social media have provided welcoming communities and access to new information to support their particular situations and life experiences. Robyn Flisfeder and Matthew Flisfeder make the compelling case that the context of parenting a child with T1D helps them, and others, to see many of the positive aspects of advances in digital media, social media, cloud computing, and algorithmic technologies and biotechnologies.

"Enabled by the Internet: A Multicultural Mother and Daughter in Japan," Chapter 10, is authored by Suzanne Kamata, an English-speaking American living in Japan. As the mother of a biracial daughter who is deaf, has cerebral palsy, and thus uses a wheelchair for mobility, Kamata has found the internet an overwhelmingly positive addition for her family. Despite numerous reports about the negative impact of the internet on contemporary youth and on family relationships, she has found that it has provided access to a plethora of apps, such as Facebook, Twitter, LINE, and Google Translate, which can ease communication for all members of her family. Internet access has enabled her daughter, a young woman with disabilities, to develop relationships, pursue interests without a caregiver's help or interference, and develop greater independence and privacy. One example is the ability of her daughter to draw her own manga characters, stories, and other artwork to share with friends via the internet (a sample illustration is featured on the cover of this collection). Another more profound example is the way in which these communications technologies are supporting her desire and ability to live independently in another city hours away from her family.

Chapter 11, "Discourses, Practices, and Paradoxes of Natural Parenting in the Digital Age," written by Florence Pasche Guignard, concludes Section III. Pasche Guignard explores the impact of internet use and communications technology on mothers who engage in natural parenting and some of the contradictions associated with it. Using three case studies (babywearing and breastfeeding, fertility awareness, and maternal entrepreneurship), she reveals how the current discourse, with an emphasis on nature and sustainability, is coupled with a high reliance on the internet by mothers who discuss, implement, and promote natural parenting. Pasche Guignard clearly illustrates how these cases reveal one of the paradoxes of natural parenting: an emphasis on nature and sustainability paired with a high reliance on internet use and communications technology.

Section IV, "Regulating Domestic Use and Surveillance: Who Is in Charge?, consists of three chapters by researchers addressing various ways of thinking through some ethical considerations associated with regulating how parents, children, and adolescents use the internet. Themes in this section address the impact and repercussions of cyberbullying, school-enforced disciplining of mothers and in turn children, and embedded corporate surveillance practices in education technology.

Chapter 12, "Mothering/Cyberbullying/Kids," is coauthored by Lisa Rosen and Linda Rubin and opens the book's final section. Drawing upon scholarly research and interviews with mothers and children about their experiences of cyberbullying, Rosen and Rubin discuss the growing concern of cyberbullying for parents and children as well as its complex and frequently painful dynamics. By focusing on the bully, the victim, and their mothers, the authors address family-level risk and protective factors for both cyberbullying and cyber-victimization. Particular attention is paid to the role mothers can play in both deterring their children from cyberbullying and supporting children who are its victims.

In Chapter 13, "'No Forwards Please': Indian Mothers on School WhatsApp Groups," Sucharita Sarkar addresses the ways in which the explosion of digital social media in twenty-first-century India has affected digitally enabled mothers who use WhatsApp. Drawing upon scholarly research, as well as interviews with other mothers and autoethnographic reflections of her participation in her fourteen-year-old daughter's school WhatsApp group, Sarkar analyses communication practices among Indian mothers as a resource for practical, needs-based connection. She reasons that although the collaborative affordances of participating in school WhatsApp groups make this a practical tool when performing neoliberal motherhood and primary caregiving, the school-authority-reinforced disciplining related to the school WhatsApp group does not allow feminist maternal conversations to develop in these spaces. Mothers who use the school WhatsApp are therefore under surveillance and effectively policed.

Chapter 14, the final chapter of the book, addresses some of the policies and their repercussions that have risen with the increased use of technology. In "Parenting in the Shadow of Corporate Surveillance:

Reflections on Children's Privacy after the Widespread Pandemic-Induced Adoption of Education Technology," coauthors Jane Bailey and Vanessa Ford focus on education technology and the human rights consequences of further embedding corporate surveillance practices into the lives of children and their families. They initially draw upon pre-pandemic research on children's privacy in a digitally networked world and highlight the foundational role played by corporate surveillance practices. They then focus on the corporate threat to children's (and families) privacy rights arising from educational technology (edtech), particularly with the mass migration to online/distance education in the wake of the pandemic. They conclude their chapter by addressing mechanisms for supporting children's privacy rights against opportunistic commoditization of children, their families, and learning environments escalated by the pandemic tide. They urge looking beyond individual responsibility towards regulations prohibiting such commoditization.

Setting Limits and Taking Control: Who Governs the Internet for the Self, Family, Nation, and Globe?

Although the first three sections in this book are not uncritical of social media and digital technologies, often noting abuse and exploitation and traps, on balance, a celebratory thread runs through them. The first section exposes some of the ways technology enables new forms of identity, caring, and connecting; the second section examines children and online learning opportunities; the third section reckons the advantages of digital technologies for promoting health and sense of wellbeing. It is the fourth section focused on ethics that calls into question whether and how the internet and social media need some form of regulation to protect users—both those who are underage as well as those who are more mature yet perhaps lacking boundaries or sense of danger. Of course, questions of regulation are emergent and contested, and so none of the chapters advocates for a particular process. We are considering regulation here because the question of regulation is implicit in those chapters that report on new usage trends to evaluate the effects of our growing reliance on communication technologies and its increasing presence in our homes and lives.

As we move into post-pandemic times, criticism of our online dependence appears to be ramping up. For example, in *Context Blindness*, Eva Berger outlines the online environment as fostering autism and giving normalcy to what we currently characterize as neurodivergent. In *Scorched Earth*, Jonathan Crary goes farther still, launching a full-scale attack on digital culture—blaming it for psychic and social decay, as users are entranced by addictive algorithms and give up any interest in real others to pursue online fixities. He suggests online culture threatens all forms of life: "It is remarkable that at a moment of unparalleled danger for the future of the planet, for the very survival of human and animal life, that so many people should voluntarily confine themselves in the desiccated digital closet devised by a handful of sociocidal corporations" (121). To the extent that there is truth in these accelerated warnings that the internet has trapped us into narcissistic isolation and dangerous connections, questions about its proper role or scale in the home are more pressing than ever. The home is a space over which we can exert some control and influence—in which we have some agency and decision making.

Yet the volume was not curated to argue the case that mothers or parents should be tasked with moderating the internet—it does not argue that the fix begins at home or that parents should be cast in the role of authoritarians in charge of governing family practices. As many chapters underscore here, and in other volumes that explore mothering and motherhood, mothers are already burdened with expectations and with work (Hays; O'Reilly), and few who write as feminists are open to delegating as motherwork the task of taming computers and technology, as they are now imbedded in our homes. Although parents may be willing to model the sort of self-regulating behaviour they wish to encourage in their children—putting phones away at night, limiting hours of online entertainment—the gist of the argument made by chapters in this collection is that broad and concerted systemic effort is needed if we are to effectively push back against the powerful force of technology, since it has taken over so many of our hours, habits, and minds. This is clearly a situation where individual actions are small compared to the systemic vision and programming that is needed.

On setting up restraints and policies to protect us as users—especially policies to guard children as underage users—we are bound to need the support of educational institutions and of government, law, and policy. In the final chapter of this volume, Jane Bailey and Vanessa Ford encourage coordinated efforts to protect the privacy rights of children:

> It is essential to think beyond the individual child, caregiver, family, teacher, and even school board and province respon-sibility to investigate and contract for legislative compliance.... Approaching the issue as one of corporate regulation helps to relieve pressure on individual adult caregivers to engage in the virtually impossible task of policing corporate privacy practices, and instead rightfully places that burden on the state.

We might extend their claim about protecting children's privacy rights to our broader claim that the internet itself needs some form of flexible regulation. Children and parents need to be given a place at a table with international and interdisciplinary experts and users seeking to develop flexible protections against online and social media abuses and invasions.

Because the internet reaches across political borders, such support is bound to be more effective if it is more global than regional or national. A collection like ours, for example, with international contributors, indicates that the internet is posing challenges to homelife that are global and shared. If we share the dangers of being radically open and overcommitted to digital worlds, we share, too, the huge advantages of finding forums for international exchange and discussion to share our experiences and observations. If we were to live in regimes that were each governed by a suite of different policies and laws, we would struggle with barriers and lose our conduit to others around the globe. Laura DeNardis captures both the drive to regulation and the concerns about offending the "invariant" freedoms that characterize the web and constitute its democratizing energy and powerful appeal. She points out that we know and expect technical norms that promote the continuance of connection:

> These technical norms include global reach, the potentiality of any end device to reach any other regardless of location, and interoperability among devices made by different manufacturers. They also include permissionless innovation in which anyone can introduce a new Internet application without a gatekeeper's

consent as well as a network marked by accessibility and general purpose support of any application or service. ("Internet Architecture")

Perhaps more importantly, we expect personal access guaranteed by "invariants," such as "collaboration among stakeholders, mutual agreement, and the principle of no permanent favourites so essential for ongoing Internet innovation" (DeNardis, "Internet Architecture"). Such regulations, as we are able to establish, will have to be flexible and responsive in order to satisfy our collective understanding of internet freedoms.

Apart from resistance to loss of freedom in terms of usage practices, there are feminist implications arising from governance questions. Our blog site, Ta[l]king Care: Family Blog Lines, picks up a line from DeNardis: "Arrangements of technical architecture are inherent arrangements of power" ("Hidden Levers" 721). As she observes, apps, online technologies, and software privilege some users over others; as Carolin Aronis observes in this volume, it is generally true of technology that it has been developed and skewed to privilege male designers and users. So the question of who steps forward to devise plans for change and regulation—for policies to enable fair access and discourage overuse—is crucial to women and other marginalized folks, who will want to participate in such discussions to avoid being disadvantaged. Mothers and parents will also want a voice to shape any regulations that may be devised to affect the delivery and rollout of media in the home. No one wants to be burdened by regulatory rules, yet most want to secure a safe, healthy, and equitable environment where they have access to the media that we need without being tethered to it.

Shoshanna Zuboff is more aware than most of the grasp and dangers of the growth of big tech. She ends The Age of Surveillance Capitalism by calling on all of us to take notice of how technology has changed our actions and expectations, throwing a yoke around our necks that inhibits free choice or action. She says we need to individually awaken and to collectively demand an end to thraldom by pronouncing "No more" (Zuboff, 525). It is particularly pertinent to our collection—which examines the question of internet home invasion from a parental and mothering perspective—that Zuboff ends her treatise by addressing her children and encouraging them to recognize how the internet controls our actions and expectations: "It's not OK to spend your lunchtime conversations comparing software that will camouflage you and protect you from continuous unwanted invasion" (521). She continues with an even more powerful appeal:

> I tell them that the word "search" has meant a daring existential journey, not a finger tap to already existing answers; that "friend" is an embodied mystery, that can be forged only face-to-face and heart-to-heart; and that "recognition" is the glimmer of homecoming we experience in our beloved's face, not "facial recognition." I say that it is not OK to have our best instincts for connection, empathy, and information exploited by a draconian quid pro quo that holds these goods hostage to the pervasive strip search of our lives. (521)

Zuboff is dire in her forecast about big tech moving in on our lives, channelling our interests down narrow lanes they approve and giving up our data as we go. Others are equally bleak. In *Dark Age Ahead*, James Bridle warns of the social dissolution and planetary degradation that accompany digital life. Yet despite deep concerns, both theorists believe it is in our human reach to regain control by recognizing the dangers and asserting human values. Zuboff ends her study calling for "collective effort" to break the cycle (525). Similarly, Bridle argues that we have some power: "Our understanding of those systems and their ramifications, and of the conscious choices we make in their design, in the here and now, remain entirely within our capabilities" (252).

In the mid-twentieth century, Canadian media theorist Marshall McLuhan predicted a world driven by technology and media. In *Understanding Media*, he forecast as our fate to live entirely "without walls"—to lose individuality and privacy and to replace these with new forms of connection and sharing (176). Nonetheless, as with Zuboff and Bridle, he imaged we could still gain control over media and technology and direct these forces to assist rather than direct our lives. In this collection, affirmations of the support role technologies can play are particularly strong in chapters by parents who applaud medical devices and advances that enrich and enable them and their children to live full and healthier lives (Kamata; Flisfeder and Flisfeder). In this, they are in line with the conclusion DeNardis draws in *The Internet in Everything*, where she recommends taking stock of the many gifts offered by medical advances, and "rejecting dystopian imaginings" to work instead on "building digital trust and security" (227, 229).

The promise of media is still there, as is the threat. Focused on technology and domestic spaces, this volume shows the potential energy of researched supports; it also pinpoints the dangers and pressures that need attention. If we are to stake some control and develop helpful strictures governing the use of technology and media in our world and homes, it is beyond the scope of individual actors—it is not a parental responsibility. Nor is it a matter of all-in-the-family household values. Exercising controls and enabling technological modifications may even exceed national policy and governance because we need protective guidelines that are flexible and responsive to a network of worldwide users—to our extended, global family.

Works Cited

Berger, Eva. *Context Blindness: Digital Technology and the Next Stage of Human Evolution.* Peter Lang, 2022.

Bridges, Lauren. "Amazon's Ring is the Largest Civilian Surveillance Network the US Has Ever Seen." *The Guardian*, 18 May 2021, www.theguardian.com/commentisfree/2021/may/18/amazon-ring-largest-civilian-surveillance-network-us?utm_term=5b6f10fd 895472ab09ec06887aa66460&utm_campaign=GuardianToday UK&utm_source=esp&utm_medium=Email&CMP=GTUK_email. Accessed 8 May 2022.

Bridle, James. *New Dark Age: Technology and the End of the Future.* Verso, 2018.

Crary, Jonathan. *Scorched Earth: Beyond the Digital Age to a Post-Capitalist World.* Verso, 2022.

DeNardis, Laura. "Hidden Levers of Internet Control." *Information, Communication & Society*, vol. 15, no. 5, 2012, pp. 720-738, doi: 10.1080/1369118X.2012.659199. Accessed 15 May 2022.

DeNardis, Laura. "Internet Architecture as Proxy for State Power." *Centre for International Governance Innovation*, 15 Aug. 2015, www.cigionline.org/articles/internet-architecture-proxy-state-power. Accessed 8 May 2022.

DeNardis, Laura. *The Internet in Everything: Freedom and Security in a World with No Off Switch.* Yale University Press, 2020.

Gershuny, Jonathan. "Revolutionary Technologies and Technological Revolutions." *Consuming Technologies: Media and Information in Domestic Spaces*, edited by Eric Hirsch and Roger Silverstone, Routledge, 1993, pp. 227-33.

Goad, David, et al. "Privacy and the Internet of Things: An Experiment in Discrete Choice." *Information & Management*, vol 8, no. 2, 2021, pp. 1-16.

Hays, Sharon. *Cultural Contradictions of Motherhood*. Yale University Press, 1996.

Hirsch, Eric. "The Long Term and the Short Term of Domestic Consumption: An Ethnographic Case Study." *Consuming Technologies: Media and Information in Domestic Spaces*, edited by Eric Hirsch and Roger Silverstone, Routledge, 1993, pp. 194-210.

Huston, Nancy. *Fault Lines*. Grove Press, 2008.

Killick, Adam. "Tech Titans like Google and Facebook are Built on a 'House of Cards.', Says Oxford Philosopher." CBC, 29 Jan. 2021, www.cbc.ca/radio/spark/tech-titans-like-google-and-facebook-are-built-on-a-house-of-cards-says-oxford-philosopher-1.5893760 Accessed 8 May. 2022.

Kumar, Deepak, et al. "All Things Considered: An Analysis of IoT Devices on Home Networks." *USENIX*, www.usenix.org/conference/usenixsecurity19/presentation/kumar-deepak. Accessed 8 May 2022.

McLuhan, Marshall. *Understanding Media*. Gingko. 1964.

O'Reilly, Andrea. "Outlaw(ing) Motherhood: A Theory and Politic of Maternal Empowerment for the Twenty-First Century." *Hecate*, vol. 36, no. 1-2, pp. 17–29.

Richardson, Megan. *The Right to Privacy: Origins and Influence of a Nineteenth-Century Idea*. Cambridge University Press, 2017.

Solove, D. J. "Conceptualizing Privacy." *Cal. Law Rev.*, vol. 90, 2002, p. 1087.

Statista. "Global IoT End-User Spending Worldwide 2017-2025." *Statista*, 22 Jan. 2021, www.statista.com/statistics/976313/global-iot-market-size/. Accessed 8 May 2022.

Statista. "Number of Digital Voice Assistants in Use Worldwide 2019-2024." *Statista*, 22 Jan. 2021, www.statista.com/statistics/973815/

worldwide-digital-voice-assistant-in-use/. Accessed 8 May 2022.

Stewart, Conor. "Percentage of U.S. Adults That Were Willing to Wear Technology That Racks Select Health Statistics as of 2018." *Statista*, 7 Mar. 2019, www.statista.com/statistics/829479/willing ness-to-wear-health-tracking-technology-us-adults/ Accessed 8 May 2022.

Ta[l]king Care: *Family Blog Lines* https://familybloglines.com

Turkle, Sherry. *Alone Together: Why We Expect More from Technology and Less from Each Other.* Basic Books, 2011.

Vincent, David. *Privacy: A Short History.* Polity Press, 2016.

Webb, Diana. *Privacy and Solitude in the Middle Ages.* Hambledon Continuum, 2007.

Williams, Raymond. *Television: Technology and Cultural Form.* Routledge, 1975.

Woolf, Virginia. *To the Lighthouse.* Houghton Mifflin Harcourt, 2001.

Zhou, W., and S. Piramuthu. "Information Relevance Model of Customized Privacy for IoT." *Journal of Business Ethics*, vol. 131, no. 1, 2015, pp. 19-30.

Zuboff, Shoshanna. *Age of Surveillance Capitalism: The Fight for a Human Future at the New Frontier of Power.* PublicAffairs, 2019.

Section I
Moms on Media: Stage and Screen

Chapter 1

Impossible Subjects: Mothers and Maternal Ethics in the Digital Space

Shelley Buerger

Feminist literary and cultural critic Jacqueline Rose opens her recently published book *Mothers: An Essay in Love and Cruelty* with the following observation:

> A simple argument guides this book: that motherhood is, in Western discourse, the place in our culture where we lodge, or rather bury, the reality of own conflicts of what it means to be fully human. It is the ultimate scapegoat for our personal political failings, for everything that is wrong with the world, which it becomes the task—unrealisable of course—of mothers to repair. (1)

Rose invokes an idea of Western motherhood that is at once all-powerful, all-consuming, and all-subsuming. There is an assumption of an inherent contradiction attendant upon the maternal that confines mothers within a symbolizing economy in which they are assigned an almost fearsome power as facilitators "of what it means to be fully human" while not being afforded any control—at the individual or cultural level—over how this symbolism is mediated. Thus, the complexity of the mother's humanity is subsumed under the status of "the ultimate scapegoat." Or as fellow feminist psychoanalytical critic Lisa Baraitser observes in her book *Maternal Encounters: The Ethics of Interruption*: "The mother, after all, is the impossible subject par excellence' (5).

In this understanding of motherhood, the personal and particular are collapsed into the cultural. Furthermore, the figure of the mother becomes a kind of palimpsest upon which "we lodge, or rather bury" our existential anxieties (Rose 1). In short, Rose and Baraitser present us with a conceptualization of motherhood, in which mothers remain strung between opposing cultural impulses. Or, as Baraitser argues, the Western mother is caught "in an ever-widening gap between her idealization and denigration in contemporary culture, and her indeterminate position as part object, part subject within Western philosophical tradition" (4). Rose's use of the terms "lodge" and "bury" to describe the social and psychic labour demanded of mothers by society casts them in the role of passive receptacle—of the signified rather than signifier, the described rather than describer. What can be a greater expression of what it means to have access to full subjective status than the ability to speak and/or tell one's own story? Yet in the schema of maternal existence outlined above, the mother has been largely silenced while still being overloaded with responsibility. The jostling impulses of denigration and idealization—if left to run unchecked not only over the Western philosophical tradition in the abstract, but also contemporary culture at the material and aesthetic level—leave little room for mothers to conceptualize and articulate individualized, heterogeneous depictions of maternal subjectivity and experience.

Baraitser takes up this point, calling for what she terms a "strategic valorization of motherhood" that engages with "the generative, surprising and unexpected" aspects of motherhood (7). She envisages this as a space to air "what is excessive (but *not* monstrous) in maternal experience" (7). Clearly this can be read as a call to liberate motherhood from the oppressive binary of denigration and idealization, but Baraitser is also aware of the fraught potential of the term "valorization": "This deliberate valorization of the generative potential of maternity may appear to be a rather alarming aim; a reductive or cheerful attempt to celebrate motherhood despite the profound psychological, emotional, relational, and financial crises (to name a few) that it so clearly provokes in so many of our lives" (7). While acknowledging the uncomfortable proximity of valorization to idealization, Baraitser goes on to argue: "If we shift from a female [or otherwise] subject position to encompass a maternal one when we have a child (be that an adoptive, birth, foster, community or surrogate child, or any other relationship in which one comes to name another as one's child), then we must surely contend with the notion that *motherhood produces something new*" (my emphasis, 8).

In recognizing motherhood as both a relationship and a subject position, Baraitser figures the maternal as a variable designation rather than one explicitly or necessarily tethered to biology. Although this conceptualizing of motherhood opens it up both as a category and a role, the interwoven and overlapping edges of these potentially opposing facets are also possible sites of conflict. The potential for such conflict is heightened with regards to maternal representation, which necessarily involves balancing the "self" of subjectivity with the relational demands of motherhood.

This chapter explores the "something new" produced by the competing obligations of maternal representation and takes as its central premise the contention that the rise of digital communication and the internet have facilitated an unprecedented animation and reflection of this something new as a space in which mothers might explore all aspects of their experiences, generative or otherwise, as well as a space that challenges the confines of idealization and denigration. I trace the unfurling of this space over the past two decades and examine the evolving digital representation of motherhood and maternal subjectivity to interrogate the impact of blogging on the cultural, social, and political status of the mother. The key question posed here is whether the original radical disruption of the mommy blog has resulted in a decisive and enduring challenge to reductive notions of motherhood. Has this unprecedented access mothers now have to vast audiences to whom they might project their particular version of maternal experience afforded them greater control over their cultural signification? Or has gaining digital control over their maternal positioning merely resulted in the canny leveraging—and therefore reification—of the patriarchal delineation of motherhood for commercial gain? What has been lost in the shift from writer/narrator mommy blogger to the Instagram influencer in thrall to corporate influences we see now?

I contend here that the evolving story of maternal writing on the internet can thus far be divided into two distinct yet overlapping waves. The first of these I map coincides with the purposing of the Internet as a site for the reimagining of the personal and of life writing that occurred in the early 2000s with the rise of blogging and social media. The second wave I map progresses from advances in technology circa 2010, such as smartphones—which increased the portability and ubiquity of the internet—combined with the emergence of new micro social media platforms, such as Instagram, which have accelerated the impetus towards the monetization and corporatization of digital motherhood. Although I have laid out a rough chronology here of maternal writing on the internet, I do not suggest that the effects and impacts I trace in this chapter can be interpreted as proceeding linearly from one fixed position (positive or negative) to another. In understanding the internet as an unsettled location, this chapter nevertheless seeks to interrogate the outcomes of the "something new" these narratives contribute to the positioning of mothers in contemporary Western discourse.

It must also be acknowledged that the most prominent, overwhelming, and complicating "new" thing motherhood produces is, of course, the child. Psychoanalytic theory from Freud and Lacan as well as the poststructuralist interventions of theorists such as Julia Kristeva locate the mother as facilitator of the child's individuation and autonomous subjectivity, primarily via the mother's willing effacement. Refusal of this process on the part of the mother is figured as a transgression of the boundaries and norms upon which the symbolic order—the dominant organizing principle of Western society according to psychoanalysis—is founded.

Kristeva positions the refusal of the mother to prioritize the facilitation of the child's individuation by relinquishing the intense dyadic relationship of the infant period as abject—"the place where meaning collapses" (2). This has portentous implications for representations of maternal experience as generative and evolving. How are mothers to establish their own particular subjectivity in the face of cultural forces that demand their silent effacement? Building on the rich contributions of writers and theorists—such as Sara Ruddick, Adrienne Rich, and Andrea O'Reilly—to the discourses of maternity, this chapter investigates the premise that the internet affords a uniquely expansive and flexible space for the exploration and representation of motherhood. If we understand the digital sphere as a place of increased representational potential, has this potential been realized in ways that have enlarged our understanding of motherhood and mothers beyond reductive extremes? Has having access to a global audience without many of the barriers imposed by traditional publishing enabled mothers to realize a new, more resonant and self-governing subjectivity?

Digital Proxies

In her book *Mommyblogs and the Changing Face of Motherhood*, May Friedman writes that "mommyblogging, as a practice, has shifted understandings of motherhood" (29). For Friedman, the blogs depicting motherhood she turned to in the early 2000s resonated precisely because they were personal and immediate. Friedman describes the experience of discovering this new format as a first-time expectant mother:

> Thus began the first blog I ever read, on my travels towards motherhood. In my pregnant and slowly expanding state, the words of a woman I didn't know seemed to hold the key to the secret reality that awaited me. I couldn't imagine the shift in identity that lay before me, and as an apprehensive traveller to this uncharted territory, I looked to blogs—part welcome mat, part travel guide—to ease my trepidation. (3)

In this depiction, the mommy blog is a place of reassurance in the face of the ambiguous liminality of pregnancy. At the moment Friedman finds herself adrift, facing an uncertain future that tests the limits of knowledge and identity, she discovers a place "part welcome mat, part travel guide" to welcome her into this "secret new reality" (3). The immediacy of recognition Friedman describes is striking, but there is also a sense that this is a recognition of something intangible, unquantifiable, and still unrecognizable. And that this new medium exists outside of traditional discourse, almost as if it disrupts these other texts with its very presence.

In fact, Friedman goes on to say that much of the appeal of these blogs lay in the ways in which they confounded not only traditional texts about motherhood but also her own academic and political sensibilities. She realized that her lived experience of motherhood had shifted the ways in which she approached these texts:

While much feminist writing had resonance ... it did not yield the intimacy and dialogue that I craved. Even the best academic writing had a conclusion, which—in keeping with all expert literature on motherhood—was often presented as a "right" way to mother. Now, in addition to being bewildered, I was also frustrated that I could not maintain my feminist idealism when it came down to the messy, real-life work of parenting. (3-4)

The most significant aspect of Friedman's unease with conventional (historical) maternal texts is what she sees as their tendency to offer prescriptive observations from an assumed position of authority. Thus, for Friedman, the printed text appears in comparison to the open fluidity of the digital space as a closed entity—fixed in its opinions and pronouncements and resistant to exchange or dialogue with readers. Friedman is not alone in this reaction. Australian academic Megan Rogers observes that "Like many maternal studies academics ... I came to read blogs on motherhood as a new mother first and as an academic second" (250).

Baraitser notes that when one enters into motherhood "reflective space is obliterated" (48). She continues: "This relentless and infinite present destroys all that is subtle, indeterminate, unknowing in one's thinking" (48). She concludes that it is "not that mothers stop being able to think. It's that we think in another order—the order of immediacy" (48). The notion of reflective space being obliterated is one most mothers will be familiar with. In many respects, the types of communication and writing engendered by the internet generally, and blogging and social media specifically, inhabit a reading space in which reaction is privileged over reflection. This is not to say that the blogs Friedman and Rogers describe are not thoughtful textual spaces but rather that the immediacy of the digital sphere primes readers to react, often in very personal and urgent ways that are usually public and therefore more akin to the call and response of conversation than the traditionally solitary experience of reading.

If my own experience of reading mommy blogs as a first-time mother is anything to go by, I would contend it is the potent combination of having one's reflective space so abruptly curtailed—combined with the feeling of narrative order mommy bloggers bring to the seemingly inarticulable details of the "relentless and infinite" and, I might add, unfamiliar present readers find themselves inhabiting—

that gives these blogs such resonance (Baraitser 48). The appeal of mommy bloggers lies in their ability to present themselves as a kind of digital proxy for their reader. Motherhood is a time of transformation and identity crisis—or, as Baraitser proposes, a process of splitting, whereby one's "old independent self/new messy maternal self are refigured" (50). This refiguring can engender feelings of loss and confusion, as mothers are socialized to feel their old self "must be mourned and then given up" (50). In acting as a digital proxy, the mommy blogger offers a solution to this identity crisis that is both soothing and seductive without being prescriptive. This is not to say these blogs depict motherhood in an unambivalent or reductive way. Rather, the mommy blogger offers a palpable representation of the "new messy maternal self," that, by leaning into ambivalence helps readers make sense of this transformation. The mommy blogger as digital proxy tempers the cultural burden Rose argues mothers must assume, while adroitly encompassing the strategic valorization Baraitser calls for.

Consider this post by Heather Armstrong of *Dooce* detailing the particularity of her maternal transformation:

> So I think I'm getting the hang of this thing, this thing being my new job as mother of a two-month-old baby. I haven't mastered this thing by any means, but I've at least come to a point where I don't panic when Jon leaves for his job in the morning, and I'm faced with spending the next ten hours ALONE WITH A BABY. For a while it felt like he was leaving me alone with a bomb, and if I turned away from it at any point during the day it would explode and destroy the whole world. Now it feels more like a hand grenade, and I just have to resist the urge to yank out its safety pin, which in Leta's case would be picking her up while she's perfectly content on her back and attempting to cradle her. There is no cradling of the hand grenade in this household, because the hand grenade will look at you like *What do you think I am, a baby? I am not a baby! I am a hand grenade!*

Armstrong uses a combination of humour and hyperbole to detail the painful transition Baraitser describes above. Although both rhetorical devices can be seen as a form of deflection, they also combine to powerfully embody Armstrong's maternal subjectivity.

This frank articulation of the "loss and shock of the maternal" is an arresting enactment—and refusal of—the obliteration of self the maternal subject experiences (Baraitser 51). Armstrong responds to the challenge to her identity by privileging her own subjectivity throughout, whereas her infant child is reduced to the status of destructive metaphor. In providing such an explicit representation of her maternal subjectivity, Armstrong also becomes digital proxy to her readers. The interactive nature of blogging, which encourages readers to see themselves as being in dialogue with bloggers, perhaps obscures the constructed nature of the textual narrative by overlaying it with the appearance of an intimate conversation. Baraitser argues that contemporary maternal literature "unwittingly figures the feminine as the lost unified subject, and maternity as the messy interdependent excess" (62). Certainly Armstrong's words conjure the "messy inter-dependent excess" of maternity, but as each blog post, like the one quoted, offers us glimpses of her daily life that are articulated as being in the present moment, readers are encouraged to feel as though they are being brought into Armstrong's world.

Armstrong's disarming use of humour makes her more accessible and desirable as a proxy by relieving her readers of the burden of any of the unpleasant emotional fallout from her maternal transformation. As Baraitser observes, being "a 'subject-in-process/on trial,' to borrow Kristeva's term is not exactly pleasant" (63). Armstrong manages here to inhabit her complicated becoming maternal subjectivity without flinching from its more portentous implications while still entertaining her readers, which brings us to the crux of the appeal of the mommy blog as a platform that embraces the personal as entertainment and cultural commentary. Friedman notes a potential for fluidity and hybridity in blogging: "[This] allows for the interruption of patriarchal tropes of motherhood, replacing them with a greater degree of heterogeneity and confusion. Such an interruption is sorely required as an antidote to the essentialising and minimizing rhetoric around motherhood elsewhere" (47).

It is worth pausing here to consider the ongoing positioning of mommy blogging as it has continued to shape and be shaped by culture over the last two decades. Mommy blogging is now as much an established part of culture as it is a reaction to it, which necessarily complicates notions of blogging as a digital disrupter of the status quo.

Although the seemingly inexhaustible space provided by the internet from which the maternal subject might speak is conducive to heterogeneity and multiplicity, I would argue that the personal focus of this kind of blogging makes it equally susceptible to self-selecting reading. The richness of "heterogeneity and confusion" (47) Friedman describes can paradoxically encourage a narrowly focused reading, as readers already unsettled by the upheavals of motherhood seek the comfort of the recognizable over the disruptions of confusion when faced with an abundance of choice. The particularity and immediacy of motherhood can mean such moments of recognition sometimes require (or encourage) the setting aside of one's previous convictions (Friedman 4).

Friedman is a thoughtful reader and early critic in *Mommyblogs and the Changing Face of Motherhood*, presenting her audience with a careful, nuanced, and considered exploration of mommy blogging as a phenomenon she is personally invested in. However, it is the personal nature of this investment—which Friedman refers to repeatedly in her discussion—that complicates her analysis. Friedman's dual reading perspectives of scholar and mother often seem poised between the kind of contradictions detailed above—whereby a more scholarly reading seeks bloggers "who self-identify across the spectrum of race, including many mothers with hybridized racial identities; who represent a wide range of sexualities and gender positions; and who have a range of different abilities" (45) and the mother who craves "kinship," which is lacking "in the embodied world of parents around" her (5).

Building on Friedman's scholarship, Megan Rogers suggests that this bifurcation of reading perspective might be most fruitfully integrated by privileging the more academic and literary aspects of blogging, whereby a reconceptualizing of blogs as maternal essays, which draw upon the techniques of creative nonfiction, would rehabilitate these digital texts from what Rogers sees as the problematic implications of the term "mommy blogger." Rogers positions this as a matter of categorization rather than a shift in terminology, but it must be noted that this conceptual framework risks erecting its own kind of representational gatekeeping. Rogers writes: "By considering together all the online writing about motherhood we fail to appreciate and understand the true worth and impact of much of the writing. Therefore, I would like to argue the term 'mummy blogger,' whether you spell it with a 'u' or an 'o,' not only has negative connotations but it covers too many styles of writing to be meaningful" (250). Although I would agree that if one's focus is blogging's challenge to a reductive status quo then not all mommy blogging will resonate, it is worth pondering how and by what standards "true worth" is measured and, further, whether such judgments can also become hostile to maternal expression and self-determination.

Of course, these reading positions need not be figured as diametrically opposed. Friedman certainly does not suggest they are, instead reconciling these disparate readings by positioning blogs as "a shared, dialogic account of motherhood" (5). However, I am intrigued by the implications of the space between these reading positions. If we see academic readings as being informed by specialized reading practices that are generally focused on detached critique and deconstruction, often from within a specific political and/or critical perspective, the fact that mommy blogs are capable of eliciting both these expert and intensely personal responses suggests that they do indeed produce something new. It can be argued that mommy blogs are a unique manifestation of the political/personal intersection in feminist polemics in that the personal often overwhelms consideration of political implications via the strong sense of identification and relatedness they provoke in both reader and writer. Although this vacillation between reading states may not be specific to maternal narratives, I would argue that the particular disruptions to one's identity and selfhood coupled with the ambivalence (both cultural and personal) occasioned by motherhood creates a singular desire for identification and recognition. The challenge of balancing this desire with the political considerations of opening up motherhood as a cultural and social category in which mothers might have control over how and why they signify lies in the ongoing ability of these digital narratives to encompass the multiplicity and heterogeneity of maternity.

Digital Subjects

Writing in 2022, I am less convinced that the internet continues to facilitate the kind of diverse representation of motherhood Friedman spoke of in 2013. Whereas once blogs functioned as archives of life writing, now the most prominent among them appear to be repositories for beautifully lit images of photogenic children artfully posed against expensive backdrops for the express purpose of selling products. Internet motherhood appears now to be a milieu most viscerally and visibly inhabited by white, middle-class American bloggers eager to encourage conspicuous consumption. This is not to say that the earlier narrative-based blogs were entirely free of financial impetus. Critics have noted that by the mid-2000s the increasing popularity of early mommy blogs like *Dooce* encouraged the professionalization of blogging as a practice which in turn led to monetization (Lawrence; Lopez; Hunter). Andrea Hunter writes:

> When mommy blogging began, bloggers felt as if the content on their blogs was so far outside of what advertisers were interested in, that they were doing something "radical" by telling stories about the raw realities of parenting (Lopez, 2009). However, this soon changed. As mommy blogs became increasingly popular, advertisers started to take notice. Eager to capitalize on the loyalty and trust that mommy bloggers had developed with their readers, marketers began seeing these bloggers as an important, direct way to reach consumers (Douglas, 2009).

Hunter's comments suggest that it is the original radical potential of the mommy blog—the facilitation of representation and connection on the mother's own terms—that ironically encouraged the shift towards monetization in which content is dictated by corporate entities.

From a commercial perspective, I would argue that the unquantifiable impression of connection and identification that animated the first mommy blogs continues to be the most valuable commodity—materially and culturally—generated by these blogs. The current crop of mommy bloggers still benefits from this remarkable store of cultural goodwill; the main difference now is that this asset is now more nakedly pressed into profitable service, giving a whole new meaning to Baraitser's "strategic valorization" (7). Facilitated by visual mediums, such as Instagram, which eschew complex narratives, the "messy real life work of parenting" (Friedman 4) has been replaced by the appearance of perfection, and the mommy blogger has been refashioned as an (admittedly more authoritative sounding) influencer with a host of new digital tools calibrated to maximize the reach of their brand.

This newer version of maternal representation offers the mommy blogger an exceptional—if disquieting platform—from which to project their maternal subjectivity. The new mommy blogger is not a digital proxy in the sense that their readers might expect to identify with them, and in the process overwrite their subjectivity with their own, but rather the mommy blogger might now be seen as a digital subject. By this, I mean they inhabit the digital world they have created for themselves with what seems to me an almost unimpeachable singularity. So concretized and pervasive is this form of maternal subjectivity that many bloggers have turned their social media feeds into lucrative sources of income capable of providing for the abundant lifestyles they assiduously catalogue. The contemporary mommy blogger has commodified and corporatized their maternal subjectivity and, in the process, it must be noted, also their children's subjectivity. This is a remarkable example of a depiction of maternal experience— seemingly controlled by and under the aegis of the maternal subjects themselves—that foregrounds motherhood to an extraordinary degree.

In a 2017 article in the *Atlantic* titled "Instamom: The Enviable, Highly Profitable Life of Amber Fillerup Clark, Perfect Mother and Social-Media Influencer," Bianca Bosker details the distinctive elements of contemporary blogging that distinguish it from the previous generation of blogs:

> If the feats these blogs capture are familiar—dressing well, attending to children—this is a key part of the appeal; the women epitomize a new breed of celebrity, as public fascination expands beyond the rich and famous to the well-off and above-average. "We're seeing people following almost idealized versions of themselves," said Rob Fishman, a co-founder of Niche, an ad network for online Influencers that is now owned by Twitter. "It's this attainable perfection."

The key word is "idealized," as Fillerup Clark admits: "We always have to think of our life as 'Where can you take the prettiest pictures?'"

There is a paradox at play in the appeal of the Instamom. As with the previous iterations of mommy blogs, Fillerup Clarke's audience is motivated by a desire for connection and relation, but whereas readers of *Dooce* were attracted by frank depictions of motherhood, Fillerup Clark's readers are enticed by a materialistic impulse of illusory fulfilment that does little to disturb the idealization-denigration binary. Beyond marketing spin, "attainable perfection" signals a shift in the dialogic call and response relationship produced by blogging and in the language used to describe it. Readers are now referred to as followers—a term that has very different connotations, especially when paired with the neologism "influencer." Followers positions audiences as acolytes rather than peers, a dynamic that is evident in the words of twenty-nine-year-old Gena Baillis, quoted in Bosker's article, who looks to Fillerup Clark to help her become a better version of herself. In Baillis's case, this better version of herself involves "purchasing nail polish, camera gear, sports drinks, healthy snacks, and workout equipment" based on Fillerup Clark's recommendations.

These notions of attainable perfection and better selves sit uncomfortably with Rose's claim that mothers are the scapegoats for all human imperfection. On the surface, the extraordinary success of Fillerup Clark's blog *Barefoot Blonde* would seem to negate the disconnect between the veneration of motherhood and the ways in which the maternal subject's right to self-determination has historically been silenced or overwritten, but what are the implications of her success if it can be principally attributed to her shrewd deployment of the tropes of white, middle-class motherhood and femininity? Fillerup Clark is under no obligation to use her blog to challenge institutional assumptions about motherhood, but the scale of her success and resultant social capital generated by this success weighs upon and shapes our understanding of contemporary motherhood. Whereas "perfect mother" might once have been understood to reinforce ossifying and paralyzing notions of maternal subjectivity, here it refers to the source of Fillerup Clark's power as an influencer. The word "influencer" also bears examining in this context. If we see it as conferring greater cultural authority on these individual mothers and by extension their version of mothering, what do we make of their impulse towards the homogenization and sanitization of motherhood? The widespread sanctioning of Fillerup Clark's endorsement of a patriarchal and capitalist delineation of motherhood is not a valorization that encourages or endorses maternal heterogeneity or diversity. Furthermore, our understanding of the mother-child relationship as being rooted in the ethics of care is compromised by this blatant display of transactional capitalism. This professionalization of the personal and the maternal is perhaps the logical conclusion of neoliberal capitalism. What could be more congruent with the tenets of neoliberalism, with its insistent focus on the individual and the nuclear family, than this digital commodification of family life?

Maternal Ethics in the Digital Space

The ethical concerns of writing about one's children has long been a point of contention within maternal discourses—a concern that has been heightened by the sprawling, perpetual nature of the internet and the insistent blurring of the distinctions between public and private. In their article "Mommy Blogging and Deliberative Dialogical Ethics: Being in the Ethical Moment," Jaqueline McLeod Rogers and Fiona Joy Green identify what they see as the most prominent ethical issues of mommy blogging: "1) the potential for corporate exploitation, 2) generic expectations governing truth telling and misrepresentation, and 3) the need to protect the privacy of subjects (particularly that of our children who are dependents and/or minors)" (32). The blogging practices of Fillerup Clark's cohort with their reliance on using their children's images to sell products are particularly susceptible to all these concerns. When analyzing the ethical consequences of the enlarged digital presence of the Instamom, it must also be remembered that the content being created is predicated upon the performance of an intimate relationship in which one or more parties are dependent minors. McLeod Rogers and Green note that the act of mommy blogging involves a choice to "move into territory fraught with ethical questions about the rights and feelings of self and others" (39). The important notion here is choice, given bloggers and Influencers are autonomous adults making these choices on behalf of their children, many of whom are far too young to grasp the (potentially lifelong) consequences of internet stardom.

McLeod Rogers and Green propose that redefining mommy blogging as "a communicative act" rather than seeing it "solely as a form of self-expression" would encourage a sense of community among bloggers in which shared ethics might be agreed upon that discourage "maverick narcissism" (40). But it is hard to see how such a project might gain traction in the influencer economy, which trades upon a heavily stylized and constructed individualism seemingly designed and directed by bloggers. Although it could be argued that the level of self-determination and self-representation Instamoms enjoy in the digital sphere represents a radical challenge to the demand for maternal effacement, the co-opting of the becoming subjectivity of children in this project risks reinforcing what Baraitser terms "the tendency for abjection to cling to the maternal" (7). This brings us back to the original conundrum confronted by all mothers whose desire to tell their stories is complicated by the interconnected and contested nature of maternal subjectivity.

In her essay "Maternal Silence," Miri Rozmarin writes of the conflict she felt at the thought of recording details of her children's lives in a journal for posterity. "I felt like I was faking something," she writes, "like I was doing it for some future trial. Especially, I was bothered about addressing my experience of my children to their future selves. I felt bad about deciding what's important enough, smart or sweet enough to document, as if I would be editing their past and by that narrowing their future" (4). Rozmarin is pinpointing here the place where she feels her maternal subjectivity should give way to her children's subjectivity, but in doing so, does she preclude the possibility of any maternal writing? Rozmarin does not offer a definitive pronouncement on this, but rather prevaricates, saying in the one instance that recognizing the child's "open future" means that "maternal subjectivity can never be fully narrated" (4). A glance at Fillerup Clark's Instagram feed—or that of fellow high-profile bloggers such as Naomi Davis (*Love Taza*) and Rach Parcell (*Pink Peonies*)—suggests that, unlike Rozmarin, they feel comfortable mediating all aspects of their maternal and digital subjectivity via images of their children.

It is here I must confess to feeling conflicted in my critique of the Influencer mommy blogging model. On the one hand, I want to resist the foreclosing of resonant depictions of maternal subjectivity, and as detailed above, the Instamoms resonance is undeniable. On the other hand, as also detailed above, the digital resonance of their children has also been enlarged to a troubling degree, creating a landscape I find alienating in comparison to that I remember from my original engagement with mommy blogs. Writing about one's child may indeed represent an unwarranted intrusion on their individuation, but from a privacy perspective, the written word affords more space in which, and distance from which, the child may still be seen as a constructed character in the narrative rather than the embodied and inescapably identifiable presence captured in photographs. Many of the earlier blogs I was familiar with used pseudonyms for both themselves and their children to protect their anonymity. This had the effect of creating a textual environment in which mothers were able to write more freely while still creating a layer of obscurity for their child. The digital footprint being created by the Instamom for their children is of another magnitude. All claims to anonymity have been discarded by the mother on behalf of their children. Indeed, given the expansive and continuous panorama of the internet, it would be impossible to gauge exactly how far these photos figuratively travel or how many times they are viewed and by whom.

The tangled, ambivalent nature of the Instamom's challenge to maternal effacement is more disquieting than reassuring. Although it is perhaps too soon to make any definitive pronouncements on the contemporaneous phenomenon of Influencer blogging, it seems to me that much of the Instamom's power resides in their ability to project their subjectivity with an individualized prominence without coming into conflict with the pathologizing parameters the symbolic order has traditionally erected to stifle maternal self-determination. The ability to conceptualize a continuous, evolving maternal subjectivity that does not slide into abjection or neurosis while still working within the aegis of the symbolic order is a project that has eluded theorists, such as Kristeva, but it is the deftness of the Instamom's ability to not only work within the potentially stifling dictates of the symbolic but also to use them to their (financial) advantage by leveraging the cultural goodwill built up by the more thoughtful and radical contributions of the previous generation of mommy bloggers that unsettles me.

However, there are signs that this cultural goodwill is not limitless. Alongside the rise in the Influencer economy, a parallel discourse has emerged on websites like *Get off my Internets* devoted to critiquing bloggers like Fillerup Clark, Davis, and Parcell. In 2019, blogger and lawyer Christie Tate published a piece in *The Washington Post* detailing her daughter's reaction to discovering an already existent digital footprint inextricably intertwined with Tate's writing and blogging on motherhood. When confronted by her daughter's demand to know why there are all these pictures of her on the internet, Tate is unable to provide an explanation that soothes her daughter's outrage: "In the moment, I stammered, trying to buy time.... When that failed, I told her the truth: that I write about our family in essays and that sometimes

I include a picture. She was not comforted." Finding herself at a point where her maternal subjectivity comes into conflict with her daughter's separate subjectivity, Tate acknowledges her daughter has the right to expect to veto pictures and some content that relates to her (a right Tate ascribes specifically to her daughter's age, implying her daughter has no right to control representations of her younger self), but she stops short of embracing Rozmarin's version of maternal silence. Ultimately, Tate concludes she cannot promise not to write about her daughter because doing so "would mean shutting down a vital part of myself" (2019). Tate frames this as a refusal of "the cultural pressure for mothers to be endlessly self-sacrificing on behalf of their children"—a stance that generated considerable (perhaps unexpected) animus on social and digital media. Writing for *Slate* magazine, Ruth Graham was particularly scathing of what she saw as Tate's "callousness" and "narcissistic self-justification." Graham's outrage seems motivated by a belief that Tate's refusal to silence herself is a glaring transgression of cultural norms worthy of denunciation and scorn. A transgression, Graham muses with dark glee, that will be corrected when children like Tate's daughter write memoirs of their own, thus restoring the natural order of mother-child relations.

Similarly, a 2019 article in *Vanity Fair* on Australian-based American blogger Courtney Adamo offers a deep dive into the incongruities of the influencer economy. The overwhelming impression one gets from Chocano's article is of the ontological vertigo induced by the surreal intersection between commercialism and maternal sensibility straddled by bloggers like Adamo: "She still considers her feed her 'personal thing,' but there's something about the stream of photos—... the styled life, the sponsored content, the kids like modern-day von Trapps—that looks like a massive ad campaign." While not as nakedly hostile as Graham's article on Tate, Chocano nevertheless conveys a palpable ambivalence towards Adamo's professionalization of her family life, observing wryly that "Wilkie, [Adamo's son] whose entire life, including his birth at home, has been documented online is having an old-fashioned childhood—and that means no screens," leaving the unvoiced accusation of hypocrisy dangling.

Articles like Graham's and Chocano's, and the enduring presence of sites like *Get off my Internets*, indicate a fraying (but not necessarily a breakdown) of the goodwill that made mommy blogging such a lucrative pursuit. They also speak to the quasicelebrity status of bloggers. Although fame and fortune are glamorous and aspirational designations, they also come with a burden of cultural, social, and even political scrutiny, as Naomi Davis found when she confessed in an Instagram post to fleeing New York City in March 2020 at the height of the city's first outbreak of COVID-19. The backlash to Davis's flight was covered in *Buzzfeed* and *The New York Times*, which suggests that for all their excesses of signification, the mother as Influencer remains caught in up in the same restrictive cultural dynamics Jacqueline Rose identified, now with the added encumbrance of modern celebrity—a weight that must also be assumed by their children. The Instamom's valorization of motherhood may be strategically beneficial to their individual financial interests, but, ultimately, I believe it has less emancipatory potential for mothers at the cultural level. Rather, the radical communicative potential of the mommy blog has been squandered by the "maverick narcissism" McLeod Rogers and Green warned of. Whereas the original iteration of mommy blogging can be read as producing something new in that it opened up a space for mothers to reshape maternal discourse, by pointing the conversation back to the threat maternal subjectivity poses to the open future of the child, the influencer/Instamom model risks reemphasizing abjection and reanimating expectations of maternal effacement.

However, given the influencer model relies upon the confluence of specific economic and commercial imperatives that will only persist as long as profitability does, perhaps there is reason to believe it will be the more complex narratives of long form writing and storytelling that encompass reflection rather than just reaction that endure. Social media's emphasis on ego and self-representation might make it a compelling vehicle for the dissemination of narcissistic and capitalist impulses specific to our current moment, but it is precisely this myopic and reactive performativity that ensures its ultimate ephemerality. Although I do not propose to make any definitive claims regarding the future of maternal representation here, I suggest we look to Megan Rogers's conceptualization of maternal essays. If such a proposal can resist veering into cultural elitism or gatekeeping, traditional formats such as the essay ultimately offer more revolutionary potential for exploring the multiplicity of motherhood as a category than the relentless contemporality of social media. In this context, the internet does not completely relinquish all claims to radical disruption in the cultural reimagining of motherhood but remains a vital part rather than the totalizing whole of such a project. Most importantly, a more reflective kind of maternal writing allows for a grappling with the complex ethics of representation in ways that do not foreclose the mother's claim to representation by framing maternal silence as the most ethical gesture.

Endnotes

1. This chapter, like Rose's book, focusses on Western notions and experiences of motherhood. However, this is not to suggest that these are in some way more superior or important. Rather for the purposes of this discussion, I am writing within my own cultural framing and experience.

2. O'Reilly in particular for her coining of the term "matricentric feminism."

3. For a more comprehensive accounting of maternal representation on Instagram see May Friedman's article "Insta-Judgement: Irony, Authenticity and Life Writing in Mothers."

4. Parcell is technically considered a fashion blogger. Her blog rose to prominence before she became a mother, but since having children, Parcell has featured them heavily on blog and in her social media posts in both a personal context and in service of her business endeavours.

5. See Judith Butler's essay "The Body Politics of Julia Kristeva" for a discussion on what Butler sees as the shortcomings of Kristeva's semiotic theory in challenging maternal effacement.

Works Cited

Armstrong, Heather. *Dooce*. 2022, dooce.com/. Accessed 10 May 2022.

Baraitser, Lisa. *Maternal Encounters and the Ethics of Interruption*: Routledge, 2009.

Bosker, Bianca. "Insta Mom: The Enviable, Highly Profitable Life of Amber Fillerup Clark, Perfect Mother and Social-Media

Influencer." *The Atlantic*, March 2017,www.theatlantic.com/magazine/archive/2017/03/instamom/513827/eb. Accessed 10 May 2022.

Butler, Judith. "The Body Politics of Julia Kristeva" in *Ethics, Politics, and Difference in Julia Kristeva's Writing*, edited by Kelly Oliver, Routledge, 1993, pp. 164-78.

Chocano, Carina. "The Coast of Utopia." *Vanity Fair*, 2 July 2019, www.vanityfair.com/style/2019/07/the-coast-of-utopia-surfer-moms-instagram-influencers. Accessed 10 May 2022.

Davis, Naomi. *Love Taza*. 2020, lovetaza.com/. Accessed 10 May 2022.

Dean, Jodi. *Blog Theory: Feedback and Capture in the Circuits of Drive*. Polity Press, 2010.

Fillerup Clark, Amber. *Barefoot Blonde*. 2020, amberfillerup.com/. Accessed 10 May 2022.

Friedman, May. *Mommyblogs and the Changing Face of Motherhood*. University of Toronto Press.

Friedman, May. "Insta-Judgement: Irony, Authenticity and Life Writing in Mothers' Use of Instagram." *Interactions: Studies in Communication & Culture*, vol. 9, no. 2, 2018, pp. 169-81.

Graham, Ruth. "That Outrageous Mommy Blogger Who Refuses to Stop Writing About Her Kid Highlights a Key Parent-Child Generational Gap." *Salon*, 8 Jan. 2019, slate.com/human-interest/2019/01/mommy-blogging-christie-tate-generation-gap.html. Accessed 10 May 2022.

McLeod Rogers, Jacqueline, and Fiona J. Green. "Blogging and Deliberative Dialogical Ethics: Being in the Ethical Moment." *Journal of the Motherhood Initiative*, vol. 6, no. 1, 2015, pp. 31-49.

Hunter, Andrea. "Monetizing the Mommy: Mommy Blogs and the Audience Commodity." *Information, Communication & Society*, vol. 19, no. 9, 2016, pp. 1306-20.

Kristeva, Julia. *The Power of Horror: An Essay on Abjection*. Translated by Leon S. Roudiez. Columbia University Press, 1982.

Lopez, Lori. "The Radical Act of 'Mommy Blogging': Redefining Motherhood Through the Blogosphere." *New Media & Society*, vol. 11, no. 5, 2009, pp. 729-47.

Lorenz, Taylor. "Flight of the Influencers." *New York Times*, 2 Apr. 2020, www.nytimes.com/2020/04/02/style/influencers-leave-new-york-coronavirus.html. Accessed 10 May 2022.

McNeal, Stephanie. "An Influencer Is Getting Tons of Hate Online for Fleeing NYC with Her Five Kids for A Cross-Country Road Trip Amid the Coronavirus Pandemic." *BuzzFeed*,30 Apr. 2020, www.buzzfeednews.com/article/stephaniemcneal/an-influencer-is-getting-tons-of-hate-online-for-fleeing. Accessed 10 May 2022.

Parcell, Rach. *Pink Peonies*. 2020, rachelparcell.com/. Accessed 10 May 2022.

Rogers, Megan. "Beyond Blogging: How Mothers Use Creative Non-Fiction Techniques to Dislodge the Mask of Motherhood." *Journal of Family Studies*, vol. 21, no. 3, 2015, pp. 248-60.

Rozmarin, Miri. "Maternal Silence." *Studies in Gender and Sexuality*, vol. 13, no. 1, 2012, pp. 4-14.

Rose, Jacqueline. *On Not Being Able to Sleep: Psychoanalysis and the Modern World*. Chatto & Windus, 2003.

Rose, Jacqueline. *Mothers: An Essay in Love and Cruelty*. Faber & Faber, 2018.

Tate, Christie. "My Daughter Asked Me to Stop Writing about Motherhood. Here's Why I Can't Do That." *Washington Post*, 4 Jan. 2019, www.washingtonpost.com/lifestyle/2019/01/03/my-daughter-asked-me-stop-writing-about-motherhood-heres-why-i-cant-do-that/. Accessed 10 May 2022.

Chapter 2

Making Time and Space: Digital/Material Divisions and Maternal Life Writing

Astrid Joutseno

In the beginning of the new millennium, mothering, like almost everything else, has become a digital phenomenon. Mommy blogging has developed into a practice that impacts mothering. Yet when it comes to mothers, the relationship between digital and material is often presented as troubling (Lehto, "Bad Is the New Good"; Kaarakainen and Lehto; Jokinen).

In this chapter, I analyze the demarcations constructed in maternal online life writing between the private and public as well as the digital and material by seeing how blogs create distinctions of time and space. (For more on maternal life writing see Joutseno) Early definitions of the internet described potential to overcome material restrictions, identity markers, and even bodies (Nakamura; Kennedy). This vision was predicated on the belief that human embodiment was separable from the digital and their relationship was that of something real and its representation. Recent scholarship in (social) media studies and philosophy of science show that digitality and materiality merge via devices and technologies, narratives and affects as well as the human user as both subject and object (Barad, *Meeting the Universe Halfway*; Coole and Frost; Sloan and Quan-Haase; Laaksonen et al.; Paasonen, "Resonant Networks"). With the development of small carriable devices, such as smart phones and laptops, as well as internet connection nearly everywhere in the Northern hemisphere, the inseparability of the virtual and material is evident in everyday practices. Katherine Hayles describes this as a cognitive assemblance formed by humans and technology merging together in varying degrees through differing practices (Hayles, *Unthought* 118-19).

For centuries, those (self)identified as women have been restricted by rigid sociocultural rules, which defined them mostly as mothers and caregivers. Mothers were denied full citizenship, human rights, as well as the right to define their own experiences (Hallstein and O'Reilly; O'Reilly, "Maternal Theory"; Rich; Bueskens, "Mothers Reproducing the Social"). In the early twenty-first century, a wide discussion on the experiences of mothers and the cultures of mothering has emerged. Finally, the voices of mothers in the Northern hemisphere have begun to be heard in various social, political, and creative contexts, and matricentric feminists continue to develop the critical analysis of mothering (O'Reilly, *Matricentric Feminism*). This discourse appears in the contexts of late capitalist racist patriarchy, the institutions of intensive parenting (Ennis) and work, as well as the ideals of good mothering (O'Reilly, *Matricentric Feminism*; Rich; Friedman, *Mommyblogs*; DiQuinzio; Cleaf, "*Of Woman Born* to *Mommy Blogged*"; O'Reilly, "Maternal Theory"). Mothering is entangled in the novel digital turn with life writing online. Despite the scientific community's understanding of the digital as an assemblance and a multidirectional, webbed entity with its own kind of materiality (Paasonen, "Ihmisiä, Kuvia, Tekstejä Ja Teknologioita"; Hayles, *Unthought*), mommy blogs present a continued affinity to separating the digital from the material. This divisional idea appears common in all corners of social media and internet-related discussions. What is embedded in the dichotomy is the idea that life offline is more real and valuable, whereas online presence is less actual and can be harmful if not dangerous. The division evokes the oppositions presented between lived and narrated, private and public, embodied and represented, as well as subject and object—the dualistic discourses that have become the foundational troubles of postmodern thought (e.g., Butler). I propose that mothering in the early twenty-first century takes shape in the interpellation of a digital/material divide, which is a construction that materializes in specific intra-actions (Barad, *Meeting the Universe Halfway*; Hayles, *Unthought*). I address the following two-part research question in this chapter:

1) How is the digital/material divide constructed in maternal online life writing with the concepts of time and space?

2) What role does this divide perform for mothering as a cognitive assemblance and from the perspective of agential realism?

To begin addressing these questions, I first present Karen Barad's theory of agential realism and then my concept of maternal double space/time. Finally, I apply these to examples from blogs while analyzing their particular formulations of time and space.

This chapter is based on my analysis of English-language mommy blogs and sites. Their writing ranges between popular pioneers in mommy blogging to less followed blogs. Some blogs have turned into multiauthor media during the study. Some are professional and commercial agents; others update without monetary gain or a large audience. I have followed the blogs for a period of six to eight years. During this time, maternal online life writing has gone through transformations, and the qualitative research practices of digital material have developed (Bassett et al.; Markham). In the course of this study, I have lost access to some material, but most of it remains online. In this chapter, I discuss examples from the blogs/sites *Cup of Jo*, *LoveTaza*, *Blog a la Cart*, and *Somewhere Slower*. My approach combines matricentric feminist perspectives on mothering, the new materialist theory of mattering, as well as media studies insights on digitality and auto/biography studies' approach to understanding life writing and subjectivity (for example O'Reilly, *Matricentric Feminism*; Barad, *Meeting the Universe Halfway*; Paasonen, "Ihmisiä, Kuvia, Tekstejä Ja Tekno-logioita"; Douglas and Barnwell; Smith and Watson, "Virtually Me"; Poletti and Rak; Hallstein et al.).

Barad's theory of agential realism provides a framework for addressing digital/material borders as a construction that serves the blogger and is born in its iterations rather than some preexisting distinction. Previous studies of mommy blogging have often either assumed a representational approach to blogs, treating them as direct translation of lived experience into digital form, or have analyzed them only as text without addressing their connection to lived experience. Both approaches simplify the role of the medium in constructing the mommy blog and its subjects. I propose that with agential realism, this division can be addressed as a materialization rather than a prescribed condition. It is the idea that the virtual is never material and therefore unreal that I argue against, finding it dangerous in the context of the world we are co-constructing. I also wish to counter presentations of the digital/virtual as a threat to a preexisting form of mothering or family life. With these extensions towards and from quantum field theory, ethics, and feminist politics, I venture to examine maternal online life writing and its resonances with Barad's theory. My aim is not so much to prove this connecting "right" but to play with it as one possible "ghostly" entangled reconfiguration (Barad, "Trans-materialities" 407). My inquiry contributes to research in the fields of motherhood, social media, and auto/biography studies. This interdisciplinary approach facilitates analysis of online life writing and mothering as intersecting activities with impact on multiple fields of study and of acting. By tracing along the leaking boundaries inscribed in theories, fields of study and the act of blogging while mothering, I wish to address the overlaps, gaps, and messy distinctions that guard contemporary mothering.

Theory, Concepts, and Methodology: The Internet and Autobiographical Subject

In addition to gender studies, I conduct this research in the context of internet and social media studies and life writing studies. Recent research in social media and digital cultures acknowledge the relationality between so-called real life and narrative as well as their mutual constitutive roles and situatedness in social, political, and historical contexts (Sloan and Quan-Haase; Morrison, "Social Media"). Digital spaces are not translational surfaces representing materiality as virtual. Susanna Paasonen emphasizes the internet as a research object/subject that troubles knowledge production (Paasonen, *Figures of Fantasy*). She proposes that the internet is not a tool or a channel for communication but is involved in the production of the research subject; it is an assemblance or "an agencement" of technologies, applications, protocols, and experiences. Crucially, the internet is defined by multimodality—that is, the interlinking of text, image, platform design, links, and other things that appear to the user/creator (Paasonen, "Ihmisiä" 33-34). The internet has its own materiality.

In comparison to previous studies on maternal life writing online and the questions of private/public or digital/material spaces, I explore the construction of these distinctions rather than assume their existence. In my view, assuming a representational relationship between the lived and its online remediation narrows the role of the internet and blogs as passive platforms onto which a projection of the life of mothers is presented in the form of life writing. This view ignores that the writing and creation of posts are practices of making auto-biographical acts, which are part and parcel of the narrated digital mother of the blogs (Smith and Watson, *Reading Autobiography*; Smith and Watson, "Virtually Me"). For example, when Jaqueline McLeod Rogers and Fiona Joy Green raised concerns over mommy bloggers sharing narratives about their children, they presented it as a case of a representational private-public problem because children may not be able to give consent for their appearance in the digital publics ("Mommy Blogging"). I understand this worry to be grounded in a dualistic model of materiality and digitality. I present the digital/material as co-constructive and agential in their existence and refer to the concept of agential realism. I also show that the construction of privacy and publicity and the sense of control the blog authors have relates to norms of good mothering but also race and class.

Just like internet and mothering, life writing and the internet have been entwined from the start. As Laurie McNeill states, "Auto/biographical acts have become an inherent element of Internet culture and practices" (160). How lives are narrated online is therefore a central concern in the fields of life writing and in social media studies. Questioning the utility in reading virtual selves as the equivalent of the lived self, Anna Poletti and Julie Rak have emphasized the importance of considering the "self as an effect of representation" and have pointed out that more than questioning what is being "evidenced through online practices," approaches rely on the chosen methodologies of reading (6). Sidonie Smith and Julia Watson conflate identities and subject positions and suggest that the autobiographical subject is "an … assemblage of subject positions through which self-understanding and self-positioning are negotiated" ("Virtually Me" 82 and 71). In these definitions, the medium is indistinguishable from the autobiographical self. I suggest that viewed with Barad's agential realism, life writing does not equal representation of the lived, but it nevertheless impacts the lived co-constructing it. This means that maternal digital life writing influences its writers and readers and their ways of living and mothering by creating insights and critique of norms, by strengthening them, or by creating new ones. I argue that blogging or digital life writing is not a testimony of life but an extension of it. It matters what blogs are read as evidence for.

Mothers and Mothering

In *Of Woman Born*, Adrienne Rich delineates mothering from the institution of motherhood. She argues that the institution (mother-hood) governed by patriarchy has ignored the experiences of mothering and thus what is known about mothering is limited. Mothering as work, practice, identity, and as a source of women's oppression or joy have been troubling and controversial concepts in the history of feminist thinking (DiQuinzio; Bueskens, "Introduction"; Green; Hollway; O'Reilly, "Maternal Theory"; McRobbie). I rely on the emergent body of work in matricentric feminism in approaching mothering as a material, cultural, social, and political activity. (O'Reilly, *Matricentric Feminism*; Hallstein et al.) In using the term "mothering," I divorce this practice from binary gender or sexual identities as well as from biological ties between parents and children. Mothering can be performed by any adult so choosing. According to matricentric feminism, mothering is socially and culturally defined activity of care, which benefits from the deconstruction of its patriarchal organization. Mothering is shared between parents and untied from gender expectations or heteronormativity (O'Reilly, *Matricentric Feminism*). At the heart of matricentric feminism is a matrifocal research position—the idea that mothers' experiences in the world are moulded by mothering in tandem with other intersecting categories, of which little attention has been paid. According to Andrea O'Reilly, mothers are marginalized as both women and mothers and remain outside the equality advancements of women without children (*Matricentric Feminism* 2). The proliferation of online mothering narratives coincides with not only the technological inventions and availability of the internet but also the intensification of mothering itself. Intensive mothering refers to the style of parenting currently held up as the standard of good mothering in the West. It is defined by the idealization of the continued presence of the mother as the sole caregiver and portrays this position and labour as natural and enjoyable (Ennis; O'Reilly, "Maternal Theory"). Intensive mothering is characterized by particular activities: cosleeping, carrying a baby in a sling, breastfeeding, status safeguarding, and controlling the child's environment in terms of safety and desired outcome (Ennis 70). These mothering ideals are also entangled in promoting whiteness, heterosexuality, cisgender identities, consumerism, and class status. These conflicted ideals (and resistance to them) permeate the blogs in this study.

Maternal Online Life Writing

Maternal online life writing comprises mommy blogs and coauthored media sites, which some blogs have turned into. In this chapter, I do not analyze social media accounts, although they too form a large part of maternal online life writing. Previous studies of digital maternal life writing studied blogging, but since in the period I have conducted my research, the scene of maternal presence online has shifted from one platform to many, I have named my research object *maternal online life writing*, not mommy blogging (Joutseno). The term addresses the multimodal, shifting quality of the material. Maternal online life writing follows somewhat in the footsteps of epistolary traditions and diary writing, but early mommy blog research identified it as a genre defined by technology and affordances of its own (Friedman, *Mommyblogs* 42; Petersen; Poletti and Rak 4-5). The personal tone is achieved through conventions of narration and the assembling of an identity autobiographically (Morrison, "Autobiography in Real Time"). The parts of this construction are text, images, video, the blog template visuals and organization, as well as the stylistic uses of first-person singular in personal narrative (Smith and Watson, "Virtually Me"; Poletti and Rak; Weller et al.). Crucially, the blogs facilitate comments from the readers and foster a conversational tone. There is no reliable estimate of how many mommy blogs exist. Even conservative estimations count them in their millions. They continue to be some of the most popular content on the internet. Blog proliferation started with easy-to-use web-design platforms, such as Blogger and WordPress, emerging in the early 2000s (Weller et al.). By the early 2010s, some mommy blogs had developed into businesses, and their writers had become famous (Cummings; Cleaf, "Our Mothers Have Always Been Machines"). At the same time, millions of mothers continued to blog without monetary gain.

Maternal online life writing facilitates self-expression and communication among those who mother (Friedman, *Mommyblogs*; Friedman, "*Mommy Blogs*"). It has become one facet of the matrilinear discourses about care, gender, and lifestyle as well as being a mother in a sociopolitical and cultural structure that used to not find the experiences and voices of mothers important. By the late 2010s, reading and writing mommy blogs had become somewhat normalized parts of contemporary Western mothering for mothers with internet access (Friedman, *Mommyblogs*; Cleaf, *Blogging through Motherhood*; McDaniel et al.). In one sense, mommy blogs are in-between spaces—they are not quite media, not quite discussion forums, nor are they social media or literature. Readers navigate to maternal life writing to find discourses but also to escape their everyday surroundings. On a blog, readers and authors alike can be seen, heard, and connect. Neoliberalism and the intensification of digital and material labour are crucial in iterating the form that blogs take (Cleaf, "Our Mothers Have Always Been Machines"; Steiner and Bronstein).

The embodied experiences of mothering are often conveyed in relation to agility regarding self and identity. It appears that the digital identity technologies, which is how some online life writing scholars have characterized blogs and social media, work well in this mode of maternal transformation (Poletti and Rak, 3–22). Since the mainstreaming of social media, writers of digital autobiographical narratives slide between social media platforms (e.g., Instagram, Facebook, and Twitter) and blogs or websites producing a presence via multiple digital nodes (Lehto, "Ambivalent Influencers"). For example, an Instagram post can provide a glimpse into a moment by presenting an image and some text, then linking it to the blog, where a new post has appeared.

The transformation of digital life writing together with the technological development impacts the narrative construction of a maternal self. For this chapter, I look into maternal life writing on blogs and sites.

Research Material

I will draw examples from English-language mommy blogs and/or sites from the US, Australia, and the UK. To identify relevant posts for this chapter, I reread the blog archives and collected posts that explicitly addressed blogging and family life or discussed issues around blogging, privacy, and shifts in how the blogger situated herself. I conducted my analysis and drew examples from these thematically collected posts. The images in the posts were mostly portraits of the writers themselves, underlining the personal tone and identifying the blogs with the mother-author. All posts include photographs. Considering them in conjunction with the text produces my analysis, although I have had to limit the description of the images, as there are so many of them. With understanding the internet as an assemblance and the mothers online as an assemblance, I consider visuals as important to the posts as the text is (Hayles, *Unthought*; Paasonen, "Ihmisiä"). Examples are introduced and ordered according to the two main tropes with which I approach the digital/material division.

I first discuss blogs that use temporal measures in their construction of a separation between the material and digital. The second part of the analysis focuses on the employment of spatial tropes in constructing borders between their digital and material family life. In my analysis, I used the practices of thematic close reading and note taking (Federico; Schell and Rawson). This meant that in addition to reading from the perspective of the chosen themes, I allowed the texts to show what arose from them and how it related to the overall analysis. My focus is on a small dataset of "thick data"—that is, I work with a small sample set with great thematic relevance.

This approach leans on the practices of auto/biography and literary studies methods. I also draw from the feminist critique of the role of big data in digital culture studies, data mining, and new technologies with emphasis on techno-fiction over differences and the unmeasurable qualities of subjectivities, which the preface to *Furious: Technological Feminism and Digital Futures* outlines (Bassett et al.). Although I analyze examples from individual posts and blogs, the examples model discourses that occur across the mommy blogs in my research material. The posts and the blogs themselves are often reactions to trends; in the blogosphere particularly, they connect by using similar vocabularies, sharing affects and views, and borrowing and circulating representational styles (Petersen; Morrison, "Social Media, Life Writing"). Even though these are facets of affinity and genre building, they are also tenets of a discourse on mothering.

The Digital/Material Divide

Most of the blogs present the digital/material divide as a question of separating the online and offline realms. I approach these separations by producing a reading with Barad's theory of agential realism. Barad provides a vocabulary for naming the material/virtual forces at play while questioning their existence as separate entities. These reconfigurations suggest what the blogs also evidence: maternal online life writing is formulated and realized in its material/virtual[1] iterations. With the help of Barad, I underline the relational co-construction of materiality and virtuality and their fluency. I take Barad's method as a generous invitation to imagining anew the (dis)connections and rewiring—much like Donna Haraway's theoretical and methodological contributions—between the concepts of relating among matter and mattering (Barad, "Transmaterialities"). I am drawn to working with Barad because they facilitate the examination of the material and virtual as fluent, relational, and co-constructive while always recognizing them as political. Their theoretical offering is to suggest that everything is already full of the potential of (dis) connection and the queer or the monstrous are always already part and parcel of a given construction (Barad, "Transmaterialities").

Agential realism is a set of concepts, which develops a quantum physics understanding of matter towards multidisciplinary (social and cultural) explorations of subjectivity and performativity with the aim of constructing a feminist ethical understanding of relating. Born from a posthumanist and postanthropocentric view of subjectivity and the agential characteristics of material (not only words or cultures or human subjectivity), agential realism offers a way to not dwell on the border—the gap between material and digital—but to engage with the performative creation of online maternal life writing and the movement or lines of causality and breaking of the virtual/material borders as they occur (Barad, *Meeting the Universe Halfway* 132-85). In short, agential realism understands subjects and objects as taking form in relation to each other. Instead of interactivity, which presupposes an entity exists before its encounter with another, Barad talks of intra-activity:

> Concepts like "life state" or "alive-ness" are not merely ideational; rather, they are specific material configurations. And the semantic and ontological indeterminacy is resolvable only through the existence of a specific material arrangement that gives meaning to particular concepts to the exclusion of others, thereby effecting a cut between "object" and "subject," neither of which pre-exists their intra-action (Barad, "Living in a Posthuman Material World" 170).

Therefore, matter and discourse are emergent only in relations, as are time and space. So instead of understanding time/space as containers of material subjects which then can be discursively represented, Barad's phenomena occur via intra-action, in which through processes of agential cuts, some things come to matter whereas others are excluded from mattering. This process is not linear and does not follow a causal contingency because quantum physics concludes that there are no given trajectories but always a renewed possibility taking place in any intra-action. Barad's aim is to deepen the reach of performativity as presented by Judith Butler. Barad suggests that performativity applies to everything: "Event and things do not occupy particular positions in space and time; rather, space, time and matter are iteratively produced and performed" (Barad *Meeting the Universe Halfway*, 393). She constructs a performative way out of the represented/real conundrum, into which analysis of mommy blogs and other digitally consumed/produced material often threatens to succumb. Barad takes interest in the "life" and "lived" that auto/biography studies locates as distinct from the narrated. She notes that the presumption of priority of living before narrating is false because there is no prior aliveness but only "specific material configurations" taking form in the cuts (Barad, "Living in a Posthuman Material World" 170).

In my analysis of the blogs, I suggest that mothering is an apparatus (constitutive and constituted of material and discursive elements), and mommy blogs form another apparatus (in intra-active relation to mothering as also a phenomenon). Barad writes the following: "Apparatuses are specific material configurations, or rather, dynamic (re)configurations of the world through which bodies are intra-actively materialized. That is, apparatuses are the practices of mattering through which intelligibility and materiality are constituted (along with an excluded realm of what doesn't matter)" (Barad, *Meeting the Universe Halfway* 169-170). Agential cuts, which are made of a set of intra-actions and are the chosen practices of a given apparatus, are what begin the separation of matter into objects and subjects. I suggest that the genre of mommy blogging is born in agential cuts. The conventions that take care of the upkeep of the genre but also, become prescriptive of mothering itself.

Whereas I apply agential realism to an analysis of the digital/ material as well as temporal/spatial rifts on online maternal life writing, Paasonen applies this consideration to digital materiality and its relationship to the research material as well as to the researcher. Similar to Hayles and Barad, Paasonen not only suggests that digital becomes its own materiality but also points out that in archiving and organizing online material, the researcher creates a new dataset, which, for example, lacks some of the elements of how one interacts with the material online (Hayles, *How We Became Post-Human*; Hayles, *My Mother Was a Computer*; Paasonen, "Ihmisiä"). Paasonen describes this as the agency of the researcher entangling with the potentiality of the material—that is, the researcher is creating the project, both its questions and possible answers (i.e., the knowledge and its object). In this sense, content cannot be separated from the medium it is produced by.

Importantly for this chapter, Paasonen underlines that the materiality that digitality produces is not the divide between the lived and represented but its own form taking with technology. For example, technological devices and software create images in the specific ways that a blog or a social media template has set for it. The notions of the specificity of a materialization conjure up the virtual/material relationality: intra-action. Hayles has articulated the underlying dichotomy as a question of analogue versus digital. She suggests that it is necessary to look at their cooperation as a producer of structures, which she visualizes as feedback loops:

Complex feedback loops connect humans and machines, old technologies and new, language and code, analog processes and digital fragmentations. Although these feed-back loops evolve over time and thus have a historical trajectory that arcs from one point to another, it is important not to make the mistake of privileging any one point as the primary locus of attention, which can easily result in flattening complex interactions back into linear causal chains. (Hayles *My Mother Was a Computer* 29-30)

The idea of the feedback loop is helpful in illustrating the relationality of material, discursive, cognitive, and semantic contact zones, which Barad's agential realism proposes.

Concern has been expressed regarding the increasing sense of fluidity between the material and virtual aided by technological devices, such as smart phones. Within the feminist critical tradition, Barad has come to be questioned for their wish to dilute dualities with the kinds of complex materializations that quantum physics proposes. Their combination of this with a yearning for a nondualistic theorizing of agency, ethics, and politics has been criticized. Their arguments involving the so-called hard sciences have been dubbed a masculinist move, a kind of analogy application of science to social science, whereas their ethics have been described as vague (Braunmühl). Barad's identification as one of the new materialist theorists has also raised questions. Ahmed has argued that new materialism is a name for a group of ignorant feminists making unfounded claims about feminism's ignorance of the body and material subjectivity, and thus presenting their contributions as ground breaking, when in fact bodies and materializations have always been at the centre of feminism. In any case, Barad's voice has been inspirational, maybe even triggering. Those who seek to engage with Barad's theorizing credit them with deepening understanding of how textuality or discourse is "alive" and material, as are inanimate things (Freitas 743-44) and how performativity is visible even on the level of the smallest particles in the world. I do not wish to propose any finalizing arguments as to the correctness of any one theory; instead, I engage with agential realism as a tool for analyzing the boundary building between the material and virtual. I argue that these boundaries are necessary for political agency, the safety of children and parents, and the construction of new modes of living for the ever-changing cognitive assemblances.

Maternal Double Space/Time

Earlier research on mothering identified it as a node of temporal transformation. Time becomes defined through the mothering practices, but it also is given meaning and value in the social constructions of care as labour or as the naturalized duty of mothers (for example Baraitser; Fannin and Perrier; Daly and Reddy). Mariana Thomas has suggested that mothering creates an experience of time as still and nonlinear; she names this maternal time and describes it as connecting the mother to a deep time of the past. Thomas argues that the "ongoingness" of time and the difficulty of putting this experience into language produce a formlessness, which, in turn, can lead to new forms of expression (73-79). Functioning as a cognitive assemblance, a mommy blogger and a mother, engaged in the activities of blogging, reading, and mothering create a particular experience of temporality. Maternal online life writing addresses this particular construct of time, as it speaks of entangled relations between time and subjects, as I show with examples. In my view, these knots are some of the new forms born in the enfolding of mothering and digitality. In conducting research of maternal online life writing, I find that time appears doubly; split into simultaneous on and offline times.

In previous studies of mommy blogging, this doubling of labour has been found in understanding mothering as carework, occurring simultaneously with the virtual labour of blogging. Both maternal and digital labour also offset the capitalist patriarchal definition of work, but in Kara van Cleaf's view, they have come to be consumed by the demands set by this prevailing system (*Blogging through Motherhood*, 14-150). A feminist breakage in this doubling of time the blogs describe would require the reevaluation of both mothering and care as well as refiguring the logic of working for wages. Lisa Baraitser has claimed that these constructs hold anyone mothering or working in a relationship to time in which it signifies a commodity (404-05). Baraitser puts together the conceptualizations of "postmaternal" by Julia Stephens and "postwork" by Kathy Weeks and arrives at postmaternal (Baraitser; Stephens). In the context of psychoanalytic approaches to the maternal, Baraitser defines postmaternal in relation to time "as the contamination of love and hate in psychic life that could be seen across the shared field of mother-child relations. Its emergence requires the time that it takes to 'get a life,' a repetitive return to the site of emotional contamination, and the mattering of emotional labour" (407). In light of these perspectives, I present maternal double space/time as the constitution of time under the conditions of the capitalist, patriarchal organization of care and labour as facets of work.

The blogs present time as an uncontrollable organizer of everyday life. Furthermore, time appears to hold particular qualities when it shows up in maternal online life writing. Similarly, spaces are evoked in the examples both as material and virtual. In the research, material questions of space occur mostly together with discussions about online privacy. I suggest that in the context of maternal online life writing, agential cuts can be understood not only as the doubling of time and space but also as the conventions of utilizing personal narrative to produce subjectivity. I present maternal double space/time as a characteristic of maternal online life writing. It impacts the experience of mothering and leads to specific practices. The doubling of time and space describes how a sense of duality persists when mothering in a digital/material continuum. In the light of my research and the following analysis of the examples, I suggest that maternal online life writing creates a maternal double space/time in which mothers tell their digital narratives while they do their mothering.

Making Time

Next, I examine how the digital/material divide is constructed through temporal shifts. In thinking with Barad, the often presented order of having an experience first and then writing about it next—writing as mediation—becomes not an inaccurate hierarchy. The treatment of text, online or otherwise, should not be from the epistemological perspective of experience's primacy because according to quantum theory, time too is capable of transforming just like space (Freitas 743-44). This is another reason for not reading posts as a mediation of experience. Instead, I trace the updates the blogs websites have undergone over the years and note how life changes manifest in the posts. I propose that the agential cuts leading to the agential separability of a mommy blogger include at least the following: honesty or realness achieved through temporal immediacy, coherence achieved via frequent posting, and presence, which is constructed also in relation to a sense of time that is continuous and predictable.

The first example from *Blog a la Cart: Love Letters to A Dead Woman* illustrates how time appears circular: In the example, the oldest daughter of the blogger reads the blog archive for the first time (Cart). Ash Cart started *Blog a la Cart* in 2009 and focused on the Cart family's life in rural Vermont. The site remains online, although it has not been updated recently. In addition to the blog and its archive, the site houses Cart's portfolio of photography and contact information. She can be hired for wedding and family photography. As part of the blog content, Cart has posted birth stories that she has photographed for her customers. After the sudden death of the author's mother in 2016 and the birth of her third child, as well as the family's relocation to a village, the blog transformed into a log of letters directed to the dead mother. Since 2016, post frequency has dwindled, and in 2018 and 2019, only one new post was published. Other than working as an advert for the narrator's photography, the blog has not incorporated advertising or followed the path of professionalization. Instead, it appears as a personal record, a love letter, and a project aware of its feminist potentialities—a recording of the everyday life so often considered dull, uncreative, uneventful, and unworthy of recording or publishing.

In the post "120 Months" from May 18, 2019, Cart addresses her oldest daughter, Sunny, on her tenth birthday. The post is mostly made of photographs (twenty-two in total) as a celebration. There is a picture from each one of her daughter's ten years and a stream of images that feature daughter and mother together at different stages of the past decade. In these images, two smiling faces stare at the camera or each other. The visuals are of special moments, celebrations, rainbow cakes, candles, and hugging. More than a stylized stream of ideals, the post is an ad-hoc selection ordered by each lived year. In between the pictures the text addresses the daughter in letterform. The blogger praises her child, describes her qualities, and offers her wishes for her future. She mentions that Sunny has now read the blog archive herself:

> I can picture you sighing and gently smiling as you read that sentence, as you have noted that that is the sentiment of all of my birthday letters to you: the onslaught of time juxtaposed by the sweetness of the present. Because, yes, you've now read this here blog, and all of the letters. And that is what I dreamed you'd do. And here we are, a decade later, and the very words I wrote for

you above all others are being processed and understood and read by your very eyes. It is a wonder to behold you grow into a person who can now relate to her mother in this way. I so adore this stage. I so adore you. ("120 Months")

Here, the maternal narrative becomes a part of a spiraling story in time. For the first time viewed by one of her subjects, Sunny, who until now, has appeared in images and via the mother's narrative perspective. We do not hear Sunny in the post this time either, but her role changes. Her meaning to the blog is reliant on her agency turned towards the maternal life writing. Cart points to this in saying that the daughter now relates to the mother in a new way. The reference the writer makes to prioritizing the blog as an archive for her children points to another function of mommy blogging: They are entangled in the making and archiving of family memory and—being public—cultural memory. José van Dijck has suggested that a multimodality made possible via digital archiving becomes part of the process of remembering through the availability and incorporation of technologies, such as digital cameras and the internet ("MyLifeBits" 124). I understand blogs as part of this novel system of memorizing—described by Paul Arthur as the dangerous enhancement of material memory with digital technologies, which do not necessarily lead to more remembering, even though the quantity of pictures can rise rapidly, but to the ephemerality of generational remembrance (Arthur). The archival motivation for maternal online life writing was especially underlined in the early phase of blogging, when it was not considered a profession or done for commercial reasons, but its traces are visible in Cart's post and her online life writing at large (Jezer-Morton).

Thinking of this post with agential realism constructs an elliptical movement that manifests as a decade. The mother of a baby begins to publish life writing online; an archive builds, and the passing of time impacts the blog, for example, when it recentres around grief over losing the author's own mother and so forth. Everyone's relation to the blog is shifting. The digital/material division on *Blog a la Cart* is born in the enfolding of the relations and agencies of family members as subjects and readers, or in relation to the dead mother of the author, to whom the life writing is directed. The changes manifest as lessening in posting frequency, a sense of time passing in silence—happening someplace else. Family life does not necessitate blogging as a structure that maintains coherence, although it does hinge on other devices related to temporality to remain intelligible. Still, in online life writing about mothering, existence is maintained by posting and a sense of honesty or "realness," which becomes an affirmation that the narrative is not a fiction. It is born in the intimate connections with mothering's unfolding.

A sense of unity between the digital and material is maintained via continuous presence online. The more regularly posts appear or social media updates are made, the more believable or lifelike the online presence becomes (McNeill 149). Both the blogger and reader begin to separate life and narrative more when temporal gaps appear. The blog *Somewhere Slower* is an example of this development. It is a popular mommy blog focusing on travel tips for families created and maintained by Courtney Adamo and her partner. In 2015 the Adamo family took a leap year travelling in the Americas and Australia while blogging about it. By 2018, the family had settled in Australia, and their posts became less frequent. The blog now updates irregularly. The author addresses the growing gap between her offline life and the increasing silence online: "It's been five months since my last blog post. I'm sure most of the readers here have given up hope of new content by now! There have been so many things I've wanted to write about, and yet I haven't found the time to do so. I would really love to share about our new home and the renovation process and design ideas we have" ("Ouahu, Hawaii: Three Quick Days"). In her discussion of the infrequency of posting, time appears as a widening barrier between living with the family in a new home in Australia and life writing. Time unravels uncontrollably, rendering the blogger incapable of posting. With the perspective of agential realism, I construe that multiple agential cuts[2] are affecting not only the mother, who is in the throes of changes, but also the blog. The phenomena are mothering and the blog, although the blog may also be an apparatus related to the phenomenon of mothering; these may overlap. Yet for the purposes of presenting subjectivity on a blog, the notion of time as an inevitable force releases the writer from fully addressing her agential role in her absence online. The infrequent posting nevertheless increasing incoherence.

The post itself is similar to others on the blog: a collage of twelve photographs, plus a banner picture above the post title. In a familiar manner, the post lists what to do, what to eat, and where to stay in

Honolulu. By constructing a costumery advice post, the narrative holds on to the idea of the blog, whereas the content and the infrequency of posting suggest a transformation—one that will appear in relation to and as intra-actions of time; the digital/material materializations of the blog/mother. Temporal predictability appears mandatory for maternal online life writing. The sense of linear time online breaks easily, and when it does, the "realness" of the life narrative is compromised. Samuel Veissiere has described how this is true for all kinds of networked online interactions, including email and social media. He discovered during stints researching in the Amazonian rainforest, where there was no internet access, that his online absence came to be interpreted as total absence from life by his kin and work associates alike (218).

The *Somewhere Slower* example shows how time materializes as an inevitable dividing instrument in online life writing. Evoked by the blogger, time also becomes a measuring apparatus, which designates transformations in the subject and object positions (*Blog a la Cart*). Finally, in the blog *LoveTaza*, time entangles with the transformation of the maternal subject grappling with narrative coherence. "Some News: I'm Writing a Book," from *LoveTaza*, addresses a division between the material and digital (Davis). The chasm appears via temporal shifting, which the writer describes as she reveals she has been writing a book of essays. The post begins with photographs of the author in a green coat posing on the steps of a Manhattan building. The images depict a cheerful fresh-faced beauty, posing dancerlike in her colourful outfit. As usual, the author appears stylish and humorous to the point of not taking herself too seriously. The writing constructs two locations of separate but linked narratives. One is the material, in which a manuscript is being put together for publication. The other is the blog, to which she pledges her faith and sounds guilty for having taken on the other assignment of life writing. The guilt expressed over the secret work is suggestive of the imperative to construct temporal immediacy online (Morrison, "Social Media, Life Writing"). The facets of life that the writer assumes will become known at some moment, negatively impact the narrative construction, and widen the gap between material and digital. Additionally, I read this as an example of the trajectory that a professional mommy blogger in the 2010s often forges. From my research project, I have learned that maternal online life writing can lead to invitations from publishers to publish a book—a memoir, fiction, journalism, and other forms of creative publishing. It is also evidence of the privileging of a published book over a popular blog, which constitutes another layer of preferring the tangible materiality over what is considered the ephemerality of the digital. The blog is transitory and shapeshifting in its entanglements with the creation of the blogger. Narrating transitions such as this one requires repeated assurances of the continuity of digital life writing. Not knowing about a behind-the-scenes book project has most likely not impacted the sense of presence that readers have experienced, but the author experiences a rupture, tearing open the linearity if time. In this section, I have shown how maternal online life writing employs time both as a necessary barrier between private and public lives and how time's passing can threaten the authenticity of the online maternal narrative. Next, I discuss spatial divisions in the same context.

Making Space

In this second analysis section, I discuss the differing strategies blogs assume to separate private life from what has become a career. This division evokes questions of space. Barad reminds that time or space are not preexistent but unfold in relation to phenomena (*Meeting the Universe* 180). My concept of maternal double space/time becomes evident in the following. The sense of spatial and temporal doubling is constituted in the separation that the narratives produce. In the examples, the material demands of mothering are often contrasted with time spent in the digital space, wherein time appears like a black hole—eating chunks from the everyday through increased online activities and connections that have to be maintained. I also discuss how normative whiteness affects the strategies regarding privacy and spaces. The needs that occurred online required material arrange-ments, such as moving to a new house, or they impacted the kinds of sharing that materialized on the blogs. In the examples I analyzed, privacy of children was mostly offered as the motivation for dividing the material and virtual. Noting that in some cases the visibility of children becomes an intentional strategy increasing safety rather than decreasing it.

The construction of work and home spaces in maternal online life writing demarcates spaces on and offline. The goal of this division is to perform better as parents by adhering to the ideals of intensive parenting as well as to avoid discussing such issues as race and class. I first discuss *Cup of Jo*, a popular mothering and lifestyle site, which was started as a blog by Joanna Goddard in 2007. In 2012, Goddard was the sole author of her blog. The post "Blogging as a Career" addresses how what began as a hobby turned into a full-time job. The post describes starting in 2007 to get over a breakup and how slowly the writing transformed. The site first made some money by hosting adds, and then in 2011, the blog became her fulltime job. Goddard humorously discusses that she sometimes gets recognized by readers, which breaches the isolation she experiences while constructing posts.

One of the negative side-effects of blogging according to Goddard is working alone from her bedroom. Goddard writes extensively about the loss of a distinction between work and leisure: "Working on vacations/Christmas/weekends/etc. since I started *Cup of Jo* five years ago, I don't think I've ever taken a vacation where I didn't spend some time working—including our honeymoon. Blogging never stops, and running your own business never stops" ("Blogging as a Career"). Goddard associates the loss of separation between online life writing and living with her working alone. It is likely that since becoming a multiauthored site, it is easier to take breaks from upkeep. Still, I view this inseparability as a function of the maternal double space/time: Since vacations and family reunions are the subjects of the life narrative, it becomes challenging to create time and space that do not serve as potential material. The family members are therefore not just present on the blog, but the blog materializes in their lives.

A need for distinguishing between the material and virtual arises in tandem with a need for privacy. In this configuration, the virtual becomes public, and the material private. In 2017, Goddard posted "A Personal Note" on her site. By this time, her blog had turned into a multi-authored site. Every now and then, Goddard wrote posts for the media in the same personal style familiar from the blog's earlier days. "A Personal Note" discloses that for a long time, the author's family had been facing troubles that were not addressed online. Without identifying the problem, she addresses discomfort when posting happy updates on social media and the site while at home her life had become difficult:

I haven't mentioned it on the site, but our family has been dealing with something for the past few years, and it has been very disorienting and emotional and hard to navigate. I had an especially hard time this winter as we were struggling to figure out a new element. I want so, so, so much to talk about it and tell you everything and connect with other parents in similar situations, and maybe I can at some point, but right now, it's not my story to tell. But I wanted to at least say something now because when I look at the blog or Instagram, it's all true (we did throw a fun dinner party, we did go to the beach), those photos show such a small part of the story. And this other thing is going on with one of our children that monopolizes my heart and brain and is the #1 worry that keeps me up at night. ("A Personal Note")

The post suggests worry about a child. Her children had been visually and narratively present on the blog from its very beginning. Now the author acknowledges the agency of her children in relation to the unknowability of the impact of her online narrative on their everyday lives. On one side of the scale weighs the pull of disclosing intimate material about struggle and "connecting with other parents in similar situations"; on the other is the privacy of her children. The post addresses the material/digital divide as a question of privacy, which brings to the fore the concerns that McLeod and Green expressed over the ethics of representing those who cannot give consent ("Mommy Blogging"). Acknowledging the vulnerability of the author or the unfinished quality of the family and their narrative is a common life writing practice, which may both protect the narrator and her subjects while renewing the contract of intimacy between bloggers and their followers (Friedman, *Mommyblogging* 77). This post produces a kind of compromise that incorporates parental affect—it may help the mother to write about her worries online—but remains silent about details concerning the children.

This compromise holds on to maternal life writing practices online while putting forwards and adhering to the notion that children have to be protected from the online publics. It holds together separate spaces or the maternal double space/time while attempting to address their messy entanglement. The notion that digitality has its own materiality via technologies entangled in its production (Paasonen, "Ihmisiä") is accompanied by the mattering of the discourses, which produce digital materiality and space. The literary production of material and digital separation generates a kind of online privacy. It treats blogs and social media spaces as publics from which children need protection. Interestingly, the author negotiates between good motherhood and being a good blogger, which require different sets of actions. In Barad's terms, whereas some materialize, others become excluded.

In the example, Goddard creates a distinction between digital and material as spaces, thus assuming one set of behaviours and discourses in one space and another set elsewhere. Maternal online life writing also addresses the desire for a separation between home and work as an issue relating to ideal parenting. The material/digital entwining of time and space becomes a problem when work and family time become inseparable. It is the presence or absence of digital devices that signals which time is running. The qualities of digitality create a specific space/time. Tasks are completed online via various applications, programs, and formats; discussions can be had without seeing faces or by seeing them on a screen. Transactions, organizing, planning, and publishing are done without entering material locations or a specific time—anything can be accessed at home while online. Nothing appears to consume effort or time. A time optimism is born out of this illusion of ease. Yet each post and social media update or email to advertisers consists of planned, written, photographed, published, and managed actions. Online presence becomes time away from home despite these two presences overlapping and taking place in the same location. A body's presence is not enough. This is what the research material solves by making arrangements via allotted space use. One mommy blog writer describes moving to a bigger home, whereby constructing boundaries between blogging (work) and family life happens spatially. Yet maternal online life writing nearly always includes pictures of children to go with stories about their current lives, so the presence of the blog in the children's lives is not easily removed.

As I showed with the examples from *Cup of Jo*, the prevalent concern is working mothers and digital devices are bad for children. The narrated resolution to separate work and family spaces is both a reaction to cultural ideals of mothering and digital devices and a generative act producing the division between material and virtual. I read these arrangements and concerns as reactions to the discourses around digitality and childhood, which insinuate the white, middle-class patriarchal idea that working mothers are harmful to their offspring (Cleaf, "Our Mothers"; Cleaf, *Blogging through Motherhood*). The concern echoes the intensive mothering ideals of being constantly present for children (Ennis). As such, it cannot be taken as a given that the presence of new technology or working from home is harmful.

Yet my research material constantly appears in negotiation with cultural scripts of mothering that suggest danger in the novel entanglements of work-life balance and parenting. The catch is that there is nothing new in labelling maternal care and creative work as inherently incompatible. In my analysis, I noted that maternal online life writing negotiates with the same set of norms and ideals that occurred previously in literature of childrearing and child psychology and underpins the intensive parenting ideals, which have continued to position women as the sole caregivers of their children (Ennis; O'Reilly, *Matricentric Feminism*).

By presenting the questions of privacy and publicity online as issues of space and time, maternal life writing is silent about the intertwining race and class questions. Yet during my research, I came to see that even in the absence of reference, space and time are constructed online in relation to race and class. The majority of the research material for this chapter was authored by white, middle- or upper-class ciswomen. When I contacted the bloggers to inform them about this study, one author asked me to remove her site from it. She cited continued racist threats as a reason for not wishing to be a part of the research. Whereas I celebrated her site as feminist, Black online maternal life writing, to my surprise, the author did not even identify her writing as mommy blogging.

The absence of this site from the examples is a loss to this project and highlights the failures in my data collection. It also gestures towards an unexpected research result: In the freely accessible, published, and commercial online maternal life writing sites, the authors have a strong sense of control. They govern the digital space as if it were property comparable to land or home ownership. Bloggers permit and deny comments (mediating post comments) or choose advertising; they wish to select outside attention and the perspective from which they are looked at. This was evident in all my messaging with the authors, who were hospitable to research but wanted to know how their life writing was being used in my research. In contrast, the kind of extreme publics of the internet and the feeling of intimacy and openness usually ascribed to blogs, mothers both partake in publishing intimate narratives and images of their families and try to retain complete control over presentation and interpretation. They do this through commercial visibility in the form of advertising while presenting their children.

Just as is the case offline, in the material world, digital privacy, safety, visibility, and space are matters of structural racism. The blogs I studied in this chapter mostly avoided situating themselves in terms of race or economic status, although there were exceptions. *Cup of Jo*, for example, gives voice to a variety of women from different backgrounds and has addressed economic issues from the perspectives of US women (often sponsored by a financial entity).

In reading the writing of the blogger who did not wish to participate in this research, I came to see how the online definitions of private and public depend on the cost of visibility. The cost can be measured in monetary terms (and often is with sponsored posts), but it is a question of social and political wellness. In the US, Black children are socially more visible than white children because they appear nonnormative (Collins). The choice of picturing them aesthetically and lovingly while also discussing the ongoing racism experienced by the family can be related to safety. The visibility of children online can be a product of necessity with economic and political consequences. From this perspective, the concern over privacy and disclosure of the white authors appears a privilege. A white mommy blogger's concern over the visibility of their children online is related to shame, and maybe fame, intra-familial relations, and the borderlines of online autonomous subjectivity—but never the threat of discrimination and violence continually experienced by Black American mothers and children.

Conclusions

With this chapter, I argue against reading mommy blogs as translational surfaces. Instead, I suggest reading them as extensions formed in intra-action. I claim that blogs are not (virtual) testimonies of (material) life; they are the actual development of that life. Yet digital life writing cannot be interpreted as corresponding to the lived material experiences of the authors. The blogs in their agential shifting explicitly discuss privacy and the temporal future, present, and past as horizons against which they project life narratives—often tentatively, as if sketching. They make stylistic, thematic, and genre-related choices in articulating spaces and times both on and offline. They respond to communal, commercial, technological, and material norms while also questioning them. They occur as the result of a circulation of influences, a set of intra-actions in a feedback loop. As such, maternal online life writing is not simple to pin down because it does not remain still. The divisions proposed in the examples uphold borders between the material and virtual, aiding in the construction of (discursive-material) boundaries to protect family members from the (semi)public spaces of the internet. Protection is needed against the harmful publicity of children, commercial interests, or the seeping of work into leisure. Protection is also needed against racism, and class distinctions as well as the acknowledgement that they exist. Divisions are erected to perform and safeguard good mothering. In this chapter I have focused on how posts achieve these protections via spatial and temporal arrangements (and how, in turn, they end up constituting space and time).

I have developed the concept of maternal double space/time to describe the construction of temporality and spatiality enfolding specifically in digital life writing by mothers. I propose that this doubling is particular to maternal online life writing and can be recognized as one of the agential cuts in its continuous production. This perspective does not presume spaces and times preexisting their descriptions or experiences. Agential realism does not negate the production of subjectivities, such as the maternal subject. Agential realism shows that maternal subjectivity produces materializations and is entangled in the becoming of the internet, the mamasphere, and mothering. When matter and discourse are always-already agential, details become important because everyone and everything are responsible.

Maternal online life writing shapes mothering. May Friedman and Silvia Schultermandl have noted how "the constraints and uneven access to quick media technologies—their role in extending surveillance, reproducing power relations, and generating new modes of exclusion—also mirror and in part amplify prevalent social inequalities, especially in a globalized context" (11). Race is entangled in the spaces and times constructed in the mamasphere. In the future, the normative whiteness of mommy blogging requires scholastic attention from the perspective of how online maternal spaces construct race and participate in racist definitions of mothering. In addition, BIPOC (Black Indigenous people of colour) maternal life writing requires attention, as it appears that there are racially divided safe spaces in mommy blogging and a strong emergence of FUBU (for us by us) culture in maternal online life writing.

In writing this chapter, I have learned that online visibility via life writing constructs a sense of control and safety. What constitutes digital private and public spaces does not follow a straightforward ethical or legal paradigm, nor is it a reflection of their definitions elsewhere. Bloggers appear to feel more in control of their online appearance than is usual in the case of book publishing for example. The maternal constitution of online space and time presents the possibility of control and the prospect of affirmative self-definition.

Endnotes

1. I am referring to the virtual as a kind of digitality here. As materiality that the internet constructs, usually defined by its non-materiality (which Barad troubles) and appearance within the frames of the Internet and computer technologies. I am therefore not quite aligning it with what Barad has called the virtual in her exploration of Quantum Field Theory (Barad, "Transmaterialities: Trans*/Matter/Realities and Queer Political Imaginings"), but not foreclosing a connection either.

2. Barad fashions an order in which phenomena are structured via intra-actions that bring about agential cuts between subject and object, and this process becomes agential separation. She explains:

   Phenomena are constitutive of reality. Reality is composed not of things-in-themselves or things-behind-phenomena. The world is a dynamic process of intra-activity and materialization in the enactment of determinate causal structure with determinate boundaries, properties, meanings, and patterns of marks on bodies. This ongoing flow of agency through which part of the world makes itself differentially intelligible to another part of the world and through which causal structures are stabilized and destabilized does not take place in space and time but happens in the making of spacetime itself. (*Meeting the Universe Halfway* 139-40)

Works Cited

Arthur, Paul Langley. "Material Memory and the Digital." *Life Writing*, vol. 12, no. 2, 2015, pp. 189-200.

Barad, Karen. "Living in a Posthuman Material World: Lessons from Schrödinger's Cat." *Bits of Life: Feminism at the Intersection of Media, Bioscience and Technology*, edited by Anneke Smelik and Nina Lykke, University of Washington Press, 2008, pp. 165-76.

Barad, Karen. *Meeting the Universe Halfway: Quantum Physics and the Entanglement of Matter and Meaning*. Duke University Press, 2007.

Barad, Karen. "Transmaterialities: Trans*/Matter/Realities and Queer Political Imaginings." *A Journal of Lesbian and Gay Studies*, vol. 21, no. 2–3, 2015, pp. 387-422.

Baraitser, Lisa. "Postmaternal, Postwork and the Maternal Death Drive." *Australian Feminist Studies*, vol. 31, no. 90, 2016, pp. 393-409.

Bassett, Caroline, et al. *Furious: Technological Feminism and Digital Futures*. 1st ed., Pluto Press, 2019.

Braunmühl, Caroline. "Beyond Hierarchical Oppositions: A Feminist Critique of Karen Barad's Agential Realism." *Feminist Theory*, vol. 19, no. 2, 2017, pp. 223-40.

Bueskens, Petra. "Introduction: The Reproduction of Mothering Turns Forty." *Nancy Chodorow and The Reproduction of Mothering Forty Years On*, edited by Petra Bueskens, Palgrave Macmillan, 2021, pp. 1-45.

Bueskens, Petra. "Mothers Reproducing the Social: Chodorow and Beyond." *Nancy Chodorow and The Reproduction of Mothering Forty Years On*, edited by Petra Bueskens, Palgrave Macmillan, 2021, pp. 265-300.

Butler, Judith. *Gender Trouble: Feminism and the Subversion of Identity*.

Routledge, 1990.

Cart, Ashley. *Blog A La Cart*, blogalacart.com/. Accessed 23 May 2022.

Collins, Patricia Hill. *Black Feminist Thought: Knowledge, Consciousness and the Politics of Empowerment*. Routledge, 2000.

Coole, Diane, and Samantha Frost, editors. *New Materialisms: Ontology, Agency, and Politics*. Duke University Press, 2010.

Cummings, Kelsey. "'But We Still Try': Affective Labor in the Corporate Mommy Blog." *Feminist Media Studies*, vol. 19, no. 1, 2017, pp. 38-52.

Daly, Brenda O., and Maureen T. Reddy, editors. *Narrating Mothers: Theorizing Maternal Subjectivities*. University of Tennessee Press, 1991.

Davis, Naomi. *LoveTaza*. https://lovetaza.com/. Accessed 23 May 2022.

Dijck van, José. "MyLifeBits: The Computer as Memory Machine." *Bits of Life: Feminism at the Intersection of Media, Bioscience and Technology*, edited by Anneke Smelik and Nina Lykke, University of Washington Press, 2008, pp. 113-28.

DiQuinzio, Patrice. *The Impossibility of Motherhood: Feminism, Individualism and the Problem of Mothering*. Routledge, 1999.

Douglas, K., and A. Barnwell, editors. *Research Methodologies for Auto/Biography Studies*. Routledge, 2019.

Ennis, Linda Rose, editor. *Intensive Mothering: The Cultural Contradictions of Modern Motherhood*. Demeter Press, 2014.

Fannin, Maria, and Maud Perrier. "Refiguring the Postmaternal." *Australian Feminist Studies*, vol. 31, no. 90, 2016, pp. 383-92.

Federico, Annette. *Engagements with Close Reading*. Routledge, 2016.

Freitas de, Elizabeth. "Karen Barad's Quantum Ontology and Posthuman Ethics: Rethinking the Concept of Relationality." *Qualitative Inquiry*, vol. 23, no. 9, 2017, pp. 741-48.

Friedman, May. "Mommy Blogs." *Encyclopedia of Motherhood*, SAGE Publications, 2010, pp. 785-88.

Friedman, May. *Mommyblogs and the Changing Face of Motherhood*. University of Toronto Press, 2013.

Friedman, May, and Silvia Schultermandl, editors. *Click and Kin: Transnational Identity and Quick Media.* University of Toronto Press, 2016.

Green, Fiona Joy. "Motherhood Studies." *Encyclopedia of Motherhood,* edited by Andrea O'Reilly, SAGE Publications, 2010, pp. 831-32.

Hallstein, Lynn O'Brien, et al., editors. *The Routledge Companion to Motherhood.* Routledge, 2020.

Hallstein, Lynn O'Brien, and Andrea O'Reilly. "Introduction." *Academic Motherhood in a Post-Second Wave Context: Challenges, Strategies and Possibilities,* edited by Lynn Hallstein O'Brien and Andrea O'Reilly, Demeter Press, 2012, pp. 1-46.

Hayles, Katherine N. *How We Became Post-Human: Virtual Bodies in Cybernetics, Literature and Informatics.* University of Chicago Press, 1999.

Hayles, Katherine N. *My Mother Was a Computer: Digital Subjects and Literary Texts.* University of Chicago Press, 2005.

Hayles, Katherine N. *Unthought: The Power of the Congitive Nonconscious.* University of Chicago Press, 2017.

Hollway, Wendy. *Knowing Mothers: Researching Maternal Identity Change.* Palgrave Macmillan, 2015.

Jezer-Morton, Kathryn. "Online Momming in the Perfectly Imperfect Age." *The Cut,* Apr. 2019, www.thecut.com/2019/04/online-moms-mommyblogs-instagram.html. Accessed 23 May 2022.

Jokinen, Eeva. *Aikuisten Arki.* Gaudeamus, 2005.

Joutseno, Astrid. *Life Writing From Birth to Death: How M/Others Know.* 2021, http://urn.fi/URN:ISBN:978-951-51-7459-8. Accessed 23 May 2022.

Kaarakainen, Suvi-Sadetta, and Mari Lehto. "Lähisuhdeväkivaltaa Ja Muita Kertomuksia – Äitien Älylaitteiden Käyttö Mediajulkisuudessa." *WideScreen,* vol. 3, 2018, widerscreen.fi/numerot/2018-3/lahisuhdevakivaltaa-ja-muita-kertomuksia-aitien-alylaitteiden-kaytto-mediajulkisuudessa/. Accessed 23 May 2022.

Kennedy, Helen. "Beyond Anonymity, or Future Directions for Internet Identity Research." *Identity Technologies: Constructing the Self Online,* edited by Anna Poletti and Julie Rak, University of Wisconsin Press, 2014, pp. 25-41.

Laaksonen, Salla-Maaria, et al., editors. *Otteita Verkosta: Verkon Ja Sosiaalisen Median Tutkimusmenetelmät.* Vastapaino, 2013.

Lehto, Mari. "Ambivalent Influencers: Feeling Rules and the Affective Practice of Anxiety in Social Media Influencer Work." *European Journal of Cultural Studies,* 2021, pp. 1-16.

Lehto, Mari. "Bad Is the New Good: Negotiating Bad Motherhood in Finnish Mommy Blogs." *Feminist Media Studies,* vol. 20, no. 5, 2019, pp. 1-15.

Markham, Annette N. "Ethics as Impact—Moving From Error-Avoidance and ConceptDriven Models to a Future-Oriented Approach." *Social Media + Society,* vol. 1-2, 2018, pp. 1-11.

McDaniel, Brandon T., et al. "New Mothers and Media Use: Associations between Blogging, Social Networking, and Maternal Well-Being." *Maternal and Child Health Journal,* vol. 16, no. 7, 2012, pp. 1509-17.

McLeod, Jaqueline, and Fiona Joy Green. "Mommy Blogging and Deliberative Dialogical Ethics." *Journal of the Motherhood Initiative for Research and Community Involvement,* vol. 6, no. 1, 2015, pp. 31-49.

McNeill, Laurie. "Life Bytes: Six-Word Memoir and the Exigencies of Auto/Tweetographies." *Identity Technologies: Constructing the Self Online,* edited by Anna Poletti and Julie Rak, University of Wisconsin Press, 2014, pp. 144-64.

McRobbie, Angela. "Feminism, the Family and the New 'Mediated' Maternalism." *New Formations,* vol. 80, no. 80, Lawrence and Wishart, 2013, pp. 119-37.

Morrison, Aimée. "Autobiography in Real Time: A Genre Analysis of Personal Mommy Blogging." *Cyberpsychology: A Journal of Psychosocial Research on Cyberspace,* vol. 4, no. 2, 2010, cyber psychology.eu/article/view/4239/3285. Accessed 23 May 2022.

Morrison, Aimée. "Social Media, Life Writing: Online Lives at Scale, Up Close and In Context." *Research Methodologies for Auto/Biography Studies,* edited by Kitrina Douglas and A Barnwell, Routledge, 2019. pp. 41-48.

Nakamura, Lisa. *Cybertypes: Race, Ethnicity, and Identity on the Internet.* Routledge, 2013.

O'Reilly, Andrea. "Maternal Theory: Patriarchal Motherhood and

Empowered Mothering." *The Routledge Companion to Motherhood*, 1st ed., Routledge, 2020, pp. 19–35.

O'Reilly, Andrea. *Matricentric Feminism: Theory, Activism and Practice.* Demeter Press, 2016.

O'Reilly, Andrea. *Matricentric Feminism.* Demeter Press, 2016.

Paasonen, Susanna. *Figures of Fantasy : Women, Cyberdiscourse and the Popular Internet.* Turun yliopiston julkaisuja, Sarja B, 2002.

Paasonen, Susanna. "Ihmisiä, Kuvia, Tekstejä Ja Teknologioita." *Otteita Verkosta: Verkon Ja Sosiaalisen Median Tutkimusmenetelmät,* edited by Salla-Maaria Laaksonen et al., Vastapaino, 2013. (accessed as a digital book with no pagination).

Paasonen, Susanna. "Resonant Networks: On Affect and Social Media." *Public Spheres of Resonance,* edited by Anne Fleig and Christian von Scheve, Routledge, 2020, pp. 49-62.

Paasonen, Susanna. "Resonant Networks." *Public Spheres of Resonance: Constellations of Affect and Language,* edited by Anne Fleig and Christian von Scheve, Routledge, 2019, pp. 49-62.

Petersen, Emily January. "Mommy Bloggers as Rebels and Community Builders: A Generic Description." *Journal of the Motherhood Initiative for Research and Community Involvement,* vol. 6, no. 1, 2015, jarm.journals.yorku.ca/index.php/jarm/article/view/40238. Accessed 23 May 2022.

Poletti, Anna, and Julie Rak, editors. *Identity Technologies: Constructing the Self Online.* University of Wisconsin Publishing, 2014.

Rich, Adrienne. *Of Woman Born: Motherhood as Experience and Institution.* Norton and Company, 1976.

Schell, Eileen E., and K. J. Rawson, editors. *Rhetorica in Motion: Feminist Rhetorical Methods and Methodologies.* University of Pittsburgh Press, 2010.

Sloan, Luke, and Anabel Quan-Haase, editors. *The SAGE Handbook of Social Media Research Methods.* Sage Publishing, 2017.

Smith, Sidonie, and Julia Watson. *Reading Autobiography: A Guide for Interpreting Life Narratives.* Second ed., University of Minnesota Press, 2010.

Smith, Sidonie, and Julia Watson. "Virtually Me: A Toolbox about

Online Self-Presentation." *Identity Technologies*, edited by Anna Poletti and Julie Rak, Wisconsin University Press, 2014, pp. 70-95.

Steiner, Linda, and Carolyn Bronstein. "Leave a Comment: Mommy blogs and the Everyday Struggle to Reclaim Parenthood." *Feminist Media Studies*, vol. 17, no. 1, Jan. 2017, pp. 59-76.

Stephens, Julia. *Confronting Postmaternal Thinking: Feminism, Memory, and Care*. Columbia University Press, 2011.

Thomas, Mariana. "The Mother Becomes Time: Exploring Altered Temporality in Contemporary Motherhood Memoirs." *Journal of the Motherhood Initiative for Research and Community Involvement*, vol. 9, no. 1, 2018, pp. 71-81.

Van Cleaf, Kara. *Blogging Through Motherhood: Free Labor, Femininity, and the (Re)Production of Maternity*. Graduate Center City University of New York, 2014.

Van Cleaf, Kara. "Of Woman Born to Mommy Blogged: The Journey from the Personal as Political to Personal as Commodity." *Women's Studies Quarterly*, vol. 3 and 4, no. 43, 2015, pp. 247-64.

Van Cleaf, Kara. "Our Mothers Have Always Been Machines: The Conflation of Media and Motherhood." *Digital Sociologies*, edited by Karen Gregory Jessie Daniels, and Tressie McMillan Cottom, The Policy Press, 2016, pp. 449-62.

Veissiere, Samuel. "The Internet Is Not a River." *Click and Kin : Transnational Identity and Quick Media*, edited by May Friedman and Silvia Schultermandl, University of Toronto Press, 2016, pp. 214-137.

Weller, Wiwian, et al. "Collecting Data For Analyzing Blogs." *The SAGE Handbook of Qualitative Data Collection*, edited by Uwe Flick, Sage Publications Ltd, 2017, pp. 482-95.

Chapter 3

The Smartphone Camera as a Maternal Technology: Reconstructing Mothers' Relationships with Their Children in the Digital Age

Carolin Aronis

Introduction

Smartphone devices seem to be everywhere; in many countries, most of the population carries at least one device that functions as a phone, a camera, and means of internet access.[1] In Western culture, mothers with these devices have become devoted to a new communicative practice that involves taking daily pictures of their own children—documenting their children's hobbies, their perceived achievements, their development, and the good and important moments in their lives—and then posting these photos on social media and messenger apps to share with friends and family. What was in the past a tool for communication from afar (i.e., the telephone) has become a tool for communication from close by; what was a sophisticated masculine device (i.e. camera) has become a mother's possession— easily handled, kept in the pocket or purse, and used in everyday life. And what required a chain of procedures and movement throughout the public space (i.e., film developing, post office, and mail delivery) is now accomplished in the seconds it takes to post a picture with a short caption. Susan Sontag writes about the place of family photos in predigital times: "Through photographs, each family constructs a portrait-chronicle of itself—a portable kit of images that bears witness to its connectedness. It hardly matters what activities are photographed so long as photographs get taken and are cherished. Photography becomes a rite of family life" (5-6). However, while Sontag reminds us that "Cameras go with family life" and that taking pictures of small children became a sign of good parenthood with the "old style" camera (5), the constant availability of the smartphone and the almost effortless practice of sending pictures to family and community members have changed the positionality of the mother within the relationship with her children.

This chapter examines how this communicative situation reconstructs the relationships Western mothers have with both their children and smartphones (cameras) and, in turn, their maternal identity. I am particularly interested in the love and care relationship mothers establish through the smartphone as well as their social and familial position in their own homes. Drawing on mothers' reflections on the practice, on autoethnography, and on media phenomenology, I explore how the actual practice of taking, sharing, and viewing pictures is involved in the relationship Western mothers develop with their children in the digital age, particularly those in the US and Israel (the two countries serving as the locale of my autoethnographic explorations). In terms of affect, I examine intimacy in relation to power, distance, and memory. I assume these concepts are interactive, following Jennifer Daryl Slack and J. Macgregor Wise, who propose examining technologies in terms of articulation and assemblage as integrally connected to the context within which they are developed and used as well as their relationships between practices, representations, experiences, and affects.

This current chapter offers a somewhat alternative perspective on communication technologies. It does not study the technology itself or how it is gendered, empowering, or discriminatory (see for instance, McGaw and Wajcman); instead, it focuses on the actual feminist framework of doing as well as the praxis of communication (Sotirin and Ellingson 115), both of which involve the technology of the smartphone and its digital camera. I use the approach of media ecology, which rarely focuses on women, let alone on mothers and their auto-ethnographic voices and daily life. Following Lorraine Code—who is interested in analyzing women's "positions of minimal epistemic authority," "women's underclass epistemic status," and the structural blocks to the acknowledgment of women's contributions to knowledge (qtd. in Mar Pereira 51)—I look to reclaim this maternal rhetorical space and maternal epistemic authority in the scholarly media ecology environment, where they are too often left academically unacknowledged and unvalued.

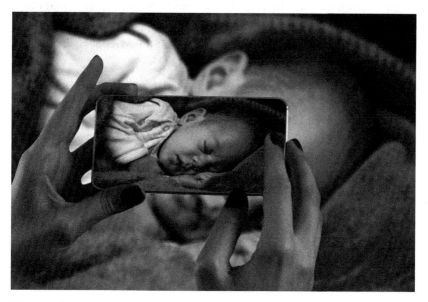

Photo by Gerd Altmann, 2011 (from Pixabay).

Below, I characterize the relationship between women and technology. Following this, I outline three perspectives on motherhood: multitasking motherhood, controlling motherhood, and loving, intimate motherhood. In the conclusion, I explain the maternal practice of sending love through taking and sharing pictures, which makes the smartphone a maternal tool. Although this broad examination of topics deserves to be covered in greater depth, I see this current chapter as an introduction to this subject of study.

Motherhood and Communication Technologies

Western culture is a child-centred society that values children's needs and wellbeing above those of others, especially those of mothers. Scholars note that the ideal of 'good motherhood' is one of an intensive motherhood that serves a child-centered society while dismissing the mother as a subject with legitimate needs and wants, as it expects her to sacrifice herself and conform to an unachievable ideal (see Badinter; Douglas and Michaels; Hays; Wall). Sharon Hays explains that this ideal is a cultural model of natural, intensive, self-sacrificing, and isolated motherhood. Therefore, discussions about motherhood often invoke binaries of ideal versus good enough mothering and good versus bad mothering (Badinter; Douglas and Michaels; Lachover; Shloim, et al.; Steiner and Lachover).

Mothers' daily lives are usually filled with exhausting commitments and high demands. Even for mothers with partners, studies indicate that mothers spend more time than fathers caring for children. Lyn Craig's study of Australian intact families is representative of mothers who work full time and still spend more time with their children than fathers and do more interactive care as well as physical care (e.g. providing meals, transporting children, giving them baths, and putting them to bed). Hence, mothers are more time constrained by their childcare duties than fathers, and many of them preserve time by multitasking (Craig 275). Yet as Susan Douglas and Meredith Michaels argue about the US culture, media representations of the impossibly perfect mother contradict the reality of actual mothers' exhausting daily lives, creating incurable frustration among mothers who consume that media. This argument holds true for Israeli media as well, especially in terms of the simultaneous media obsession with cases of 'bad' mothers in reports of maternal neglect, rebellion, unprofessional motherhood, and even maternal infanticide (Aronis, "*Reconstructing mothers' responsibility and guilt*"; Steiner and Lachover). These media images, which reinforce social attitudes, contribute to mothers' insecurities and the need to embody the ideal of "good mothering" in order to conform to expected norms while also needing to take care of themselves—either for the sake of their children or as a matter of survival.

Technologies, and especially communication technologies, have played an important role in this complex positionality of mothers within the family, in front of their children, and in their larger communities. Historically, it was usually men who dominated the development, ownership, and "sophisticated" operation and assemblage of technologies, frequently leaving women to be the end users, if they were involved at all.[2] As Michelle H. Jackson writes in relation to other scholars' work (Kidder; Kirkup and Keller; McIlwee and Robinson; Schwartz Cowan; Wajcman), "The study of culture in dozens of technological contexts consistently reveals the dominance of masculinist ideologies of mastery and control" (149). Judy Wajcman points to the exclusion of women from "technological domains and activities" and illuminates how "concrete practices of design and innovation lead to the absence of specific users, such as women." Via science and technology studies (STS), Wajcman seeks to expose the "constitutive power of tools, techniques and objects to materialise social, political and economics arrangements" (150-51).

The newspaper, camera, radio, and television were all men's developments and design. In these moments in history—and where most Western women have held unprivileged and discriminatory positions in society and in the home as compared to their male counterparts—men gained control and power over media technologies and environments as both producers and directors or as social actors, with the exception of women working in subordinate roles.[3] In the mid-twentieth century, in predigital times, women were not expected to be part of public life and had limited social relationships (e.g. Friedan). Radio brought media technology into the domestic sphere (Moores), but women were constructed as mere users and as not having any understanding of the design and operation aspect of new technologies (Marvin; Moores; Wajcman). Carolyn Marvin shows how women were constructed as reliant on men's skills and developments and how "technical ignorance" (23) was a virtue of the good woman. As Wajcman argues, femininity was reinterpreted as incompatible with technological pursuits.

Gender was embedded in technology itself. Technologies of the home served the needs of cleaning and cooking for the family (Wajcman). For instance, Marvin shows how the first texts in the emergent field of electrical technologies "stigmatized the unempowered: the rural, the female, the nonwhite" (17), and created two separate groups of 'insiders' and 'outsiders.' Moreover, this discourse presented women as consumers of men's labour, as interested in fashion and in talking for no important reason.

Against this history, the smartphone camera, along with messenger apps and social media, has in many ways liberated women from their role of inferiority regarding "masculinist" technology. These new technologies have allowed women and mothers to possess and operate nongendered technology as tools for managing motherhood and their social life.[4] Interestingly, research shows that the smartphone plays a crucial role in everyday communication and interaction of mothers with young children (Chan et al.; Chen, Zhou, and Han). My aim in this piece is not to evaluate how smartphones and social media benefit or harm children, mothers, or society. Instead, I explore the actual operative communicative acts of mothers' relationships and identity as developed through the practice of taking pictures of their own children and posting them to a small or large community online. As Jackson offers, technologies encompass the understanding of identity, interaction, and communication, and they exhibit gendered characteristics of women's access, voice, and empowerment. I focus in this chapter on mothers and mothering.

Ethnographic Observations of Maternal Use of Smartphones

In the following, I briefly unpack the steps taken in the communicative situation of picturing one's own child/ren and sharing the photos online with friends and family, which seems prevalent among mothers.[5] Through my observations of many mothers in the US and Israel over the last decade, I have identified a pattern and rhythm that serve as a reference point for my arguments[6]:

1. *Recognizing the moment for taking a picture or the potentiality in initiating one*: When with or near their children, mothers will usually either recognize a moment that is worth capturing (e.g., the children on their first day of school, the youngest child playing creatively with a new toy, or the child accompanied by an unusual guest) or will initiate a potential moment (e.g., thinking of how nice it would be if the child poses with friends on the last day of school with their teacher or holds the country's

flag on independence day and smiles at the mother photographer). This first step depends on the mother's attention and her ability and desire to recognize a moment that is worth a picture. These are determined by what values she wants to enhance for her children's identity and understanding of the world.

2. ***Initiating the moment of taking a picture:*** I identify two practices, both of which involve the mother's act of picking up her smartphone. In the first case, the mother, without any announcement or interruption of the child, snaps a photo and thus keeps the situation authentic. The second option involves a clear announcement of a change in the frame (for framing, see Goffman), for the situation to be announced as "picture taking" instead of the other activity in which the child is currently engaged (e.g., "Let's take a picture" or asking, "Can I take your picture?"). It is that moment when the child understands that they should stop what they are doing, or sometimes keep doing what they are doing, and give attention to the mother and camera for a situation that will be captured.

   The initiating moment could also be more planned and involve arranging the child and the whole setting for the picture (e.g., bringing them in front of the Christmas tree or going to a certain place for the purpose of taking pictures). In this case, it is even more dependent on her active initiative to create the situation for the picture in order to capture and even curate their precious moments to be remembered.

3. ***Picture taking:*** This is the actual act that involves holding the device in between bodies, as a mediator (Latour) between the mother and the children, as a screen that creates a barrier and connection. Taking the picture requires touching this barrier/connector.

Photo by Eugen Visan, 2017 (from Pixabay).

4. ***Viewing and evaluating the pictures***: After releasing the children back to what they were doing before being paused for the picture, mothers will find a time, later on, usually in between other tasks (or through tasks), many times in front of the children, to view the pictures and evaluate their suitability for sending/posting. Here, they address the potential audience (i.e., family members and friends) and the values the mother would like to perform through the picture (e.g., beauty, joy, good health, love, as well as other traits of "good motherhood").

5. ***Sharing and posting the picture:*** This involves sorting through the new digital images, which are now data and take space in her phone's storage, the mother will share one or a few of the pictures via messenger apps and social media with family members and friends, adding a caption or a short description.

6. ***Waiting for endorsement:*** After posting, the mother waits, sometimes anxiously, to get responses from others she cares about. She will count the "likes" and other performances of love and endorsement for her children or for her.

In the meantime, the children are unaware of this whole complicated process of communication, which centres on them and circulates around and throughout the world.

During my time in the US and in Israel, I have come to know mothers who take pictures of their children several times a day or a few times each week or month. It often depends on how much time the mother spends with her children, which activities are worth a picture, her availability and time to focus on taking pictures, the social norms of expecting or not expecting picture taking in certain places, her own values of how much to involve the device in her relationship with her children, and, lastly, the responses of the children. For instance, Wendy Wisner writes about her tendency to take pictures of her three-year-old son all the time. She reflects on a day she hung out with him in a playground: "There I was on my phone, taking pictures of him. I probably took 50 or so. I don't know what it was about today, but I had this nagging feeling that I had to capture it all" (Wisner).[7] In contrast, A., a Jewish Israeli mother, tries not to use her smartphone as much in front of her children, but when quarantined through the COVID-19 pandemic, she found herself taking countless pictures of her three sons doing special jumps on the trampoline in their yard, dressing up, the youngest taking his first steps, the middle one helping make food, etc.

Many children in Western society became familiar with this practice. Unlike what I myself remember from my own childhood, complaining with my sisters and friends about our mothers taking our pictures, today I could hardly see my own daughters, their friends, or other children rolling eyes or getting upset with their mothers for photographing them. It seems to me that our children usually do not feel embarrassed, as they willingly participate in this ritual. They know when to stop what they are doing and put on a smile for us. Many of them will even ask us to take their picture when doing something funny or impressive or wearing something special.

However, this practice raises important ethical, philosophical, social, and cultural questions. Do mothers have the right to capture their children's image, use their children's innocence, and post the image online? Who has power within the relationships and how does it relate to the capitalistic, consumer practice of accumulating images and contacts as data? In what sense are we objectifying our children and scrutinizing them in order to please others? Children do not have their own phones, money, or relationships with a broader community, so they cannot do the same. Additionally, in what sense does this address the responsibility and moral care mothers owe their children as their caregivers? These important questions (or even imperatives) are not to be left aside, and some scholarship has already developed an important discussion in this regard (e.g., Feeney and Freeman; Phelan and Kinsella). However, I am interested here in unfolding additional aspects of this practice. In the following, I focus on the momentarily communicative act and relationship that the mother establishes with her children and her community, along with her position and operation within the normative expectations of "good motherhood," as a controlling authority over her children and as developing love, care, caregiving, and identity through the use of the smartphone camera and the posting apps. My goal in this piece is to add to the complex understanding of this phenomenon when focusing on the mother as the studied subject.

Three Perspectives on Motherhood: Multitasking, Controlling, and Loving

In a way, the following three perspectives run parallel to one another and/or overlap. I develop the third perspective more than the others, as it has had less attention from scholars working in feminist studies, media ecology or phenomenology.

1. Multitasking Motherhood

In her study on mothers and fathers in the Australian intact family, Craig found that mothers preserve time in childcare by multitasking (274). She defines multitasking as a "double activity"—activities that are done at the same time as other tasks (270). For instance, she shows that often when fathers play with or talk to their children this is the only thing they are doing. Although interactive care is the childcare subcategory that is most valued by parents, mothers more often do it at the same time as other activities, in other words—they multitask (271). In this regard, I argue the use of the smartphone discussed in this chapter can be seen not only as multitasking but also as a more complex multirole act. It is a practice that includes practices of thinking (not only doing) and dividing attention as well as moving quickly back and forth between tasks. In this instance, the mother is expected to care for her child and to capture the important moments in their life.

The use of the smartphone to take and share pictures of one's own children with a community who responds to them—and also knowing that the children depicted will view the photographs—have developed some (new?) maternal roles that are often practiced, taken, and embodied concurrently. What does it take for a caregiving mother to take pictures of her children in the midst of watching them, preparing meals, picking them up from school, giving them baths, putting them to bed, and interacting with them, educating them, and soothing them? Mothers' busy lives, already multitasked, do not allow for the privilege of practicing mothering on only one level. They are expected to be with their children, to nourish them, to care for and take care of them (Badinter; Douglas and Michaels; Hays; and Wall), and at the same time, they are working towards preserving their moments via photos that are shared with others.

Thus, in order to perform these expectations, and specifically to take pictures of their children, mothers observe the situation from the "outside," serving as an observer or researcher of her own children's lives in order to recognize when a special moment arrives. They practice a dual role of doing care and doing "research," like an anthropologist who lives with the studied community and becomes part of the informants' lives and environment but still holds an observer's view and takes constant notes, photos, and evidence. It is a skill that mothers seem to be gradually socialized into with a smartphone camera constantly in their hand. After recognizing the moment to be captured, the mother actively initiates the picture and can be seen as a professional photographer who just knows how to capture their subjects' precious moments. It is within this practice of choosing what to capture and how to capture it that she follows (or embeds) her maternal values into the picture, family memory, or message to the public.[8]

Along with the roles of a caregiver, anthropologist, and photographer, she could also be perceived as a journalist who reports on the children's new achievements and on changes in their lives to the public (however small). Reporting to the family, to the close community, via social media and messenger apps that her daughter has graduated, or that her son is finally walking, positions the mother in the journalist or reporter role. Along with this, the mother also holds the role of commemorator of her children's lives and as a builder of their history. She arranges the composition of the photo, its aesthetics, and later on will add a caption that will construct its message, sometimes very creatively. In this regard, I suggest seeing her also as an artist and a curator of the photos of her children's lives.

Photo by 460273, 2014 (from Pixabay).

Sending pictures of her children to relatives, friends, and people in her community encourages excitement towards the children (also towards her, through compliments on her good work as a mother or a photographer or anthropologist). Hence, she also serves as an advocate for her children—for what they have done, learned, achieved, or how smart, beautiful, and cute they are. She becomes a recruiter of love for and interest in her children from the community. It is a practice in which she invites and collects compliments, endorsements, and likes from people who view the pictures she sends. Whereas the following section on controlling motherhood demonstrates this practice from a different point of view, I would like to point here to the practice of recruiting love and endorsement of one's own children, as, for instance, reflected by Morin Gabso's statement on why she sends her family pictures of her children: "I would like my family members to learn about my children, to know who they are and what they do, to be proud of them and excited about them, and to give them some loving attention."

Mothers engage in multitasking or maintain multiple roles or levels of relationships not only through doing but also through thinking, recognizing, and paying attention. This adds to her multitasking behaviour when taking care of her children and her exhausting day. The availability of the smartphone camera seems to never truly allow the mother to dedicate herself to listening to her children's story, laughing together, or going on a walk, as she always has more and more roles to accomplish in order to satisfy the ideal of the good mother in the digital era.

2. Controlling Motherhood

Langdon Winner calls for us to reveal forms of power and authority within artifacts and technologies—media/communication technologies included. He argues we should pay attention to the characteristics and design of technical objects and their meanings and practices as they relate to a particular community. In this regard, it is clear that the characteristics and design of the smartphone (camera) allow mothers to gain power, authority, and control over their children. This technology gives the power to take a picture to those who can own a device and have the authority to use it. Not the children. The children are usually not asked for permission to take or distribute their pictures. Their vulnerability is sent out violently as Sontag suggests about any picture taking (14-15). And as Foucault notes on the panoptic culture (170–230), mothers create a culture of surveillance through their devices and teach their children how to adhere to norms, how to perform, and how they never own privacy or solemn peace. Like the Elf on the Shelf (the Christmas doll which is positioned in the home and "reports" on kids' behaviour to Santa Claus to determine whether they should receive presents) or God in the Judeo-Christian tradition, who can see but is unseen, the mother holds a sense of higher authority. Within the home, she observes her children and exercises an automatic functioning of the power of surveillance that disciplines and creates an imbalanced machinery of the gaze (Foucault 170–230).

The device and its actions are imposed on the child in an unequal relationship, in which they know they are seen and exposed to the gaze of the mother and to the potential capture by the smartphone camera.

It leaves children vulnerable, watched, screened, examined, and scanned by others as well as by those who will receive these photos through a frame or in a moment that does not necessarily represent who the children truly are. As Sontag writes: "To photograph people is to violate them, by seeing them as they never see themselves, by having knowledge of them they can never have; it turns people into objects that can be symbolically possessed" (Sontag 14). Sontag compares the language used to talk about older cameras (e.g., shooting) and the actual practice of photographing to a violent act. Hence, cameras are tools for violence and power (8). Although smartphone cameras do not impose a practice of looking through the viewfinder (as in the site of a gun) to shoot the picture, they do cause people, and in this case children, to transform, as in any picture taking, from a rich mode of life into a two-dimensional image that is frozen in time and represents only a single moment in the subject's life.

Photo by Askar Abayev, 2020 (from Pexels).

Moreover, it should be noted that taking photographs, especially by mothers who usually lead the family bonding and memory creation, reconstructs the family history by commemorating selected moments from particular angles and points of view, within selected frames and composition. In addition, photo taking teaches children to smile, to pretend they are happy (Kochemidova), to perform for the future and for others, and to satisfy and address the mother's narrative of the family and its values. It encourages "aesthetic consumerism" (Sontag 24). Privilege, authority, and power are imposed on the relationship between the mother and the child in ways that are starting to be clearer and clearer. As mothers, we have learned to advertise ourselves (or our children), look happy, consume images, experience the world through voyeurism, and make sense of the world via one momentary snapshot. We have learned to make people (and specifically our children) stand, pose, and objectify themselves so we can get our result, income, or product. The smartphone camera is not an egalitarian, democratic, or decentralized technology if we consider the children's point of view (Mumford qtd. in Winner 29). Although this is an important aspect to unpack in regard to mothers taking pictures of their children, I would like to offer in the following an alternative point of view.

3. Loving, Intimate Mothering

Wisner writes as follows: "My kids are pretty much the best thing I have in this world.... I believe that someday my kids will thank me for all the pictures I've snapped, for the beauty I saw in their every gesture, and for preserving those ordinary, extraordinary moments of their childhoods." In a blog by a mother who self-identifies as "momarazzi," Jenn Press Arata writes: "The instant gratification of capturing these fleeting moments of my daughter's childhood creates a tangible time capsule to hold on to these never-again moments, forever.... These photographs are my gift to her. I want her to see the joy in her face when she pets animals, her expression as she blows kisses or smiles a toothless grin." Is it possible to understand this type of picture taking as an act of love and intimacy(without scare quotes)? Can we allow ourselves as scholars to develop an emotional understanding of this phenomenon instead of a purely rational one that takes a judgmental stance on mothers' behaviour? Many of the mothers I talked with and observed find picture taking to be an act of love and care and an empathetic investment in their children. They find that taking pictures of their children preserves a moment for the child and/or the mother to enjoy in the future. Mothers want to capture a glimpse of their children's current existence, to capture memories (their own and their children's) in order to look backward at their precious child's moments, and to allow their children to reflect on who they were and how their childhood was.

This practice is about thinking of their children when they are older and of the person they will become, promising a construction of their past and a way to learn about their earlier life. As Arata writes: "I want her to see the house she came home to from the hospital before we moved into a new one, and the room she grew up in, the brand new toys she played with that will one day be vintage. I want her to have a way to reflect on her upbringing if she chooses to have kids of her own one day." Roland Barthes defines this as the "Studium," a body of information that provides interest in the details and "requires the rational intermediary of an ethical and political culture" (26). As is seen in Arata's statement, the mother thinks of the potential need her child will have as an adult to learn about the past and is looking to create a record that will satisfy that need for her child and her potential grandchild. It is an act of care and love that is sent forwards to unknown times.

Mothers often find this practice of photographing the child to be intuitive and unexplained—something almost natural that they do to capture, frame, remember, or cherish a moment while life keeps going. As mentioned earlier, Wisner writes about how she takes pictures of her son without following any rational and planned decision but because of "this nagging feeling" that she had "to hold onto it even as I saw it slipping by." Gabso, a Jewish Israeli mother of three children, told me: "I take pictures of my kids all the time, when I cook, when I take care of one of them, through every phase of my day. Because the smartphone is so available, it allows me to be very spontaneous, without thinking or planning much."

In addition, the actual act of taking the picture already participates in this practice of love: To take your child's picture is to spread love, attention, care, and interest their way—immediately or in the future. When I asked my youngest, seven years old, what she feels when I take a picture of her, she answered: "Love. I feel that you love me." Although it touched my heart to hear such words, it was also an important moment for me, as I usually feel guilty for bothering my daughters with my picture taking, imposing performative expectations on them in their daily lives, and pausing their activities and excitement. A few days later, I asked her more questions about it. She explained that she feels cared for, that I am giving her attention, that what I want to capture in the photo is often something she created, and she feels proud of herself because I do not photograph everything she does: "When you take pictures of my magnet buildings and my artwork, you think it is good, and you don't take pictures of all of them." It seems to me that she sees the smartphone camera as a compliment and as a tool used to provide loving attention. After these instances, I noticed that my daughters usually like it when I take their picture, so long as it is not in an unexpected place in front of other people—then they feel embarrassed by attracting so much attention (e.g., at the entrance to the building of their summer camp, on the first day since the COVID-19 quarantine started, wearing their face masks in front of several camp staff members).

Although it is important to try and understand whether picture taking truly means love in our society, reflecting on other mothers' explanations as well as my own, it seems that mothers take pictures of their children to preserve moments that the child and the mother (and maybe other people in the family) might want to remember. The photos also teach children about their mother, what she saw, what she was excited about, and how she loved them. Wisner writes about her father photographing her when she was a child:

> I remember finding the whole thing kind of grating on my nerves. There was an obsessive quality to the whole thing, a magnifying glass on me, scrutiny of my every move. And yet, I felt loved and appreciated then too. My dad would take breaks to play with me. He was a good listener, a great playmate. And now, I am extremely happy to have piles and piles of gorgeous, carefully considered photos of my childhood, through the lens of my father's eye. I look at some of the photos and want to cry. They capture everything that was beautiful about my childhood.

It is this intimacy that people may realize later on that brings evidence of love—what the father or mother found in their children and the love that they wanted to capture. Arata, for instance, wants her daughter to learn about the love she herself felt for her: "Most of all, I want her to experience even just an ounce of the pride and joy I get to feel watching her grow up."

Photo by Tanalee Youngblood, 2017 (from Unsplash).

Mothers like Arata and Wisner also want to share these moments with family members and friends who will send their love and interest back to them and their children. They will give a moment of attention to the child and often to the mother by responding warmly to the shared image. Reflecting on when she sends pictures of her daughters to family members, S., a Jewish Israeli mother who currently lives in the US, told me, "I send most of the pictures [of my daughters] to my parents and siblings, and I feel more connected to my family when I share the pictures."

Pictures and picture taking are (only) a sign of love. As mothers, we want to capture our love for our children. However, in practice, we know that it is not possible. Many of the actions we take are just echoing love—reminding us of it, symbolizing it, and not embodying it (like presents, notes, words, hugs, and kisses). A picture and even the actual act of photographing have become a sign of love and a way to capture a sense of it. Or as Arata writes, "Although I know I'll never be able to freeze time, I most certainly can frame it." Mothers have learned to express their love with certain acts, artifacts, and practices—a matter of expression and symbolization that is never the actual love itself, which is never truly reachable.

Moreover, in seeing photography as an expression of love, what can be seen as an imposition on the child can also be seen as allowing them to practice social relations through picture taking. Through their performance to/for the camera, the mother or other potential viewers when their picture is taken, they learn to be kind to the person who is looking at them; they also learn the importance of capturing happiness and allowing others to see them and hold part of them. It is a vulnerable position, and it is theatrical. They learn to imitate and copy, to be part of society, and to be proud of who they are, as they are, and as Ervin Goffman explains, all of us in our nature would like to be liked, appreciated, counted as competent, and to maintain our positive face. Sontag explains that "to take a photograph is to participate in another person's (or thing's) mortality, vulnerability, mutability" (15). As mothers, that is what we do every moment. We hold these vulnerabilities of our children, empower them, and help them find peace and serenity through their journeys. An integral part of a mother's relationship with them is exactly what photography is all about.

Conclusions and Discussion

The smartphone camera may become a maternal tool—a tool of care and love that both allows the mother an overt control over her children's history, memory, and behaviour and puts pressure on her. "Good mothering" in the digital era requires her to multitask. She must be at the same time a thoughtful caregiver, an observer, an anthropologist, a journalist, and an artist. The smartphone camera provides technology in the mother's hand, through which she produces her complex relationship with her children and her community and engages in intimate interactions from nearby and far away.

Assemblages of Love

Following Slack and Wise, who propose examining technologies in terms of articulation and assemblage, incorporating Latour's emphasis on how technologies are actually mediators and practice political transformation, translation, delegation, and prescription—I see the smartphone and picture taking and sharing as assemblages of love. The relations developed between the mother, smartphone, children, and community members can be seen as creating a fabric of connections. They are an assemblage of passages and routes that start with the mother's attention and relation to her children and are mediated through the smartphone and its camera to the child who feels loved. That child echoes this love back to the screen and to the mother, and she then extends it when sending the picture to people who view it, feel affinity to the child, and develop interest in them. These community members will later send their loving words and attention back to the mother and the child. This multiplicity of relations, where elsewhere I call "travel" ("Communication as Travel"), allows people to reflect on the routes of communication (McLuhan) and the intertwined, tangled ways of connections that may be called paths of love.

Some of my previous work (*"Mediated Public Intimacy"*; *"Communicative Resurrection"*) deals with the practice of intimacy at a distance, specifically through mediation. I argue that intimacy needs distance, the public, and the mass environment in order to occur, as it is a movement towards the Other. Intimacy is a practice of becoming closer, and it holds a tension with distant conditions. Could photography, as well as the actual photos, be seen as holding distance and gaps between the past and the future, between the photographer and the children? Similarly, Sontag explains that photographs create a sense of the unattainable, "desirability is enhanced by distance" (16). Through photography, we may bring the public into our relationships and into the moment. Yet we practice multiple relations or routes for love—sending it towards our children and community, receiving it back, or directing it to the future. This practice of picture taking and sharing creates a distanciated intimacy between mothers, their children, and the community. Holding distance and gaps between the past and the future, as well as between the photographer and the children, is the essence of enhancing intimacy in the current technological, digital world.

The Smartphone Camera as a Maternal Technology

Understanding mothers within the sociotechnical system of a patriarchal technological environment where they have been historically constructed as an "outsider" (Winner) can allow us to understand the relationship between mothers, their smartphone cameras, and their children. Mothers in Western culture live in a world where they are too often accused of not satisfying their children if they dare to think about themselves and their own wellbeing. They live in a world in which people find fault in how mothers behave, act, and treat their children and blame many social problems on them (Caplan; Douglas and Michaels; Ladd-Taylor). Nevertheless, mothers have used technologies to take care of their children and to keep themselves sane throughout history (from the thermometer to the blender and the pacifier; from listening to radio to using telephones for escapism and as a new way to contact and connect with their children). Smartphones give them easy access to knowledge, help them build authority and credibility in front of their children, and are also used for the creation of history, memory, and affection for their children.

Additionally, the politics of involved media technologies—or even the large sociotechnical system—could be understood through the concept of affordances (Norman) and of agency (Slack and Wise). Affordance is the relationship between the properties of an object and the capabilities of the agent that determined how the object could be used. As mothers, we have learned (or were socialized) to organize ourselves by touch. We have learned to communicate by our fingers, eyes, thoughts, and intentions. Throughout history, we were hardly asked for our opinion in regard to public issues, but we were expected to maintain the whole household and nourish everyone, often in silence (see for instance the ideal wife and mother in nineteenth-century US and in the 1960s). The smartphone, and especially the camera, is a tool in our hand. It responds to touch, with no words; it can go with us wherever we (need to) go; it allows us to gain knowledge, community, and a sense of public life. Taking a picture of a momentary gesture of our children and sending it to family members with a couple of words resembles how we have learned to love our children, to find peace in the little details, to redo and rethink relationships, to make sense of the world, and to live life through the prism of longing and absence (longing for the past, the fear of losing the slippery moment, and the thought of satisfying an unknown future).

The smartphone allows us (even encourages us) to keep our "traditional," intensive mothering roles and to be available to others, not to take breaks, not to prefer one thing over another, and to care and operate in multiple levels of relationships. The smartphone has become "natural" in our hands, touch, and care for others. It has become part of our maternal practices, of our love, and of our management of love. The smartphone (camera) keeps it just between us, our hands, eyes, and our children. On the one hand, it has become a maternal tool that empowers an intensive, "good motherhood," and conforms to an unachievable ideal of motherhood. On the other hand, it undermines the taken-for-granted association of men with machines and technologies as well as the standard conceptions of innovation, production, and work that have been the subject of scrutiny against women. As Wajcman argues, "The politics of technology is integral to the renegotiation of gender power relations" (151).

Photo by moritz320, 2018 (from Pixabay).

Personal Reflections on Writing This Chapter during the Pandemic

This chapter was written before and during the COVID-19 period. The worldwide situation in which many working mothers, including academic ones, found themselves back home—with or without a job—has created significant challenges to home life, family, and careers (see for instance, Guy and Arthur on academic motherhood during COVID-19). However, something interesting evolved during this time for this particular research and writing. I found myself physically and emotionally very close to my daughters, who spent many hours at home, practicing new styles of learning and being. I took pictures of them having a playdate on Zoom or presenting to their class through a computer. Back then, it seemed to me ridiculous, sad, and strange, and definitely moments to capture. Today, more than a year into the pandemic, I find no reason to capture these situations in front of the computer. Through time, I have actually found myself taking more and more pictures of my daughters outside the home, with friends (and masks), trying to capture some moments of sanity and fresh air. Many of my friends, and this is reflected also by some of the interviewees mentioned in this chapter, found themselves spending more time with their children and hence able to take more pictures of them, and especially to share them with family and friends they missed seeing in person even more than before. The pandemic, especially for mothers working from home, has built up larger expectations and obligations to our children, to our employers, and to our faraway families. In a way, the pandemic and its new life setting have emphasized the practices I point to in this chapter and their meanings.

Endnotes

1. For instance, following a survey from 2020, there are 3.5 billion smartphone users in the world, and the majority of the population in more than thirty countries own a smartphone. In the United Kingdom, United Arab Emirates, Germany, and the United States between 79 and 82.9 per cent of the population carry a smartphone (bankmycell).

2. See for instance the domination of European and US men in the invention and development of technologies, such as steamboats, airplanes, trains, cars, gas-turbine engines, printing presses, and typewriters as well as the telegraph, telephone, photography, and cinematography (Buchanan et al.). Although we are increasingly learning about some ignored parts of history where women did play a crucial role, this does not change men's domination in the field or the constant masculine erasure and neglect of women's work, needs, and potential use in relation to technology. See for instance, Carrie Meyer on practices of masculine erasure of farm women using gas engines and influencing this technology's design in the US Midwestern barnyards in the early 1900s. See also Judith McGaw on technology and women's work in and outside the home.

3. See for instance women's service work in the telephone industry (Lipartito).

4. By "nongendered" technology, I mean technological artefacts that were not developed to necessarily address specific family or domestic needs of women or mothers, such as breast pumps or the vacuum cleaner.

5. This chapter is written from a somewhat privileged position—one in which mothers can spend time with their children to take their pictures (and not work long hours outside of the home or the country) and/or have access to smartphones and family members and friends who are interested in receiving such photos. I recognize that these privileges are not enjoyed by all mothers in Western culture or elsewhere. For many people, mothering itself is a privilege. I carry this sensitivity with me while studying this topic.

6. This chapter is based on multiple methodologies, including studying posts and articles by mothers who write about the practice of taking pictures of their children in public blogs, conversations with friends and family members who are mothers, observations of mothers in my living environments, mostly in the US and Israel where I have spent the last ten years, as well as autoethnographic reflections of my own practices of motherhood. Critical feminist family theory calls to centre awareness and research of the personal/familial as political and to develop feminist auto-ethnographic explorations of family identities, practices, and

cultural discourses (Sotirin and Ellingson 115). Following this, I emphasized aspects of vulnerability, self-reflexivity, and praxis. I also used my communication studies background in studying motherhood and media technologies to analyze "picture-taking [as] an event in itself" (Sontag 11) and as a communicative act that reconstructs relationships and identity.

7. Some of the sources I use are taken from the mothers writing on the website *ScaryMommy*, which collects personal writings and reflections that are "a fresh and unfiltered perspective on parenting." Wisner is a mother who works as a writer and as the associate editor of *ScaryMommy*. See the website here: www.scarymommy. com/category/parenting/motherhood/.

8. Some mothers value friendship, so they take pictures of their children with friends; others value generational relationships, so they capture moments with grandparents; others value creativity, so they capture different artworks and projects; and so on. For instance, S. reflects on moments she captures: "I'm looking to capture their happiness and natural behavior and their interaction with one another, and the background—the places we've been." The values inherent in picture taking could be developed further in future work.

Works Cited

A. Private correspondence. Israel–Fort Collins, August 2020. Phone.

Arata, Jenn Press. "Why I Take Too Many Pictures of My Daughter." *Scary Mommy*, 30 Oct. 2015, www.scarymommy.com/why-i-take-too-many-pictures-of-my-daughter/. Accessed 12 May 2022.

Aronis, Carolin. "*Mediated Public Intimacy: Practices of Popular Media in Establishing Intimacy with Audiences.*" PhD dissertation, The Hebrew University of Jerusalem, 2015.

Aronis, Carolin. "Communicative Resurrection: Letters to the Dead in the Israeli Newspaper." *Journal of Communication* 67 (6), 2017, pp. 827-850.

Aronis, Carolin. "Communication as Travel: The Genre of Letters to the Dead in Public Media." *Explorations in Media Ecology* 18 (1–2) 2019, pp. 23-42.

Aronis, Carolin. "Reconstructing Mothers' Responsibility and Guilt: Journalistic Coverage of the 'Remedia Affair' in Israel." *Discourse & Communication* 13(4), 2019, pp. 377-397.

Badinter, Elizabeth. *The Conflict: How Modern Motherhood Undermines the Status of Women.* Metropolitan Books, 2011.

Bankmycell. "How Many Smartphones Are In The World?" *Bankmycell: Blog*, 15 Nov. 2020, www.bankmycell.com/blog/how-many-phones-are-in-the-world. Accessed 12 May 2022.

Barthes, Roland. *Camera Lucida: Reflections on Photography.* Hill and Wang, 2010.

Buchanan, Robert Angus. "History of Technology." *Britannica*, www.britannica.com/technology/history-of-technology. Accessed 12 May 2022.

Caplan, Paula J. "Don't Blame Mother: Then and Now." *Maternal Theory: Essential Readings*, edited by Andrea O'Reilly, Demeter Press, 2007, pp. 592-600.

Chan, Ko Ling, et al." Using Smartphone-Based Psychoeducation to Reduce Postnatal Depression among First-Time Mothers: Randomized Controlled Trial." *JMIR* mHealth uHealth, vol. 7, no. 5, 2019, p. e12794.

Chen, Huan, Liling Zhou, and Shufang Han. "Protest and Protect: Chinese Urban Mothers' Perception of Smartphone (Tablet) in Their Everyday Lives' Communication and Interaction with Young Children." *Journal of Asian Pacific Communication*, vol. 27, 2017, pp. 99-120.

Craig, Lyn. "Does Father Care Mean Fathers Share?: A Comparison of How Mothers and Fathers in Intact Families Spend Time with Children." *Gender & Society*, 20(2), 2006, 259–281. doi:10.1177/0891243205285212.

do Mar Pereira, Maria. *Power, Knowledge, and Feminist Scholarship: An Ethnography of Academia.* Routledge, 2017.

Douglas, Susan J., and Meredith W. Michaels. *The Mommy Myth: The Idealization of Motherhood and How It Has Undermined All Women.* Free Press, 2005.

Feeney, Stephanie, and Nancy K. Freeman. "Smartphones and Social Media: Ethical Implications for Educators." *YC Young Children*, vol.

70, no. 1, 2015, pp. 98-101.

Foucault, Michel. *Discipline and Punish: The Birth of the Prison*. Second Vintage Books, 1977.

Friedan, Betty. *The Feminine Mystique*. W. W. Norton & Company, INC, 1963.

Gabso, Morin. Private correspondence. Israel–Fort Collins, August 2020. Phone.

Goffman, Ervin. *The Presentation of Self in Everyday Life*. Anchor Books, 1959.

Guy, Batsheva, and Brittany Arthur. "Academic Motherhood during COVID 19: Navigating Our Dual Roles as Educators and Mothers." *Gender, Work & Organization*, vol. 27, 2020, pp. 887-99.

Hays, Sharon. *The Cultural Contradictions of Motherhood*. Yale University Press, 1996.

Kotchemidova, Christina. "Why We Say 'Cheese': Producing the Smile in Snapshot Photography." *Critical Studies in Media Communication*, 22(1), 2005, pp. 2–25.

Jackson, Michele H. Exploring Gender, Feminism and Technology from a Communication Perspective: An Introduction and Commentary. *Women's Studies in Communication*, vol. 30, no. 2, 2007, pp. 149-56.

Lachover, Einat. "Why Women Still Can't Have It All": Israeli Media Discourse on Motherhood vs. Career. *HAGAR—Studies in Culture, Polity, and Identities*, vol. 11, no. 2, 2014, pp. 105-26.

Ladd-Taylor, Molly. "Mother-Worship/Mother-Blame: Politics and Welfare in an Uncertain Age." *Maternal Theory: Essential Readings*, edited by Andrea O'Reilly, Demeter Press, 2007, pp. 600-67.

Lipartito, Kenneth. "When Women Were Switches: Technology, Work, and Gender in the Telephone Industry, 1890–1920." *The American Historical Review*, vol. 99, no. 4, 1994, pp. 1075–1111.

Marvin, Carolyn. *When Old Technologies Were New: Thinking about Electric Communication in the Late Nineteenth Century*. Oxford University Press, 1988.

McGaw, Judith A. "Women and the History of American Technology." *Signs*, vol. 7, no. 4, 1982, pp. 798-828.

McLuhan, Marshal. *Understanding Media: The Extensions of Man*. McGraw Hill, 1964.

Meyer, Carrie A. "Farm Women and Gas Engines: The New Technology in the Barnyard." *Indiana Magazine of History*, vol. 114, 2018, pp.115-44.

Moores, Shaun. "From 'Unruly Guest' to 'Good Companion': The Gendered Meanings of Early Radio in the Home." Ed. Caroline Mitchell, *Women and Radio: Airing Differences*, edited by Caroline Mitchell, Routledge, 2000, pp. 116-25.

Norman, Donald. *The Design of Everyday Things*. Basic Books, 2013.

Phelan, Shanon K., and Elizabeth Anne Kinsella. "Picture This ... Safety, Dignity, and Voice—Ethical Research with Children: Practical Considerations for the Reflexive Researcher." *Qualitative Inquiry*, vol. 19, no. 2, 2013, pp. 81-90.

S. Private correspondence. New York–Fort Collins, August 2020. Phone.

Shloim, N., et al. "'It's Like Giving Him a Piece of Me.': Exploring UK and Israeli Women's Accounts of Motherhood and Feeding." *Appetite*, 95, 2015, pp. 58-66.

Slack, Jennifer Daryl, and Macgregor J. Wise. *Culture and Technology: A Primer*. Peter Lang Publishing, 2015.

Sontag, Susan. *On Photography*. Penguin Books, 2017.

Sotirin, Patricia J., and Laura L. Ellingson. "Critical Feminist Family Communication Theory: Gender, Power, and Praxis." *Engaging Theories in Family Communication: Multiple Perspectives*, edited by D.O Braithwaite, E.A Suter, and K. Floyd, Routledge, Second Edition, 2018, pp. 110-21.

Steiner, Linda, and Einat Lachover. "The Mommy Wars: On the Home Front and Waged Abroad. *Feminist Media Studies*, vol. 16, no. 5, 2016, pp. 869-85. doi:10.1080/14680777.2015.1137337.

Wajcman, Judy. "Feminist Theories of Technology." Cambridge *Journal of Economics*, vol. 34, no. 1, 2010, pp. 143-52.

Wall, Glenda. "Moral Constructions of Motherhood in Breastfeeding Discourse." *Gender and Society*, vol. 15, no. 4, 2001, pp. 592–610.

Winner, Langdon. *The Whale and the Reactor: A Search for Limits in an*

Age of High Technology (second edition). University of Chicago Press, 2020.

Wisner, Wendy. "I'm That Mom Who Takes Too Many Photos of Her Kids." *Scary Mommy,* 7 May,2016, www.scarymommy.com/mom-taking-pictures-kids/. Accessed 12 May 2022.

Chapter 4

Whose Story is It? Sharenting in Blogs by Some Mothers of Autistic Children

Daena J. Goldsmith and Amalia Ackerman

"Sharenting" is a term coined to refer to the online content parents share about their children and their parenting. Judging by the results of several recent surveys, they share quite a lot. Among social media users, 89 per cent of mothers say they have posted photos, videos, or information about their child (Auxier et al. 56). By age two, 92 per cent of US children have an online presence, and a parent's first post typically happens when the child is around three months old (Businesswire). Most parents feel they are doing a good job in what and how much they choose to post (Family Online Safety Institute), but they also say they worry about revealing private information and sharing photos (CS Mott Children's Hospital). One in five admit they have posted something about their child that the child has found embarrassing, has asked the parent to take down, or may find embarrassing in the future (Family Online Safety Institute).

In a blog post entitled "Online Privacy," one blogger[1] reflected:

You see, blogs and Facebook pages and online discussion forums have largely replaced the coffee klatches and play date talks and living room chats of the past. This is where we do our talking: about ourselves, our kids, our pets, our lives. It's where we bitch about our spouses and complain about, well, everything. We've gotten comfortable here. I'd argue that we've gotten a little too comfortable here. Or a lot.

Because, as much as this might feel like one, it's not a living room and we're not in a friend's house. This is a public format on a digital platform with an infinite memory. And when we write here about the intimate aspects of our kids' lives, we are sharing those details with anyone who happens upon them now or seeks them in the future—their teachers, their classmates, their classmates' parents, the postman, the pastor, the creepy guy down the street. We are sharing the details of our children's lives with ALL of them.

This isn't a world that our parents had to navigate. It's all new stuff. So we don't tend to think of the long-term implications of social networking and blogging and commenting in online forums. But they are real and they are nearly unfathomably far-reaching.

Although this is not a world our parents had to navigate, ours is not the first generation to grapple with new understandings of the boundaries between public and private. Contemporary ideas about the sanctity of family privacy arose in conjunction with the idealization of the nuclear family; in other times and places, childrearing was not considered a private enterprise engaged in spaces outside of the public eye and distinct from economic production (Thurer 142-48). Participation in social media can prompt us to question our assumptions about privacy, acknowledge limits to individual control of information, and figure out new ways to navigate a context in which public-private boundaries are blurred (Marwick and boyd 1052).

Like coffee klatches and living room chats, online sharenting serves important purposes. We celebrate family life and share it with friends and family near and far (Damkjaer 213-14). We make sense of our experiences and document them in the online version of a journal or scrapbook (Blum-Ross and Livingstone 116). Seeing what others post and reading their reactions remind us that we are not alone, and we find information, support, and validation for mothering (Lupton, Pedersen, and Thomas 731). As we write this chapter, COVID-19 has limited our access to coffee shops and our friends' kitchens, making virtual connections more important than ever and sharenting even more alluring.

However, there are risks of doing this online. There are rare but frightening cases of what happens when the "creepy guy down the street" (or across the globe) accesses children's information or images. More common, yet still significantly problematic, are outcomes of embarrassment, interpersonal conflict, or diminished trust between parents and children (Family Online Safety Institute). Sharenting creates a "digital dilemma": "To represent one's own identity as a parent means making public aspects of a (potentially vulnerable) child's life and yet because they are the parent, they are precisely the person primarily responsible for protecting that child's privacy" (Blum-Ross and Livingstone 112).

The dilemmas of sharenting extend beyond reconciling the needs of individual mothers and children. The intimacy and support that come about through sharenting can create a community to which one feels a responsibility (Blum-Ross and Livingstone 122). Likewise, as norms for online behaviour are still taking shape, "an ethical gaffe is not an isolated personal self-promotional misstep ... but damaging to the development and ethos" of the larger collective constructed from user practices (McLeod Rogers and Green 36). These communal dimensions of sharenting are consistent with feminist theorizing about relational approaches to privacy.

We explore this communal dimension to sharenting among a subcommunity of mom bloggers who wrote about their lives with autistic children across a period spanning from 2004 to 2017. These bloggers experienced a heightened need to share stories as well as a high level of self-reflection about the risks of sharing, not only for them and their children but also for other mothers and for adult autistics who had a stake in what they shared and how. The principles and practices these mothers developed, as well as the collective, conversational process through which they developed them, are instructive for those navigating this new aspect of mothering.

The Mamasphere circa 2004 to 2017

Mom blogs—journal style personal blogs chronicling the everyday ups and downs of motherhood—became popular in the early 2000s. By 2012, there were an estimated 3.9 million mom blogs (Laird), one-third of all bloggers were mothers (Nielsen Newswire), and 18.3 million internet-using mothers said they read blogs at least once a month (Walters). Some high profile mothers monetized their blogs, and this has negatively shaped many readers' perceptions of the genre (Borda 138; Hunter 1314). However, most mom blogs are spaces for self-expression, mutual support, and community for an audience that is at once intimate and public (Morrison 37).[2] The longer posts, slower pace, and reciprocal reading and commenting that characterize blogs facilitate narrative sensemaking and social support (Nardi, Schiano, and Gumbrecht). Although many moms blog less frequently now and use Facebook, Instagram, or Twitter for daily updates, their endeavour to find others who are going through similar life experiences persists across time and adapts to technological change.

Concerns for privacy and authenticity emerged as mom blogs rose to prominence (Goldsmith 120). Many early mom bloggers began writing when their children were small. As those children grew old enough to read (and possibly object to) what their mothers were writing, the internet was developing powerful search tools, and users were becoming aware of the reach and persistence of online text and images. A few high profile cases of uncivil discourse, doxing, and trolling prompted caution (Loe, Cumpstone, and Miller 190). Bloggers and readers discussed the risks and rewards of public storytelling, the ethics of posting about children, and the obligation to write authentically. This self-reflection had an even greater urgency for mothers of autistic children, who wrote during a period of intense public attention to autism and the emergence of autism self-advocacy groups. Mothers writing about autistic kids were caught up in online controversies about how to conceptualize autism and whether and how to represent a mother's experience. Online conflicts erupted among parents with differing beliefs about cause (e.g., MMR vaccines) and the efficacy and ethics of treatment. Autistic self-advocates criticized parents who framed autism as a tragedy, posted accounts that violated children's privacy, and contributed to negative stereotypes.

The nature and evolution of the mom blog coupled with the

distinctive challenges of writing about an autistic child make blogs by mothers of autistic children written during this period of time (2004–2017) a productive site for examining sharenting. These mothers had a pressing need for the sensemaking and support they found from storytelling in a community of reciprocal reading. Yet they wrote during a time in the history of social media and of autism when the ethics of telling their stories publicly were called into question.

Our analyses are part of a larger project tracking a sample of blogs by mothers of autistic children over a decade-long period.[3] We selected from the larger dataset fifty-five posts that included reflection and discussion about sharenting and/or engaged in strategies responsive to privacy and other concerns. We each read and annotated posts independently and met to distill principles and practices we saw. Then we returned to the posts and our notes to refine our analysis and select illustrative cases. We found discussions of sharenting principles revolved around different claims to story ownership that produced ethical dilemmas and a range of practices for responding.

Sharenting Principles: Whose Story Is It?

In contrast to individualist notions of privacy, we align with feminist theorists who conceptualize privacy as relational and contextual (Bannerman 2187-88). Decisions to share personal information take into account relationships and reasons for sharing: Information we feel comfortable sharing (or having shared about us) in one social context may not be appropriate for sharing in another. As family members manage these boundaries, the information they share is often co-owned because stories of family life implicate multiple actors (Petronio and Venetis). Parents writing about children have both "privileged access to and implicit power over" their child's story (Couser 17), and this complicates the ethical assessment of risks, benefits, consent, and representation (Couser 17-33). "Mother" is a relational identity, blurring the boundaries between what part of a story is hers to tell and what part belongs to her child. Recipients of a story also become co-owners of information because they can choose whether and what parts of a story they might retell (repost) in another context.

Storytelling in social media further challenges a notion of privacy as a purely individual decision to restrict access within clearly defined private and public spheres (Marwick and boyd 1052). Depending on the platform, the audience for a story may encompass contacts from many different spheres of our lives (friends, family, or professional contacts), and this complicates sharenting decisions. Once posted, a story may be reposted, tagged, or accessed by friends of friends, and posts from an earlier time can be reintroduced, making it difficult to anticipate who might eventually become co-owners and in what context they will encounter the information. Alice Marwick and danah boyd encourage scholars and social media users alike to attend closely to how users develop practices, negotiate norms, and establish trust.

A feminist approach to sharenting conceptualizes privacy as relational—the self who is revealed is formed in and connected to others, and she exercises agency through networks of relations (Bannerman 2188). Our analysis of these blogs revealed a keen awareness of (and debates about) the interests of multiple owners of a mother's story. Decisions about whether and how to tell stories were grounded in reasoning about relationships and how sharenting honoured or violated them. As they articulated claims to story ownership, concerns for privacy were not only about who had a right to share (or not) but also about the relational expectations and functions of sharing (or not). What was at stake was not simply control of information about an autonomous self but constructions of selves-in-relation.

The Mother's Story

A journal-style mom blog is always the mother's story, as she writes about events in her daily life and how she felt and thought about them. Mothers describe the benefits of telling their stories. For example, one blogger thanked her readers, saying: "I don't have words...big enough, broad enough, deep enough to tell you how blessed I feel by this community, by each and every one of you, who come here to laugh with me, learn with me, celebrate with me, cry with me, fight, scrap, claw and pray with me day in and day out. Your words lifted me today. Your presence here lifts me every day" ("Of Leaky Eyes"). Shannon Rosa explained how writing a "laundry list" of events from a difficult ten-day period was what she needed to do "in order for this site to be a functional journal" ("Intense 10 Days"). Although she said she did not want to be "a whiny git," it was important for her "to get all this down, even in raw form" so that she could look back, learn, and "try to do better."

Telling one's story risks embarrassment or negative evaluation yet self-knowledge, social support, and intimacy with readers depends upon that vulnerability. Stephanie Klein believed in "writing as honestly as I can" as if in a private diary. She asked herself: "Am I being authentic? Is this how I'd say it if it was just me?" She felt this gave her a right to share: "When it's yours to experience, can't you do with it what you'd like?" Some comments on this post noted that disclosing publicly rather than in a private journal or among a few intimates increases the stakes to a blogger and her child; even so, many who responded presumed that the story is the mother's to tell. One praised Klein for being "so real, so honest" and being a role model for her to live her own life and not the one others wanted her to live. Another succinctly stated: "You're blogging for yourself; it isn't a public service and shouldn't be judged as such."

The Child's Story

Writing about mothering puts a child somewhere in the story, often as the central character or source of action. Some posts focused mostly on the mother's experience; others described a child's experience, and a few attempted to articulate the child's perspective. Nonetheless, when mothers write about a child, they are always mediating their child's story in some way.

Some posts reflected upon how a child's "co-ownership" of stories constrained honesty. Writing about one's child could risk exploitation or identity theft, but concerns were more often about embarrassing the child or revealing information that could limit future job prospects or opportunities. It can be valorous to allow oneself to be vulnerable in the service of honest disclosure, but embarrassing one's child or exposing a child to risk violates a mother's obligation to protect. In addition to what others might think, mothers must also consider the hurt an older child or young adult might feel from someday reading a mother's account and concluding that "He made his family's life difficult just by being who he is" (comment on "Online Privacy").

Bloggers articulated several principles for determining when it is acceptable to disclose the child's story, including asking the child's consent and/or considering, "At that age, would I have been comfortable with my mom posting this online for everyone I know and the world to see?" ("One Question"). Some bloggers claimed that these were simple and sufficient guides, but complications arose in applying them. For example, one blogger asks her daughters before telling personal stories about them. She reported on her non-autistic daughter telling her to stop asking: "It's not that I don't want you to write about me.... I just get uncomfortable when you ASK me if it's okay. It's okay. Just please stop asking" ("Of Leaky Eyes"). We suspect her daughter's trust developed from a respectful history of asking, yet this example highlights how seeking consent invites children into a decision-making role they may not want.

Several bloggers insisted that autistic children have the same right to consent as non-autistic children, yet autistic differences in social and communication skills can complicate obtaining consent. In his work on the ethics of life-writing, Thomas Couser cautions parents who write about disabled children that "The granting of consent...[does] not foreclose the possibility of ethical conflict" (13). He posits that even if disabled children consent, they may "not fully imagine, and thus not censor, the way [they are] being presented to a reading public" (65). One blogger described these complexities in her conversations with her son. When asking his consent, she reminds him "that people he knows read the blog" ("Protecting Him Online"). When her son suggests topics for her blog, she sometimes declines. Her multistep process includes his consent plus her own "multiple what-if analyses, being mindful of his privacy both now and in the future, appropriate barriers between him and the internet, and evaluating information through the lens of my personal values." This maternalistic protection may seem obvious for younger children, but with an older child, it could run afoul of a mother's desire to respect and presume competence. One commenter described a late teen who communicated that he would be fine with posting videos of self-injurious behavior. She asked: "Do we presume competence as in, he says yes, so it's yes? Or do we presume competence as in, he deserves privacy that [a non-autistic] kid would want even if he says he is comfortable?" (comment on "Online Privacy").

For many bloggers and commenters, conflicts between the values associated with the mother's story versus the child's story must be resolved in favour of protecting children. As one mother explained, "My desire to talk about *my* challenges, *my* fears, my own insecurities about the process, cannot ever trump her right to privacy" ("Autism, Puberty, and Respect"). Telling a story as a *mother* invoked and privileged responsibilities to the child.

Our Story

Blogging creates relationships with audiences that are always present, even when they are not recognized. An audience co-owns a story in several senses. First, once they have information, they control whether or not to share it. Second, they influence the story through the storyteller's anticipation of what the audience needs to know or wants to hear and through the audience's interjection of comments and questions. Although interaction is asynchronous, past responses and anticipation of future ones shape how bloggers tell stories and comments on a post become part of the story, too. Third, readers who are mothers or autistic may feel ownership of how their group is represented by an individual mother's or child's story.

Three different audiences said they had a stake in the stories these mothers told, including regular readers (many of whom were also bloggers connected through reciprocal reading), mothers of autistic children (or, more broadly, disabled children), and autistic adults.[4] Co-ownership with these audiences complicated the mother's and child's rights to a story, and there were also conflicts of interest among these audiences.

Our Story: Community of Bloggers and Readers

Readers read for the same reasons mothers blog: to make sense of experience and find support and validation. When bloggers withheld information to protect an older child's privacy, some readers accused them of the following: "You aren't giving them the support that they need, that you gave them in the earlier years" (comment on "Online Privacy"). One reader credited "blogs and tweets and Facebook" with teaching her about autism and advocating for her son. For this reader, these stories changed everything by showing her that her son and family were not alone: "And they did it by showing me the joy, but acknowledging the challenges and how they had worked through them." She reported a sense of loss when another mother's and child's story became unavailable: "Today, given the RIGHTFUL recognition of the right to privacy for our kids, that wouldn't happen. In fact, it isn't happening for me any longer, and so we are now wandering rather alone through puberty and its attendant challenges" (comment on "One Question").

The blogger-reader relationship can create an insider perspective to which bloggers appeal to justify writing about topics that might otherwise be seen as inappropriate: "You know what I mean. You know what I intend." For example, Klein defended the humorous intent behind nicknames that others found offensive: "Who loves that little tater tot more than his own mother? Why can't I call him whatever the hell I want when everyone knows it's said with love? And people do know that." Conversely, reciprocal readership can enable opaque references that still make sense to regular readers. For example, in a post celebrating her son's role in a school play, Jean Winegardner acknowledged the following: "The experience as a whole wasn't perfect. In fact, I just wrote and deleted seven long paragraphs about the issues I have with the way everything went down for Jack. What it boils down to is that often inclusion isn't what we want it to be, especially in after-school activities" ("Jack's Debut"). A commenter responded: "I get every single syllable of this. That which is said and that which wasn't. Truly. Every syllable."[5]

Our Story: Other Mothers

Many regular readers are mothers of autistic children who say these are "our" stories, too. One commenter said she read because of "the brave, honest, raw emotion that hits me right at my core to tell me my family is not alone." She continued: "By sharing your truth, you are sharing ours as well. By giving it a space and a voice, you tell us all that it's okay to struggle..." (comment on "Truth"). Claiming ownership in another mother's story validated difficulties and offered hope.

Telling "our story" also represents mothers of autistic children to an outside world that misunderstands, stigmatizes, and fails to provide adequate support. Telling their collective story, "warts and all" could "[let] people see what it is like to live with and love" disabled children and writing about acceptance "begets others' acceptance in the long run" (comment on Klein). For example, Martine O'Callaghan used a story about the challenges and the fun of getting around with her son to discredit the accusation that parents seek an autism diagnosis to "cash in" on government benefits ("To Mr. Bigot"). Commenters replied with their own stories of stigma, mother-blaming, misinformation, and limitations of state support.

Our Story: Autistic Adults

Just as mothers may identify with one another's stories, adult autistic readers may find their story in a child's story. These blogs represent autistics to outsiders, and as Amy Sequenzia explained, portraying autistic children in their most difficult and vulnerable moments "can, and will affect how we are treated, and the expectations about us." Conversely, writing that includes autistic strengths and the rewards of family life with autism can promote acceptance. Writing about her son's afterschool program for children and adults with disabilities, Kristina Chew observed, "Theirs, and Charlie's, are faces that are too easily hidden because society prefers not to see them; because society is bothered by 'them'" ("Something").

Because they are the adults autistic children will someday be, some autistic readers claimed they were better able than a non-autistic mother to ascertain "If I were autistic, would I want to share this story?" One blogger said her sharenting had evolved in response to comments by autistic adults and through reading their blogs. In "Dear Jennifer," she described thinking before posting: "Will Jennifer think this is okay to share?" She explained: "Your life experience as an autistic woman, just like my twelve year-old daughter will soon enough be, leads you to a different, and often more stringent, set of criteria for what is acceptable to share and what's not."

Finally, claiming an autistic child's story as "our story" can come from a desire to amplify autistic voices rather than presuming that non-autistic parents and medical experts are the authorities on autistic experience. For example, Jennifer (the same of the "Dear Jennifer" post) reminded parents, "You are not your child's voice.... You are just the one who can amplify their voice the most." She urged parents to take advantage of insights from autistic adults: "Listen to your child's adult peers.... Disabled advocates have lived through your children's futures" ("It's Not All About You").

Sharenting Practices: What Is a Mother to Do?

Multiple ownership claims create challenges for online storytelling: How can mothers authentically tell their own stories (and gain the benefits this provides for individual mothers, communities of reciprocal readers, and mothers of disabled children) while respecting their children's claims to their stories and the implications for representing autistics? We observed a variety of practices that balanced the interests of multiple story owners.

One solution was to segment topics and audiences. Some bloggers designated "unbloggable" topics (e.g., meltdowns, aggression, toilet habits, and sexuality) that were better disclosed in private online spaces or trusted relationships offline. As one blogger put it, "Get a girlfriend" to whom you can express frustration or dark humour (as reported by Rosa, "Blogging about Our Children"). Another blogger clarified that "not sharing publicly doesn't mean not reaching out privately" by sending a private message, creating a closed Facebook group, starting an email list, or talking to "the mom you see every week in the waiting room at speech therapy" ("Untitled"). Some argued that adult autistics should be the ones to write about highly personal topics. An autistic reader called this combination of private contact with other parents and information from willing autistic adults "the best of all worlds" (comment on "One Question"). However, some readers resisted this solution, saying that when hard stories are told only in private, they become unavailable to those who need them most, especially parents of newly diagnosed children who lack a network of autism-wise private contacts. Raw honesty is what drew many readers to these blogs, and this can be a temptation to bloggers who seek to expand their readership (McLeod Rogers and Green 42-46). The expectation that autistic adults will reveal otherwise "unbloggable" topics is also imperfect; there are still risks. and they are borne by autistics, although at least it is done with consent by adults.

When mothers did post about personal topics, writing about both positive and negative emotions and experiences was one way to remain true to their story while acknowledging other story owners. They said this bittersweet balance is what constitutes telling one's story honestly. As Chew observed: "There are lots of tough moments when, indeed, [self-injurious behaviours] occur, and there are lots of happy, lovely times when it just feels good to be alive, going through the daily journey of our lives together" ("It's the End"). Perhaps because public perceptions of autism tend to be negative, bloggers who include positive experiences can be accused of "wearing rose-coloured glasses" (Chew, "Telling It") or "making autism seem like it's all sunshine and lollipops" (Rosa, "The Bloody Shirt"). We observed many skillful examples that plausibly wove together positive and negative parts of mothers' and children's stories.

One example is Winegardner's post celebrating the last day of school ("Happy Dance"). She alluded to challenges but also lovingly described the interests each child developed over the year, portraying autistic attributes in a positive light. Her child who "isn't particularly verbally expressive" has "a lot going on inside [his] head" and instead of bemoaning his intense interest in Mario Brothers she marveled at his ability to find and catalogue information well enough to "write a three-volume biography of them." Of her son who had "the rockiest year" she wrote: "I am awed by how brave [he is] ... how much he's learned. I told him how proud of him I am." That school posed significant difficulties was clear from the conclusion of the post: "For those of you who have kids who struggle in school, who work SO goddamn hard to get through each day, and who do so with strength, resolve, the skin of their teeth, or just plain sticktoitiveness, please join me in celebrating the last motherfucking day of school!" The ice cream shop where they always go on the last day is "weird" and "kind of grungy" but "makes all of us happy"—a metaphor for the blend of positive and negative in her story of resilience and happiness at a summer-long respite from the challenges of mainstream schooling.

If a particular post was imbalanced, mothers sometimes revisited it in a postscript the next day. For example, Rosa reworked a story about moving to a house that could accommodate her son's needs: "I realized that it portrays [Leo] negatively. So let me rephrase in a way that is truer to our intentions" ("Moving"). Balance, not tragedy, is her truth.

She described gaining "enough space for [Leo] to be [Leo], year round" so that being active could alleviate his "horrible winter downward behavioral spirals." She makes brief reference to problematic behaviour, but then emphasizes: "We hate seeing him be so miserable, when we know what a sunny, happy boy he can be." Other attributes of the house were portrayed as making everyone happy. She admitted: "This move will drop us into hell for a month or so, but then we'll all be as close to heaven as we're likely to get." She concluded by reporting her son's recent expressions of affection, his hard work to curb problem behaviour, and her telling him "how wonderful he is."

We observed two approaches to writing about difficult topics. One was to allude to a child's behaviour but without elaborating upon painful details, as Winegardner did in her last day of school post. Many bloggers used metaphors, such as "rocky," "rough," or "stormy." Another example came from Rosa's description of her son's behaviours as ways "his frustration [at communication difficulties] has been manifesting" and as "ways we need to be very careful to help him redirect and learn to control for his own social and participation-in-society wellbeing" ("Intense 10 Days"). Her audiences do not need vivid detail to imagine what those behaviours are likely to be.

A contrasting approach described difficulties briefly and matter-of-factly, normalizing and contextualizing them in daily life. In "Autism and Authenticity," Chew reflected: "In addition to being '100 per cent honest' about Charlie and our life here, I have also always tried to be upbeat and write about how life with autism is awful, joyful, and good. I frequently ask myself, how am I portraying Charlie? Am I misrepresenting him?" She continued with this description of "the truth about Charlie today":

He hit his head once on the carpet at 9:00 a.m. at school. He did his share of talking the rest of the day. He was very happy when Danielle picked him up at his afterschool program; he worked well for an hour and a half with his therapist; he hung out in our backyard with a Capri Sun and a bowl of chips and got mad at me when I asked him too intently about using the bathroom.... Charlie was puzzled when I told him it is Rosh Hashanah tomorrow, and there is no school. "School tomorrow. Backpack." He smiled and sang a Wiggles song: "On your holiday, on your holiday, we love to have a very good time." We love to love you, lovely Charlie, and may the good times grow.

Chew touches on behaviours that could be portrayed as deficits (e.g., self-injurious behaviour, regulating bodily functions, difficulty with disrupted routine, and echolalia), but instead she narrates an ordinary day in which Charlie also communicates, enjoys activities, participates in self-care, and brings joy to his mother. Small details (e.g., afterschool pick up, Capri Sun and chips in the backyard, bedtime, and the Wiggles) liken their story to those of other mothers and children. In another post, Chew's matter of fact description of a meltdown in a park was sandwiched between simple pleasures that occurred before and after ("Why Charlie"). She juxtaposed that story to a news account of a child killed in a car accident and concluded: "Sometimes it seems that 'autism' can become synonymous with 'tragedy' and this cannot be right.... That moment when Charlie became a tiger—seemed as if he were having a seizure—ended with a crying boy in my arms, a boy who stumbled up and shuffled and ran eagerly home, a boy with his whole life still to be lived.... Charlie is not a tragedy." To tell her story and Charlie's story while authentically representing autism involves resisting overdramatizing the ups and downs of their everyday life.

These examples of bittersweet narration are also noteworthy for focusing as much or more on what is difficult for the child as they do on what is difficult for the mother. Problematic behaviour is shown to stem from a child's understandable frustration at not being able to communicate or from navigating a world not built for autistic cognitive and sensory abilities. Whether Winegardner's passionate tribute to her children's resilience, Rosa's exploration of the causes of Leo's distress and accommodations to alleviate it, or Chew's determination to accurately interpret her son—each attempt to understand their child's perspective on the events of their shared days. They admit this is an imperfect telling of the child's story. Says Rosa at the outset of her description of Leo's rough ten days: "I don't know why." And Chew wonders, "Am I misrepresenting him?" Nonetheless, they acknowledge multiple owners of the stories they tell.

They do so in the service of being better mothers. In "The Bloody Shirt," Rosa told how her son tripped and fell while walking to a cafe to get a scone. He was upset at a bloodied palm and knee, but she knew it would be worse if they departed from their announced plan, so they went ahead in bloodied clothes and then had an enjoyable day at the beach. Rosa wrote: "Autistic people would never claim their lives are without challenges, so I can't say that for Leo either. But even when times are rough, there are choices parents can make—based on doing our best to understand what our autistic kids need, as opposed to what we ourselves prefer—that lead to much happier outcomes for everyone." Doing her best for Leo referred to her mothering choices and to her blogging practices. She said ten years ago that she would have forced him to go home and change clothes: "And then I would have blogged about how hard it all was *for me*. Learn from me, don't be me. At least not ten-years-ago-me."

Conclusion

As sharenting has become more common, critics have called for an end to it and have blamed parents (especially mothers) who share (Livingstone and Blum-Ross 103). That sharenting continues, even as awareness of risks becomes more widely known, suggests that simple proscriptions are inadequate. Blaming individual mothers overlooks the powerful incentives to share that are built into social media (Marwick and boyd 1054) and evokes a long history of devaluing women's domestic experience (Green and McLeod Rogers 260-62). It also overlooks the relational nature of privacy and ways our stories implicate one another; recognizing this shifts our attention to the principles and practices we develop for managing co-ownership (Marwick and boyd 1063). Instead of blanket condemnation or rigid ground rules, mothers who share need "reflexive practices that encourage self-examination and allow some space for diversity of opinion and approach" (McLeod Rogers and Green 33).

Our analysis focused on a subcommunity in which this kind of self-reflexive practice and communal debate occurred. What emerged was an appreciation for co-ownership of personal stories. As these mothers articulated principles that governed sharenting decisions, they considered not simply individual rights to control information but the relational impacts of telling a story and telling it in a particular way. Correspondingly, what was shared was not only information about a particular mother or child but also information about "mothers like us" or "autistics like us" that invoked relational obligations and broader cultural conversations.

Many mom bloggers experience the digital dilemma of how to obtain support for mothering without compromising a child's privacy, but this tension is magnified for mothers who blog about autistic children. Blogging may be a lifeline when following a diagnosis mothers find themselves in need of information and experience that are often not available in their own personal network. Writing can achieve narrative sensemaking, comments can provide social support, and connecting with other bloggers can yield insight and affirmation. However, writing publicly implicates a child whose cognitive and social differences complicate obtaining consent and whose autism is still a source of stigma in the broader society. In the face of this dilemma, mothers might well decide not to blog at all.

Our analysis points to what might have been lost had these mothers elected never to blog. Several bloggers mentioned how their thinking evolved through the process of blogging and through interactions with strangers whom they might not have otherwise met. If her blog had not been public, would the author of "Dear Jennifer" have met Jennifer? Autism acceptance and the voices of autistic adults are still minority voices in the larger cultural discourses surrounding autism. Mothers who gained new perspectives from multiple audiences were able to amplify autistic voices and speak to other mothers. Their record of changed thinking gave them credibility to say things "in a way that I could have heard it when we were beginning this journey" ("Perfect Addendum").

Having decided to blog, mothers faced dilemmas about how to write publicly in a way that is "thoughtful, not scrubbed" ("Thoughtful"). If stories are too sanitized, then the individual and communal benefits of blogging are diminished. A blog that tells only of positives and victories can marginalize, "[making] those who are really struggling feel like there is something wrong with them" (comment on "Thoughtful"). Yet writing about difficulties can "demonize autism [and] allow it to be built back up into the mythical, mystical, larger-than-life monster that we've worked so hard to prove it not to be" ("Thoughtful"). It was a precarious balance and questions lingered. Am I putting my needs ahead of my child's, or am I helping to make myself and others into the parents our children need us to be? (Rosa, "For New Autism Parents"). As one blogger explained: "I feel my writing and posting co-opts my own girls' experiences, stories, and souls for the sake of educating and supporting others about our life.... I've struggled constantly about what that all means—and have thought so often about stopping. But I blog on" (comment on Winegardner, "Me Too").

One mother's story can be part of a larger collective challenge to unrealistic expectations of all mothers (Friedman 15, 152; Goldsmith, "Narrating" 115-18) and can ally with the cause of autism acceptance (Goldsmith, "Mom Blogging"). However, it took communal conversation and attention to one's storytelling to pursue these benefits. These efforts constitute maternal labour and run counter to recent developments in social media, such as the convenience of posting quickly from mobile devices, the temptation to monetize, the limitations on length imposed by platform design and user norms, and expectation of immediate sharing and responding. Responsible sharenting may require a kind of countercultural intention that resists mother-blaming critics while actively communicating with multiple audiences about principles and practices for online storytelling.

Endnotes

1. Posts that are publicly available as this article goes to press are attributed to bloggers by name and a URL is provided, in order that these published authors are given credit for their words. Posts that are no longer publicly available are identified only by the title of the original post, unless I was able to contact the author and received permission to identify her by name.

2. This was particularly true in the particular time and community we studied. These blogs had modest followings, and their structure and content were not designed to generate lots of income. This is consistent with May Friedman's (148) observation that because mothers on the margins (including mothers of disabled children) are of less interest to marketers, their writing may be less likely to succumb to pressure to generate followers or write in ways that accommodate embedded advertising.

3. The larger study is a longitudinal examination of twelve case studies. The first author started a typical case sample of nine blogs selected from those a reader would have found in December 2012 by searching blog aggregators and indexing sites (Google blog

search, Technorati, and BlogHer) using combinations of "mother," "mom," "autism," and "Asperger." She took the first ten URLs from each search, deleted duplicates, and included only journal-style blogs written by a mother of an autistic child that had been in existence for at least one year with typical posting frequency of at least once monthly. From these, she selected nine for maximum variability in mother and child demographics, including child age and gender, manifestations of autism (e.g., ways of communicating and need for support), schooling arrangements (e.g., home schooling, inclusion in classroom or self-contained program), mother's race and neurotypicality (when the information was available), and country of origin. Three blogs were eventually added whose authors commented on and linked to blogs in the original sample and who further diversified mother demographics. In 2012, the first author began reading backwards in the blog archives to the beginning of each blog (the earliest started in 2004) and continued reading through June 2017. This sample encompasses several thousand posts with comments; posts from additional blogs were snowball sampled, as they were linked in posts from the case studies. Textual analysis was contextualized with ethnographic data, including participant observation at the 2013 and 2020 BlogHer conferences and depth interviews with four of the twelve case-study bloggers.

4. These audiences can overlap (e.g., a regular reader could be a mother of an autistic child who is herself autistic).

5. Our own engagement with this exchange further illustrates how opaque references can carry additional meaning for regular readers. One of us recognized the first name of the commenter and the style of the comment and connected it to another blog in our sample, in which the commenter had written her own post about her autistic daughter's participation in a play.

Works Cited

"Autism, Puberty, and Respect." 18 Dec. 2013. Post no longer publicly available.

Auxier, Brooke, Monica Anderson, Andrew Perrin, and Erica Turner.

"Parenting Children in the Age of Screens." Pew Research Center, July 2020.

Bannerman, Sara. "Relational Privacy and the Networked Governance of the Self." *Information, Communication & Society*, vol. 22, no. 14, 2019, pp. 2187-2202.

Blum-Ross, Alicia, and Sonia Livingstone. "'Sharenting,' Parent Blogging, and the Boundaries of the Digital Self." *Popular Communication*, vol. 15, no. 2, 2017, pp. 110-25.

Borda, Jennifer L. "Cultivating Community within the Commercial Marketplace: Blurred Boundaries in the 'Mommy' Blogosphere." *The Motherhood Business: Consumption, Communication, Privilege*, edited by A. T. Demo et al., The University of Alabama Press, 2015, pp. 121-50.

Businesswire. *Digital Birth: Welcome to the Online World*. 6 Oct. 2010.

Chew, Kristina. "It's the End of the World as We Know It." *We Go With Him*, autism.typepad.com/autism/2010/01/writing-about-difficult-things.html. Accessed 18 May 2022.

Chew, Kristina. "Something To Be Bothered About: Seeing Disability (#75)." *We Go With Him*, autism.typepad.com/autism/2005/09/big_brown_dog_f.html. Accessed 18 May 2022.

Chew, Kristina. "Telling It Like It Is: The 3 Fries Day (#39)." *We Go With Him*, autism.typepad.com/autism/2005/07/telling_it_like.html. Accessed 18 May 2022.

Chew, Kristina. "Why Charlie Might Sometimes Be a Tiger, but Never a Tragedy (#15)." *We Go With Him*, autism.typepad.com/autism/2005/07/why_charlie_mig.html. Accessed 18 May 2022.

Chew, Kristina. "Autism and Authenticity; Why the Truth Hurts and Helps (#96)." *We Go With Him*, http://autism.typepad.com/autism/2005/10/autism_and_auth.html. Accessed 18 May 2022.

Couser, G. Thomas. *Vulnerable Subjects: Ethics and Life Writing*. Cornell University Press, 2004.

CS Mott Children's Hospital. "Parents on Social Media: Likes and Dislikes of Sharenting." *National Poll on Children's Health*, vol. 23, no. 2, 2015. https://mottpoll.org/reports-surveys/parents-social-media-likes-and-dislikes-sharenting. Accessed 18 May 2022.

Damkjaer, Maja Sonne. "Sharenting = Good Parenting? Four Parental

Approaches to Sharenting on Facebook." *Digital Parenting. The Challenges for Families in the Digital Age*, edited by Giovanna Mascheroni et al., Nordicom, pp. 209-18.

"Dear Jennifer." 28 Dec. 2015. Post no longer publicly available.

Family Online Safety Institute. *Parents, Privacy & Technology Use*, 2015. www.fosi.org/policy-research/parents-privacy-technology-use. Accessed 13 May 2022.

Friedman, May. *Mommyblogs and the Changing Face of Motherhood*. University of Toronto Press, 2013.

Goldsmith, Daena J. "Mom Blogging as Maternal Activism: How to be an Ally to Autism Acceptance." *Journal of the Motherhood Initiative*. vol 12, no. 2, 2021, pp. 7-22.

Goldsmith, Daena J. "Narrating an Open Future: Blogs by Mothers of Autistic Children." *Writing Mothers: Narrative Acts of Care, Redemption, and Transformation*, edited by BettyAnn Martin and Michelann Parr, Demeter Press, 2020, pp. 109-26.

Green, Fiona Joy, and Jaqueline McLeod Rogers. "When Story Time is Over: Mothering Adult Children by Practising Productive Silence." *Middle Grounds: Essays on Midlife Mothering*, edited by Kathy Mantas and Lorinda Peterson, Demeter Press, 2018, pp. 258-77.

Hunter, Andrea. "Monetizing the Mommy: Mommy Blogs and the Audience Commodity." *Information, Communication & Society*, vol. 19, no. 9, 2016, pp. 1306-20.

"It's Not All About You." *Giraffe Party*, imapartygiraffe.com/its-not-all-about-you/. Accessed 18 May 2022.

Klein, Stephanie. "Is 'Special Needs' a Retarded Term?" *Stephanie Klein.com: Stories of My Life*. stephanieklein.com/2008/07/is-special-need/. Accessed 18 May 2022.

Laird, Sam. "The Rise of the Mommy Blogger," *Mashable*, mashable.com/2012/05/08/mommy-blogger-infographic/#3rK10qfzikq6. Accessed 18 May 2022.

Livingstone, Sonia, and Alicia Blum-Ross. *Parenting for a Digital Future: How Hopes and Fears about Technology Shape Children's Lives*. Oxford University Press, 2020

Loe, Meika, Tess Cumpstone, and Susan B. Miller. "Feminist Parenting Online: Community, Con-stestation, and Change." *Taking the*

Village Online: Mothers, Motherhood, and Social Media, edited by Lorin Basden Arnold and Bettyann Martin, Demeter Press, 2016, pp. 180-95.

Lupton, Deborah, Sarah Pederson, and Gareth M. Thomas. "Parenting and Digital Media: From the Early Web to Contemporary Digital Society: Parenting and Digital Media." *Sociology Compass*, vol. 10, no. 8, 2016, pp. 730-43.

Marwick, Alice E., and danah boyd. "Networked Privacy: How Teenagers Negotiate Context in Social Media." *New Media & Society*, vol. 16, no. 7, 2014, pp. 1051-67.

McLeod, Rogers, Jacqueline and Fiona Green. "Mommy Blogging and Deliberative Dialogic Ethics." *Journal of the Motherhood Initiative*, vol. 6, no. 1, 2015, pp. 31-49.

Morrison, Aimée. "'Suffused by Feeling and Affect': The Intimate Public of Personal Mommy Blogging." *Biography*, vol. 34, no. 1, 2011, pp. 37-55.

Nardi, Bonnie A., Diane J. Schiano, and Michelle Gumbrecht. "Blogging as Social Activity, or, Would You Let 900 Million People Read Your Diary?" *Proceedings of the 2004 ACM Conference on Computer Supported Cooperative Work*, 2004, pp. 222-31.

Nielsen Newswire. "Buzz in the Blogosphere: Millions More Bloggers and Blogreaders." 8 Mar. 2012, www.nielsen.com/us/en/insights/article/2012/buzz-in-the-blogosphere-millions-more-bloggers-and-blog-readers/. Accessed 13 May 2022.

O'Callaghan, Martine. "To Mr Bigot." *Autismum*, autismum.com/2012/02/04/to-mr-bigot/. Accessed 18 May 2022.

"Of Leaky Eyes and Privacy." 20 Feb. 2014. Post no longer publicly available.

"One Question." 26 Aug. 2015. Post no longer publicly available.

"Online Privacy—Part a Million." 13 Jan. 2015. Post no longer publicly available.

"Perfect Addendum." 30 Mar. 2016. Post no longer publicly available.

Petronio, Sandra, and Maria K. Venetis. "Communication Privacy Management Theory and Health and Risk Messaging." *The Oxford Encyclopedia of Health and Risk Message Design and Processing*, Oxford University Press, 2018, www.oxfordreference.com/view/10.1093/

acref/9780190455378.001.0001/acref-9780190455378. Accessed 18 May 2022.

"Protecting Him Online." 6 Dec. 2017. Post no longer publicly available.

Rosa, Shannon. "An Intense Ten Days." *Squidalicious*. www.squidalicious.com/2013_04_01_archive.html. Accessed 18 May 2022.

Rosa, Shannon. "Blogging About Our Children With Special Needs: Real Recap." *Squidalicious*, www.squidalicious.com/2008/07/blogging-about-our-children-with.html. Accessed 18 May 2022

Rosa, Shannon. "For New Autism Parents: On Gratitude." *Squidalicious*, www.squidalicious.com/2012/07/. Accessed 18 May 2022.

Rosa, Shannon. "Moving: Towards a Positive Frame of Mind." *Squidalicious*, www.squidalicious.com/2007/05/moving-towards-positive-frame-of-mind.html. Accessed 18 May 2022.

Rosa, Shannon. "The Bloody Shirt." *Squidalicious*, www.squidalicious.com/2014/07/the-bloody-shirt.html. Accessed 18 May 2022.

Sequenzia, Amy. "Social Media and Privacy for People with Disabilities." *Autistic Women & Nonbinary Network (AWN)*, awnnetwork.org/social-media-and-privacy-for-people-with-disabilities/. Accessed 18 May 2022.

"Thoughtful, Not Scrubbed." 17 Apr. 2012. Post no longer publicly available.

Thurer, Shari. *Myths of Motherhood: How Culture Reinvents the Good Mother.* Penguin Books, 1994.

"Truth." 13 Mar. 2012. Post no longer publicly available.

"Untitled." 2 Sept. 2015. Post no longer publicly available.

Walters, Ekaterina. "Marketing To Women: 30 Stats To Know." *Media Post*, 28 Mar. 2012, www.mediapost.com/. Accessed 13 May 2022.

Winegardner, Jean. "And the Happy Dance Was Danced All Around." *Stimeyland*. Post no longer publicly available.

Winegardner, Jean. "Jack's Debut." *Stimeyland*. Post no longer publicly available.

Winegarder, Jean. "Me Too." *Stimeyland*. Post no longer publicly available.

Section II
Kids on Media: Windows and Doors

Chapter 5

The Kids' Bedrooms

Victoria Bailey

I used to rock rock

kiss squeeze

lay them down

smooth their hair

hum heart songs

'til they fell asleep

sigh inhale sigh again

tip-toe out of the room

stepping over the creaky floorboard

gently close the door

and pause

listen to their breath

deep and slow

in what felt like

a timeless space

and now I knock on doors

and ask

are you talking to anyone

is your camera on

is your mic on

are you in class

are you streaming

before entering their room

because it used to be our space

and I miss it.

Chapter 6

Mothering, Digital Media, and the Privatization of Risk: Negotiating Boundaries of Use with Academic Expertise, Tweens, and a Global Pandemic

Janis L. Goldie

Mothering in our constantly shifting and often unfamiliar digital environment is a challenge. Keeping up with digital trends, new games or applications, as well as the shifting threats that digital media use can pose to children and adults alike is a daunting task, alongside the constant physical and emotional care demanded of mothers. One might assume that having more knowledge in this realm would be powerful and simplify these parental challenges. Yet as an academic mother with teaching and research expertise in digital media and privacy, I am constantly struggling to negotiate my knowledge with my praxis in the home.

In this chapter, I outline the dialectical tensions of mothering two tweens while holding academic expertise in digital media and privacy.[1] I examine the apparent divides between what the research on digital technology, privacy, and surveillance suggests I should do in terms of parenting around digital media use and how I mother amid the expectations from my children, their peers, and other parents. Ensuring that I permit my children spaces to use and learn from digital media, while at the same time educating and setting boundaries around use, is further complicated by the global COVID-19 pandemic that erupted at the time of writing. Suddenly, digital media use occurs beyond the leisure time outside of work, school, or extracurricular activities and is now the only viable means through which these activities, as well as social interaction with friends and extended family members, can operate so that "the whole infrastructure of childhood ... has moved online" (Livingstone). Although this chapter does not offer a prescriptive one-size-fits-all solution for parents struggling to manage how their children use digital media, it does offer autoethnographic insight into one academic mother's struggles to negotiate practical use of digital technology amid an (over)awareness of its pitfalls—insight that may resonate with other mothers.

After briefly outlining the pertinent literature on parental mediation of digital media, I present the theoretical framework—which is informed by research on mothering, guilt, and neoliberalism—that shapes this discussion. Next, I review the autoethnographic methodological approach taken, discuss the background and context of my particular situation, and then present an in-depth and reflexive examination of the experience of navigating the risks and rewards of digital media, both before and during the pandemic. I argue that the neoliberal demand to privatize family happiness and risk places an impossible burden on mothers to negotiate the tensions between the risks and rewards of privacy and use of digital media for tweens. This has been notably heightened with the stress of a global pandemic and intensified use of digital media. This chapter highlights the need to expand our understanding of the complexity and contextual nature of parental mediation practices and then examines the need to move away from privatization of risks for mothers and families more generally in the digital media realm.

Parental Mediation of Digital Media

Though originally used to understand how parents monitor and guide children's television use, parental mediation theory is now applied to understand the way that parents mediate the use of the internet and digital media among their children (Livingstone and Hepsler). This robust body of literature examines the monitoring practices, rules, and creative strategies parents employ to try to balance the perceived disadvantages and advantages of digital media use for their children. Parental mediation is understood to occur currently when governments are increasingly unable or reluctant to regulate the media and communication environment so that private family regulation becomes the necessary default while the proliferation of media goods and use have skyrocketed in the home (Livingstone and Hepsler). Although the terms vary slightly, a significant portion of the parental mediation literature stems from the three broad categories of parental regulation used to understand television (Nathanson). Broadly speaking, parents use the following strategies:

1. **Active mediation:** talking about media content while the child is engaging with (watching, reading, listening to) the medium;

2. **Restrictive mediation:** setting rules that restrict use of the medium, including restrictions on time spent, location of use or content (e.g., restricting exposure to violent or sexual content), without necessarily discussing the meaning or effects of such content;

3. **Co-using strategies:** signifies that the parent remains present while the child is engaged with the medium, thus sharing in the experience but without comment on the content or its effects. (Livingstone and Hepsler 583)

The research findings within the parental mediation literature show that parents utilize a range of strategies, that social rather than technical techniques are preferred, and that increased monitoring does not naturally correlate with reduced risks for children and teenagers (Livingstone and Hepsler). Ethnographic studies highlight that when watching parental mediation of digital media use in a long-term and in-depth manner in homes, "media rules are highly variable across and within families, regularly undermined in practice, and more often [focused] around exposure than content" (Mazmanian and Lanette 2273), which points to the importance of conceiving the issues in a situated perspective. Other factors at play in affecting parental mediation of digital media use in the literature are parenting styles (Eastin, Greenberg, and Hofschire), parents' knowledge and confidence about technology (Fletcher and Blair; Shin; Shin and Li), parental stress

(Warren and Aloia), and time and socioeconomic status (Jeffery). Some studies have shown that complete restrictive or banning practices are easier to enforce and follow than contextual rules (Hiniker, Schoenebeck, and Kientz). In addition, several technological tensions exist in the home between parents and children such as their desire for mutual, uninterrupted attention (Blackwell, Gardiner, and Scoenebeck). In terms of parental mediation around privacy risks in particular, studies have investigated the role of parental mediation on the information disclosure of teens (Shin, Huh, and Faber) and have generally found that when parents actively mediate children's online experience, lower levels of personal information disclosure exist (Lwin, Stanaland, and Miyazaki). However, other studies have noted that although direct intervention strategies to mitigate privacy risk reduce teen exposure to online risks, such interventions also appear to suppress teens' ability to engage with others online and to learn to cope with online risks (Wisniewski et al.).

In all, within the parental media literature, the assumption that "clear rules around media use are the ideal for family functioning appears to influence the design and focus of much of the research around family technology use" (Mazmanian and Lanette 2274). The research focuses on how parents are or should mediate, taking this as the natural starting point (Vaterlaus et al.). In this vein, the research on parental mediation has predominantly focused on how parents restrict or reduce media exposure or mitigate its negative effects, with a dearth of research on the way that parents encourage or enable children's use (Livingstone et al.). Ignoring or downplaying the benefits of digital media use to children in the research means that there is not currently a strong understanding of the way that parents are optimizing use as well.

Catherine Page Jeffery argues that parents are faced with two different yet popular discourses around digital media at present—that children's use of digital media is rife with risk but is also crucial for the development and future opportunities of children. Negotiating this dialectical tension means that parents "are navigating a socially constructed tightrope, balancing a desire for the advancement of their child's digital skills to help them realize their potential, with protecting them from the concomitant risk that technological development necessarily engenders" (Jeffery 6). Such a social situation "responsibilizes parents for protecting and cultivating their children's development and protecting their children from harm while simultaneously fostering their independence and autonomy" (Jeffery 14). Jeffery continues: "It is perhaps not surprising, therefore, that parents continue to grapple with the competing expectations and demands of parenting in the digital age" (14). The conflicting discourses centred on the risks and rewards of digital media use and parenting are further confounded by gendered expectations of parenting.

Mothering, Guilt, and the Privatization of Risk

Contrary to the parental mediation literature, which does not focus on gender, this chapter pulls from feminist literature on mothering, guilt, and its connection to the current neoliberal risk society as a theoretical framework. This framework is embedded in ideologies about "good mothering"[2] and the inherent guilt, shame,[3] and stress that results in never being able to live up to the impossible ideal. As Jean-Anne Sutherland explains, "That mothers experience guilt and shame in relation to their roles as mothers is the most prevalent finding in mothering research" (310). Moreover, maternal guilt is such a taken-for-granted aspect of mothering in our culture and so pervasive in popular discourse that it is often considered to be a "'natural' component of motherhood" (Sutherland 310). This is distinct from fathers within the research. Even when both parents are equally responsible for childcare, mothers reportedly experience vastly higher levels of guilt in studies on heterosexual relationships, which is referred to as the "guilt gap" (Hays).

The guilt that accompanies mothering is rooted in cultural and institutional processes so that it occurs at the macro-, meso-, and microlevels (Sutherland). At the macrolevel, the good mother ideology, also known as intensive mothering, is child centred and time consuming. Here, the all-giving and all-present mother is the ideal (Hays). Sometimes also referred to as the "perfect mother" (Orenstein), the "new momism" (Douglas and Michaels), or the "mommy mystique" (Warner), the terms similarly espouse a "model of motherhood that asks women to give fully of themselves at all times, physically, emotionally, psychologically and intellectually" (Sutherland 313). Intensive mothering has three underlying components to its ideology:

that motherhood completes a woman; that mothers are a child's best caretaker; and that mothers must devote themselves completely to their children in an all-consuming physical, intellectual, emotional, and psychological manner (Sutherland). In this way, the "guilt that mothers feel today is part of a long cultural history of gendered discourses that frame children as mothers' responsibility" (Collins 3).

The myth of mothering is exacerbated by an institutional model of working outside the home that is gendered and operates in a direct way against what is expected of so-called good mothers. Despite women's employment, mothers must still shoulder a larger share of childcare and remain as leaders of the household and parenting—carework that is undervalued and under-rewarded in North America. Responsible for "a majority of the household tasks from the practical (e.g., feeding, clothing) to the complex (e.g., stimulating intellectual growth)" (Sutherland 315), mothers report stress and guilt as they try to reconcile the impossible ideology of intensive mothering with individual needs, family, and workplace needs

The privatization of the family and mothering is key to this discussion, as it ties intimately into the privatization of risk as well. Julie Wilson and Emily Chivers Yochim argue that mothering encompasses two unrelenting and connected modes of affective labour:

> On the one hand, there is the caring work associated with proper government of children: establishing and maintaining family rules and rituals, providing cognitive development activities, promoting good health, developing an effective approach to discipline, showing adequate love and attention, and attending to mundane housekeeping tasks like laundry, cooking, and cleaning. On the other hand, there is the rigorous self-work attendant to the government of mothers: ongoing self-reflexivity and affective regulation of one's own life as a mother. (39)

Here, families must be self-reliant but are carefully guided and governed by social expectations and rules. And mothers are "regarded as self-responsible agents of home and family life *and also* as potentially deficit gender subjects in need of perpetual government" (Wilson and Yochim 40). The connection to family autonomy and government of mothers through copious amounts of professional and popular advice means that mothers are responsible for sorting through the conflicting accounts and creating personal regimes of family government and rules. This situation is exacerbated by neoliberalism, through which social supports and security systems have been dismantled; individual citizens are required to accept personal responsibility for their fate so that self-actualizing citizens hold the social world together rather than the welfare state. Advanced neoliberalism "heightens maternal responsibilities, anxieties, and impossibilities, vastly expanding the scope and stakes of mothers' loads" (Wilson and Yochim 59). As the authors explain:

> Neoliberalism entails an ongoing intensification of mothers' lives; to maintain a self-determined autonomous family in an insecure world, new knowledges and risks must be incorporated into everyday family scenes and managed via mothers and their efforts at privatizing happiness. Mothering becomes ever more rife with anxiety and impossibility, as social responsibility for family life comes to rest ever more squarely on mothers. Indeed, privatizing happiness entails a double movement composed of both the widening of what it takes to be a "good" mom and the condensation of responsibility onto mothers and their women's work. (Wilson and Yochim 33)

Because of family autonomy and gendered governance, it is mothers who feel the increased pressure of managing the privatized risks associated with children and the family within advanced neoliberalism. Privatizing risk means that mothers are asked to attempt to control the uncontrollable. The expectation for mothers to manage and be responsible for the individual happiness and risks of families and children—within an increasingly uncontrolled and risk-driven society full of conflicting discourses that mothers' must sift through, weigh, and act on—is an unachievable task and one laden with guilt and shame when its inevitable failure results. Understanding the current social climate in which good mothers operate helps us better understand the challenges of managing the risks and rewards of digital media use.

Autoethnography

This section uses autoethnography as its method—"an approach to research and writing that seeks to describe and systematically analyze (graphy) personal experience (auto) in order to understand cultural experience (ethno)" (Ellis, Adams, and Bochner 273). It joins auto-biography and ethnography and connects one's life to broader cultural practices, values, or beliefs to help cultural members (insiders) and cultural strangers (outsiders) better understand the culture. Frequently relying on a first-person narrative to produce texts of "thick description," autoethnographers seek to ensure their research is accessible and evocative to reach a wider and more diverse audience (Ellis). Furthermore, autoethnographers acknowledge the inherent nature of subjectivity, emotionality, and the researcher's influence on research (Ellis, Adams, and Bochner). Although many forms of autoethnographical approaches exist,[4] this study follows a personal narrative approach, which proposes "to understand a self or some aspect of a life as it intersects with a cultural context, connect to other participants as co-researchers, and invite readers to enter the author's world and to use what they learn there to reflect on, understand, and cope with their own lives" (Ellis, Adams and Bochner 279-280). By sharing my personal mothering choices and practices,[5] and thus becoming vulnerable to broader academic and social judgments, I am furthering opening myself up to potential elements of social shame and guilt. Nonetheless, I hope that by illuminating the tensions between pragmatically mothering digital media use, amid and despite my academic existence, that insiders and outsiders alike are able to use my personal experience for reflection and for wider cultural benefit.

Background and Case

To situate this autoethnographic study, it is important to note that I speak from a privileged position. I am a white, cisgender forty-three-year-old female, who was raised in small-town Ontario with middle-class roots. Currently, I am full professor in, and chair of, the Communication Studies Department at Huntington University, a federated partner of Laurentian University in Sudbury, ON, Canada. I completed my master's degree in virtual communities and privacy in 2003, a time when exploring issues of digital media and the related privacy issues was a burgeoning issue (Goldie). Since joining Huntington University as an assistant professor, I have continued to teach and research in critical digital media studies. Through this, I am astutely aware of the problems around protecting one's privacy with data collection and tracing through social media platforms and applications—such as Google, Facebook, or Instagram (Draper and Turow; Solove; Vaidhyananthan)—and related issues around shaming, harassment, and abuse that befall online users (Klonick; Marwick and Caplan) as well as the specific challenges to children's privacy via such issues as sharenting, digital rights, and the datafication of children whose lives have been tracked and traced since birth (Lievens et al.; Bulger et al.). In all, I research and teach about digital concerns and problems for all users, including "the threats to childhood— bullies, scammers, groomers, fake news manufacturers and manipulators of all kinds" (Livingstone).

I am also a mother to two tweens: a ten-year-old son and a twelve-year-old daughter. Unlike many of their friends' parents—who seem to have less restrictions and concerns around which applications are okay to use, whether accounts can be public or private, how much time is appropriate for device use, and when and where digital media can be accessed—my children have faced more restrictions from the get go. Undoubtedly, this is tied to my academic background and knowledge on these issues. A great deal has changed in our household as a direct result of COVID-19 and the need for our family to stay at home, however. Suddenly, all of our work, schooling, socializing, and leisure activities moved online, which has had important implications on the management of digital media use in our home and speaks to the evolving and challenging nature of mothering.

Mothering Digital Media

The close monitoring and limit of how much "screen" time the children get in a day has been a consistent practice in the home. This is a situational rule rather than a hard and fast one, and the time and content they consume has varied as they have matured. Like many parents (Mazmanian and Lanette), the time permitted often depends on the day and context. For example, if family or friends are over to visit, use is discouraged. No devices are permitted at family meals, and if someone tries to use a device at the table for instance, including parents, they need to put two dollars into our travel fund. If one of the children had a lot of time on a device the day before, perhaps because of rainy weather or not feeling well, for example, then use is normally limited the following day. If there are chores or homework to do, these activities are prioritized. And if it feels as though they have been sitting or playing too long, we bump them off to do something else or head outside. Although the amount of time they have to use their devices and the kind of content they can view have varied over the years as they have gotten older, limits remain.

We live in a rural area, where the Wi-Fi is poor, so it can only be used in common areas like the living room, kitchen, or the basement. This means that I can more easily monitor their use and content. I can usually see and often know what they are doing online. I sometimes check in on the TikTok videos they are watching or making, asking who they are playing Fortnite with, or who they are FaceTiming with. I sometimes play along or watch alongside them when time permits.

In terms of mediating content, I have put restrictions on which games or applications they can download, and they are required to get permission before downloading anything new. I will check the suggested age limit of the applications as well as the nature of the game, for example, and ensure that it is what I would consider appropriate. What is appropriate, of course, has also changed as they have aged. In some cases, because I manage their Apple IDs as part of the family system, they cannot download anything without my password. I have always been incredibly strict about YouTube, only permitting YouTube Kids, and even then, closely monitoring their consumption. Instead, their television/video content predominantly occurs via NetFlix, Disney+ or Amazon Prime applications. This allows for better monitoring of content and avoids traditional commercial advertising, and my constant warnings about the terrible things that can be accessed via the rabbit holes of YouTube, I think, are generally heeded.

The tweens know that in the games they are permitted to play, they are only allowed to interact with people in their lives they already know. This is another protective mediation strategy informed by my knowledge of the research tied to exploitation and abuse. They are not allowed to play with strangers, or interact with, or follow anyone that they have not met in person or know from school, sports, the neighbourhood, or the family.

Whenever possible, I remove advertisements from applications and increase the privacy restrictions on all devices and games to the highest level they can go and still permit their use. I also ensure that people outside of their communities are not able to connect with them, so that with an application like Roblox or Minecraft, for example, the ongoing commentary or chat function is turned off while they are playing, and they are not able to play or communicate directly with anyone other than friends. I ensure that all their accounts are private rather than the public-by-default nature of most applications, and we often will use fake names, ages, or birth dates, for example, to avoid digital tracing of their use for privacy protection measures. When email addresses are needed to register new accounts or games, I enter one of my junk email accounts created specifically for this purpose to limit the tracing of their online habits and practices.

These are some of the mediation practices used in our house to mitigate risks while enabling use of digital media for the tweens prior to COVID-19. Upon closer reflection, it appears that most of the practices we follow are restrictive according to the parental mediation literature; there are clear restrictions on time and use, content, access, social interactions, and privacy concerns. However, the category restrictive mediation does not properly capture our experience, as media content as well as the potential pitfalls and issues that can arise with digital media use are constantly discussed in our house (active mediation) both during and outside of use. Finally, co-using strategies are also in place so that participating in gaming or social media application occurs while discussing the content. It appears that the parental mediation categories are too rigid to explain the practical application of mediating digital media use, at least in our house, and further that we follow—all at the same time—active, restrictive, and co-using parental mediation strategies alongside persistent dialogue. I suspect that because my children have grown up accustomed to my concern for their privacy and safety online—and with discussions of the perils and pitfalls—they do not often (visibly or verbally) resist these practices in our house, even if they are frustrated or privately unhappy with them.

My constraints against personal cell phones have not gone as smoothly. My daughter, recently in grade seven, was the only person in her class, as well as the only one in her broader social circle, without a cell phone. In fact, many of her friends from sports or school, who were far younger than her (i.e., as young as eight or nine years old), owned their own cell phones—high-end, new model, data-loaded smartphones. She was 12 years old. She had an iPad and an iPod that she could use social media applications with, as well as text, FaceTime, etc. How was a phone needed on top of this and why? This was a major point of contention for my daughter. Our rule was that she could get a cell phone when she was sixteen as I was hoping to keep her off excessive social media use for as long as possible. I had already seen firsthand the way her friends could not put the phone down, even when they were socializing, eating, or doing activities together and was well aware of the research showing the harms of social media use on self-esteem and self-development, especially for young women.

Despite these problems, I soon started to question my perspective when it became clear that she was the only person her age who did not have a phone in our broader social circle. I began to wonder if I was being unreasonable because of my academic perspective and started to question whether my knowledge and concern for risks were hampering her social development and independence. She was starting to go places with her friends on their own, and we would rely on her friends' cell phones to tell me when to pick them up or meet them, for instance, which hardly seemed fair or appropriate but rather hypocritical. She also always carries an EpiPen with her because of a severe food allergy, and I started to realize that the phone might be a safety necessity when we were not around. After many discussions, I eventually adjusted the rule from needing to be sixteen years old to needing to have a job to pay for it, hoping that working for the phone would enhance an increased sense of responsibility and help avoid entitlement. I told her that I would give her my old phone when I was ready for a new one but that she would have to pay for data monthly if she wanted any. With the new possibility of a phone in reach, it did not take long for her to find a job, and she had just started her training when COVID-19 arrived, and everything changed.

Mothering Digital Media during and after COVID-19

The first case of COVID-19 arrived in Sudbury, Ontario, on March 10, 2020, on the Laurentian University campus, and within two days, campus faculty, staff, and students were required to stay home to work, and teaching transitioned to an online remote emergency fashion. The following week, the children went on their March break to not return for the rest of the school year. My husband was also mandated to work from home for the next few months, so suddenly all four of us were at home, twenty-four hours a day, seven days a week, constantly anxious about the pandemic and attempting to continue our day-to-day school, work, and health routines as much as possible. Although this chapter was not originally intended as a discussion of the effects of the pandemic on mothering, the impact that it has had on our digital media use and mediation cannot be understated. In short, as I will show, all my intended and well-informed digital mediation strategies—in particular my more restrictive practices— went out the window.

Within the first month of quarantine, both my daughter's iPad and iPod began to break down. After watching her struggle with frustration for some time and realizing that her social interactions were severely hampered at a time when she was already excessively distanced from her friends, I ordered myself a new phone and gave her my old one as promised. She was, of course, shocked and happy and has used it nonstop ever since to connect with her friends, watch videos, and game. The contextual nature of my about face around the cell phone is notable. Before COVID-19, I was worried about keeping her away from a cell phone for as long as possible. Suddenly, I was more concerned with enabling her use of digital media—in a time of great stress and social isolation—rather than restricting her from the device. It was also a time of enhanced parental involvement, as we were spending lots of time together, so her use was easily monitored, and the rules remained. No phones or devices were allowed during mealtimes, nor were they allowed into bedrooms at night. When speaking with others, phones had to be set aside to facilitate focused conversations. Passcodes had to be accessible and known.

Whereas my daughter was now relying on her cell phone to connect with the friends she was so desperately missing, my son was lacking social interactions because his friends all gamed online, something we had never really permitted or that he had even shown a desire to do. After learning that online gaming accounts could be restricted in various ways, we decided we would get him set up so that he could speak and play with his friends. I ordered a gaming headset and after hours (and hours!) of account creation, new passwords, and changing security settings, he was able to play games like Roblox, Minecraft, and, eventually, Fortnite with his friends synchronously. This was quite life changing for him. Suddenly, he could chat and reconnect with his friends, some of the most important people in his life. I know that many people worry about the excessive time children spend video gaming, but for us in this time and context, gaming online was our son's only way to connect with his friends. It also allowed him a chance to work collaboratively and offered mental stimulation and strategic thinking opportunities. It was an excellent social, emotional, and mental outlet.

The addition of the cell phone and online gaming in our house brings me to the biggest challenge of all mothering digital media during COVID-19. The time our family, but especially our children, spend online has probably quadrupled. Prior to self-isolation, the kids would maybe get one hour a day on a usual weekday between school, homework, and sports or friends with digital media and on weekends a bit more. Now, with my husband and I both trying to work full time at home and my taking the lead on homeschooling, they were left to their own devices to entertain themselves, so to speak. Between when they woke up and when I took a break from work to get them started with school, they were most often online. My daughter was usually chatting with friends or watching TikTok, gaming or Netflixing with friends, whereas my son had joined the legions of people officially infatuated with Fortnite—honing his newly developed skills at the game by playing alone, with friends, and when not playing, watching YouTube videos of other people playing. I usually ensured they got off their devices for some physical activity and outside time, and then we would return to our laptops for schoolwork, for another two to three hours. After that, we would enjoy some more activity or outside time, but they really wanted to return to their devices for social time with friends. I needed to return to work as well. Living during the pandemic meant that keeping them off digital media was a constant, daily challenge— one that during summer holidays and an absence of schoolwork left me feeling fatigued and almost fatalistic. They went outside and did something active for most of the afternoon every day, but upon reflection, I was left feeling guilty with the amount of time they were online.

My guilt was enhanced, I think, because of my expertise in this area. I am aware that this is not the ideal scenario for development. However, I'm also aware that the reality is situational. With the pandemic, there were not a lot of traditional options to keep the kids entertained and connected. There were no sports, no camps, no water parks or amusement parks, no trips, no music concerts or movies. We are lucky to live on a bigger property with access to water and many fun things for the kids to do outside, but even that can get monotonous. Yes, they went outside and were physically active. Yes, they read novels and played boardgames. Nevertheless, they spent a significant portion of their day on their devices. This was a real—and new—struggle for me as a mother.

Because we were isolating in our homes, naturally, the children's entire lives moved online, and access issues also proved challenging. This resulted in several issues. First, because of the poor connection speed of internet in our rural setting, the four of us were constantly battling for Wi-Fi. This demand was far too much for our poor internet connection. We had to take turns for meetings, when other family members were not permitted to be online while someone was in a Zoom meeting. My husband was forced to use his work cell phone's hotspot to get anything done, as he was always fighting an uphill battle with everyone else in the house. We began to work out a schedule: I worked online in the morning, doing everything I needed to do at the crack of dawn before the kids got up until about noon, when we switched to their online needs in terms of schooling. As a result, new rules about access emerged throughout this time. Rather than restricting the amount of time, access started to be focused on enabling or permitting access. We negotiated when family members could use the internet, privileging work and school over FaceTiming with friends or video games, for example, but we made sure to allow time for the latter as well.

Restrictions on interactions online have not changed; my children are still only interacting with people they know. However, my mediation practices around privacy protections have also been severely undermined. I typically put the highest possible protection level on all the kids' devices and applications. This proved to be impossible with online gaming, and I am uncomfortable with not having found a feasible alternative. For my son and daughter to easily and consistently access and use online multiplayer games, such as Animal Crossing, Fortnite, or Roblox via Xbox or Nintendo Switch, I had to make their profiles and accounts virtually public, with a few exceptions in terms of friending. If I tried to restrict their accounts or profiles at all, some new issue would arise (e.g., they could not hear or speak to a friend, they could not play this game, or they could not make this character). In this, much like my challenges with the amount of time the tweens use their devices, I have changed my digital media strategy notably. Again, I feel like I have no other option and feel a level of guilt in allowing my children to be tracked in a way that I know to be problematic. In all, I go back and forth with feelings of shame around the loosening—or really, the collapse—of my pre-COVID-19 digital mediation practices. I wish they were spending more time offline, but I cannot also manage their choices all day long, every day. It is an uphill battle in a time of personal and professional stress.

At the same time, they are socially and mentally developing in their digital practices. I can certainly see the value and entertainment factor in the digital media applications they are using. For example, my daughter uses TikTok to learn dances and express herself, alone and with her friends (even though her account is private). Fortnite—while a kind of *Hunger Games*-themed online gaming phenomenon where the last person standing wins, seems perhaps simple and violent—is also collaborative and strategic and requires a fast level of thinking and dexterity that is surprising. The kids have taught me to play, and I have enjoyed it—both playing with them and understanding their references to the experiences they are having in this domain.

Conclusion

After exploring my mothering strategies around digital media use in an in-depth reflexive manner, both before and during a pandemic, it is clear a significant shift occurred. My pre-COVID-19 strategies focused on lessening the risks of digital media use for my tweens via restrictive practices around time, access, content, and privacy rules, for example. This was predominantly informed by the research and literature on digital media that I am familiar with as a professor in communication studies. However, during the isolation period, I began to focus more on enabling the rewards of digital media use, lessening restrictive practices, and increasing co-use strategies. Interestingly, in both phases, the active element of mediation—where discussion occurs around risks and rewards—was always in place and took place during media use, co-use, and when not using media via restrictive strategies in contrast to the parental mediation categories as defined. Perhaps parental mediation strategies typically adopted and tested in the research on digital media may need to be expanded or reconsidered to better include the contextual and situational nature of parenting strategies. Because I am well versed in these domains due to my academic experience, I can speak knowledgably about both the risks and rewards. Yet despite my teaching and research expertise, balancing the risk and rewards of digital media use in a pragmatic fashion—alongside social expectations from my children, their friends, other parents, etc.—remains extremely difficult, and is currently exacerbated because of the pandemic.

What explains the shift in focus from risk to reward in my mothering strategies around digital media use during this time? Situational factors are crucial here. Living, working, attending school, socializing, and leisure activities all suddenly needed to be done at home for our family with the onset of a global pandemic. This was not a normal situation. The kids suddenly could no longer physically see their friends as being together was not an option. I was tasked with being their mother and their grade four and grade seven teacher with no training and few resources. They were forced to entertain themselves for hours a day, as it was impossible for myself and my husband to both work full time and attend to their every need. This meant that more digital media time was inevitable and that new ways of connecting were necessary for mental and emotional health. I was also forced to suppress my concerns about privacy to enable their social interaction opportunities, and I became more involved in the games and applications they used.

I think it is fair to ascribe a lot of the shift to the situational context of the pandemic. I could also ascribe it to the increased time I am spending with the children during our social isolation and my ability to monitor and participate in their digital media use in a more intimate fashion. Perhaps now, more than ever, I am able to see the benefits, and my parenting strategies have adjusted accordingly. These are all part of the explanatory puzzle, indeed. But I think that the largest component of the shift, upon consideration of the social expectations of mothers, is that I am "buckling under more and more social responsibilities" (Wilson and Yochim 64). Faced with the intensive mothering model during a pandemic, I am now expected to work full time, act as caretaker full time, as well as teach two different grades in elementary school and be responsible for the happiness, entertainment, and mental and physical health of my children with little to no social, family, or state resources. I no longer have the stamina or will to negotiate every day with my children about their devices or to limit their experiences to protect their privacy. Managing the risks associated with digital media use is seen as a privatized risk in Canada, one in which it is up to individuals to protect themselves. As we have seen from the theory on mothering, privatized risks (and rewards) for children and their digital media use are largely the domain of mothers. Mitigating these conflicting ideologies has always been challenging, but during the pandemic, it is, in my experience, impossible. The privatization of risks—both of digital media use and health risks in this case—is simply too much. As Wilson and Yochim elaborate: "Mothers are overloaded and overrun as they teeter on the precipices of privatized risk and happiness ... chasing increasingly precarized promises of family autonomy, mothers stay tethered to ever-mounting mother loads and, perhaps more insidiously, to the pernicious idea that it is their responsibility, and theirs alone, to realize the impossible and securitize the family" (64).

Placed in such a situation, it is perhaps not surprising that fatalism or digital resignation sets in (Draper and Turow). In all, the neoliberal tendency to privatize family happiness and risks forces mothers to negotiate the tensions between the risks and rewards of digital media use, even with scholarly knowledge. Though notably aggravated during a time of heightened global health concerns and increased use of digital media, the tension will likely continue to persist. By reflexively examining my own personal mothering strategies, it seems as though a more complete model of parental mediation practices is needed to better understand this issue and that state-centred regulation of digital media is needed to help relieve families—and particularly mothers—of managing these issues, especially regarding privacy protections and rural broadband access.

Endnotes

1. It is often repeated that privacy is a complex concept with no single agreed upon definition. Dating back from Aristotle's distinction of the public sphere of political activity to the private sphere of the family and domestic life, and later tied to S. Warren and L. Brandeis's conception of privacy as the "right to be let alone," many attempts at definitional clarification have been made. My use of the term "privacy" in this chapter is informed by Judith DeCew's cluster concept, which includes "1) interests in control over information about oneself, 2) control over access to oneself, both physical and mental, and, 3) control over one's ability to make important decisions about family and lifestyle in order to be self expressive and to develop varied relationships" (3.6). This approach, highlighting the important social dimension of privacy, argues that not only does privacy have intrinsic and extrinsic value to individuals but also, importantly, has instrumental value to society (Solove). It rejects the privileging of informational privacy approach often employed in technology studies, as well as commodification approaches, among others, for overlooking the important multifaceted and contextual role that privacy plays in protecting liberty, autonomy, self-expression, and development for the betterment of society. In this way, it also pushes back against the public-private dichotomy as an either/or distinction, which is problematic from a feminist perspective (MacKinnon; Allen), as both are inherently connected.

2. It is important to note that the majority of the "good mothering" literature is rooted in studies focused on white, middle-class mothers and that motherhood cannot be examined without attention to race, ethnicity, social class, and sexuality. Although the "good mothering" concept does appear to cross intersectional boundaries, what a good mother looks like varies across these intersecting identities and needs further examination (Sutherland).

3. Sutherland helpfully distinguishes between guilt and shame, noting that "the negative self-evaluation that results from guilt

stems from some specific act or behavior," whereas "shame involves a negative evaluation of the self, a more core reaction to public disapproval, with a focus on the entirety of the self" (311). Both shame and guilt involve reflexivity so that a transgression of the self is perceived to have occurred from behaviours or actions or beliefs that are socially expected.

4. For a full list, see Ellis, Adams, and Bochner.

5. Relational ethical issues come into play here, as my children and husband are discussed in this research project. To this end, I have discussed and shared my work with my children and my husband (within our heterosexual, nuclear family) to provide an opportunity for them to respond or suggest adjustments as needed.

6. It is important to remember that this is my personal reflexive view of the mediation work in our house. It would be fascinating to hear how my children both view and practice this. I am sure it's quite a different tale.

Works Cited

Allen, A. *Uneasy Access: Privacy for Women in a Free Society*. Rowman and Littlefield, 1988.

Blackwell, Lindsay, et al. "Managing Expectations: Technology Tensions among Parents and Teens." *Proceedings of the 19th ACM Conference on Computer-Supported Cooperative Work & Social Computing—CSCW '16*, ACM Press, 2016, pp. 1388-99.

Bulger, Monica, et al. "Where Policy and Practice Collide: Comparing United States, South African and European Union Approaches to Protecting Children Online." *New Media & Society*, vol. 19, no. 5, May 2017, pp. 750-64.

Collins, Caitlyn. "Is Maternal Guilt a Cross-National Experience?" *Qualitative Sociology*, Apr. 2020. *Crossref*. doi:10.1007/s11133-020-09451-2.

DeCew, Judith, "Privacy", *The Stanford Encyclopedia of Philosophy*, spring 2018 edition, plato.stanford.edu/archives/spr2018/entries/privacy/. Accessed 14 May 2022.

Douglas, Susan J., and Meredith W. Michaels. *The Mommy Myth: The*

Idealization of Motherhood and How It Has Undermined Women. Free Press, 2004.

Draper, Nora A., and Joseph Turow. "The Corporate Cultivation of Digital Resignation." *New Media & Society*, vol. 21, no. 8, Aug. 2019, pp. 1824-39.

Eastin, Matthew S., et al. "Parenting the Internet." *Journal of Communication*, vol. 56, no. 3, Sept. 2006, pp. 486-504.

Ellis, Carolyn, et al. "Autoethnography: An Overview." *Historical Social Research / Historische Sozialforschung*, vol. 36, no. 4 (138), 2011, pp. 273-90.

Fletcher, Anne C., and Bethany L. Blair. "Implications of the Family Expert Role for Parental Rules Regarding Adolescent Use of Social Technologies." *New Media & Society*, vol. 18, no. 2, SAGE Publications, Feb. 2016, pp. 239-56.

Goldie, Janis L. "Virtual Communities and the Social Dimension of Privacy." *University of Ottawa Law & Technology Journal*, vol. 3, 2006, pp. 133-68.

Hays, Sharon. *The Cultural Contradictions of Motherhood.* Yale University Press, 1996.

Hiniker, Alexis, et al. "Not at the Dinner Table: Parents and Children's Perspectives on Family Technology Rules." *Proceedings of the 19th ACM Conference on Computer-Supported Cooperative Work & Social Computing—CSCW '16*, ACM Press, 2016, pp. 1374-87.

Jeffery, Catherine Page. "Parenting in the Digital Age: Between Socio-Biological and Socio-Technological Development." *New Media & Society*, Feb. 2020, p. 1461444820908606.

Klonick, Kate. "Re-Shaming the Debate: Social Norms, Shame, and Regulation in an Internet Age Focus on Cyberlaw." *Maryland Law Review*, vol. 75, no. 4, 2016 2015, pp. 1029–65.

Lievens, Eva, et al. "Children's Rights and Digital Technologies." *International Human Rights of Children*, edited by Ursula Kilkelly and Ton Liefaard, Springer, 2018, pp. 1-27.

Livingstone, Sonia. "Digital by Default: The New Normal of Family Life under COVID-19." *British Politics and Policy at LSE*, London School of Economics and Political Science, 5 May 2020, blogs.lse. ac.uk/politicsandpolicy/. Accessed 14 May 2022.

Livingstone, Sonia, and Ellen J. Helsper. "Parental Mediation of Children's Internet Use." *Journal of Broadcasting & Electronic Media*, vol. 52, no. 4, Nov. 2008, pp. 581–99.

Livingstone, Sonia, et al. "Maximizing Opportunities and Minimizing Risks for Children Online: The Role of Digital Skills in Emerging Strategies of Parental Mediation." *Journal of Communication*, vol. 67, no. 1, Wiley Subscription Services, Inc., 2017, pp. 82-105.

Lwin, May O., et al. "Protecting Children's Privacy Online: How Parental Mediation Strategies Affect Website Safeguard Effectiveness." *Journal of Retailing*, vol. 84, no. 2, June 2008, pp. 205-17.

MacKinnon, C. *Toward a Feminist Theory of the State.* Harvard University Press, 1989.

Marwick, Alice E., and Robyn Caplan. "Drinking Male Tears: Language, the Manosphere, and Networked Harassment." *Feminist Media Studies*, vol. 18, no. 4, Routledge, July 2018, pp. 543–59.

Mazmanian, Melissa, and Simone Lanette. "'Okay, One More Episode': An Ethnography of Parenting in the Digital Age." *Proceedings of the 2017 ACM Conference on Computer Supported Cooperative Work and Social Computing*, ACM, 2017, pp. 2273-86.

Nathanson, Amy I. "Identifying and Explaining the Relationship Between Parental Mediation and Children's Aggression." *Communication Research*, vol. 26, no. 2, Apr. 1999, pp. 124-43.

Orenstein, Peggy. *Flux.* Anchor Books, 2000.

Shin, Wonsun. "Empowered Parents: The Role of Self-Efficacy in Parental Mediation of Children's Smartphone Use in the United States." *Journal of Children and Media*, July 2018, pp. 1-13.

Shin, Wonsun, and Benjamin Li. "Parental Mediation of Children's Digital Technology Use in Singapore." *Journal of Children and Media*, vol. 11, no. 1, Jan. 2017, pp. 1-19.

Shin, Wonsun, et al. "Tweens' Online Privacy Risks and the Role of Parental Mediation." *Journal of Broadcasting & Electronic Media*, vol. 56, no. 4, Oct. 2012, pp. 632-49.

Solove, Daniel J. *Understanding Privacy,* Harvard University Press, 2008.

Solove, Daniel J. "I've Got Nothing to Hide and Other Misunderstandings of Privacy 2007 Editor's Symposium." *San Diego Law Review*, vol. 44, no. 4, 2007, pp. 745-72.

Sutherland, Jean-Anne. "Mothering, Guilt and Shame." *Sociology Compass*, vol. 4, no. 5, 2010, pp. 310-21.

Vaidhyanathan, Siva. *Antisocial Media: How Facebook Disconnects Us and Undermines Democracy*. Oxford University Press, 2018.

Vaterlaus, J. Mitchell, et al. "'They Always Ask What I'm Doing and Who I'm Talking to': Parental Mediation of Adolescent Interactive Technology Use." *Marriage & Family Review*, vol. 50, no. 8, Routledge, Nov. 2014, pp. 691-713.

Warren, Ron, and Lindsey Aloia. "Parenting Style, Parental Stress, and Mediation of Children's Media Use." *Western Journal of Communication*, vol. 83, no. 4, Aug. 2019, pp. 483-500.

Warren, S., and L. Brandeis, "The Right to Privacy," *Harvard Law Review*, vol. 4, 1890, pp. 193-220.

Wilson, Julie A., and Emily Chivers Yochim. *Mothering Through Precarity: Women's Work and Digital Media*. Duke University Press, 2017.

Wisniewski, Pamela, et al. "'Preventative' vs. 'Reactive': How Parental Mediation Influences Teens' Social Media Privacy Behaviors." *Proceedings of the 18th ACM Conference on Computer Supported Cooperative Work & Social Computing—CSCW '15*, ACM Press, 2015, pp. 302-16.

Chapter 7

Parents, Technicians, Curators: Shrinking Space and Time in Early Parenthood

Andrew McGillivray and Angela McGillivray

Soon after our son Oliver was born in January 2018, Andrew photographed him with his smartphone. Oli, as we call him, had only been in the world for a few minutes before his image was captured in time. After taking the photograph, Andrew then sent it to Oliver's maternal grandparents by SMS (short message service), bridging the considerable distance between us, at St. Boniface Hospital in Winnipeg, Manitoba, and them, at their home in Gimli, Manitoba. As a result of the SMS, Oliver's grandparents were able to share in the birth experience. From the moment of his birth, Oli has been subject to technologies that bind time by capturing and preserving images and experiences for future reference and also to technologies that bind space by transmitting information over physical distance. John Durham Peters, our principal theorist, aptly points out that people "have always interacted across distances of time and space, but digital media inten-sify opportunities and troubles in person-to-person dealings" (*The Marvelous Clouds* 6). As he grows up, Oli is increasingly able to manipulate these space- and time-binding technologies and is beginning to understand what each type of technology can do.

Oli is now a toddler and technology continues to connect our space with the spaces of our out-of-town family. Photographs and videos are sent regularly through SMS and uploaded to Angela's now-private Instagram account. To keep Oli connected to his extended family, and especially following the COVID-19 stay-home orders, we are now proficient users of Apple's FaceTime application, which enables us to hold synchronic remote video calls on a regular basis with our smartphones, opening up our home to virtual visitors. Initially, Oli's grandparents requested the video calls, but now our technologically adept toddler asks to see "grandpa's face" or "grandma's face." As his understanding of the technology increases, Oli associates the act of communicating with his relatives via video call with the smartphone, the medium used to bridge the space between us and them. However, through the smartphone, "communication has become disembodied," specifically, "the rise of the concept of 'communication' is a symptom of the disembodiment of interaction" (Durham Peters, *Speaking into the Air* 228). Although we regularly communicate with extended family through digital devices, we have also cautiously and carefully reintroduced in-person visits on occasion, as COVID-19 stay-home orders are adjusted, to ensure that the disembodiment of interaction does not become the norm for our family. As we mediate our voices and bodily images through digital communications technologies in our discourse with family, we also recognize that the unique in-person experience is lost. We hope for a future for Oli that is not reliant on the voice or video call, and we recognize the role we need to play in ensuring that inperson communication and interaction continues to be part of our daily lives.

In addition to its role in our communications, new media is also the primary instrument we use to collect and store our family memories. Oli has a digital museum of memories many gigabytes in size, composed of thousands of images, videos, and sound recordings. By accessing our digital collections on a computing device, we can easily recall not only the exciting milestones—such as Oli's first sounds, his first steps, and his first words—but also mundane, daily occurrences that we have committed to photo or video. Oli also enjoys looking through photos and watching videos of himself, and one of his signal phrases to indicate he wants to access his evolving digital archive is "Oli's in there," which he declares as he points to a device, whether a desktop computer, laptop, tablet, or smartphone. As he has become more familiar with the technology, he is able to press the home button to open the iPad Mini and navigate through these archives on his own. Not long ago, we heard music coming from the iPad Mini and realized he had figured out how to start up a slideshow.

This chapter focuses on two aspects of technological intervention into our home: the influence of technology on our shared and individual experiences of space and time. Considering these two aspects in terms of James Carey's views of communication, we can apply both the transmission view—focusing on how technology can be used to transcend space and distance—and the ritual view—focusing on time and the "symbolic process whereby reality is produced, maintained, repaired and transformed" (19). Technology space-binds our home by connecting us in real time to people in other physical spaces and time-binds us by enabling recall of various moments in our past through the collection of digital memories housed via compact digital storage.

Throughout this chapter, we also contextualize the challenges we currently experience in relation to these two aspects of technological intervention. As parents living in a world in which newer media appears year after year and becomes increasingly accessible to our young son, our challenges are parallel but also more complex and more rapidly evolving than those faced by parents during earlier moments of revolution in communication technology, especially early space- and time-binding technologies, such as the telegraph and the telephone, on the one hand, and the phonograph and film, on the other. Durham Peters, who advocates for a look into the past to understand our current circumstances, argues the following:

> As we live through something of a digital revolution in our own time, revisiting old shocks can be highly illuminating. The urgent questions about communication today—the telescoping of space-time (e.g., the Internet) and the replication of human experience and identity (e.g., virtual reality)—were explored in analogous forms in the era of the telegraph and photograph, the phonograph and telephone, the cinema and radio. (*Speaking into the Air* 143)

Advances in communication technology "in claiming to bring us closer, [have] only made communication seem that much more impossible" (143) or, at the very least, have led us to question and analyze the relationship we have with digital technologies as well as the relationships we have with others and ourselves as mediated by these technologies. In what follows, we outline what we see as two major aspects of our young son's relationship with new media—the video call and the digital archive—and attempt to speculate on how his involvement with these media will influence both him, as a child, and us, as his parents. We also remain mindful of our role as mediators, imposing our own limits on how and when Oli engages these digital technologies. Both our behaviour as mediators and Oli's own engagement with digital media will influence his development. If he becomes accustomed to communicating through digital media, we are concerned that his appetite for in-person interactions might be affected; likewise, if he is able to endlessly curate his own memory machine (i.e, via the iPad Mini), filling it with photographs and videos of himself which he can then watch and view as he pleases, we must take care to ensure that he is still able to live in the moment and enjoy real-time experience.

Sharing Space

When thinking about how our own childhoods differed from our son's, Andrew often thinks about *The Jetsons*, the space-age cartoon television show, which was produced first in the 1960s and then again in the 1980s. When watching the syndicated show in the late 1980s, Andrew was fascinated by how the families depicted in the show had television-like telephones in their work and living spaces. In the show, these devices were actually called Visaphones—"visa," from the Latin "videre," meaning to see, combined with the shortened form of "telephone"—and enabled the cartoon characters to hold real-time video calls like the now ubiquitous FaceTime, Skype, and Zoom applications, among many others. For Andrew, as a youth, this space-age science-fiction technology seemed as out of reach as the commonplace space travel also depicted in the cartoon series. He would never have imagined a world where we could see the face of another in real-time, speaking to one another in dialogue over video as if on a phone call. Instead, the screen was a device for broadcasting, with information flowing unidirectionally, solely to the viewer.

Now, "new technologies are undeniably integrating more swiftly into society than ever" (Tarasuik and Kaufman 89)—reaching an audience of fifty million that took the telephone twenty years, the television thirteen years, the internet four years, and the iPad a mere three months. Linda Cundy similarly notes that although more recent technological advances have been compared to the rise of the printing press, or even the advent of the telephone, both of these advances took longer than recent technologies to have a major influence in our lives and appear in the homes of people across the world (18). Even though we could not begin to fathom being able to make a video call from a computer device that fit in our pockets in the 1980s, in the early 2020s, video calling from our smartphones is a regular part of our lives and something to which our son Oli is incredibly accustomed as a toddler.

Interestingly, although the concept of the videophone and video call has existed in some form for decades, video calling was not truly accessible to or well-used by the general public until quite recently. From the satirical image "Edison's Telephonoscope" by George Du Maurier, which appeared in the December 9, 1878, issue of *Punch* magazine (Roberts, n.p.), to Alexander Graham Bell's 1891 article introducing the concept of the "electrical radiophone," which would allow one to "[see] by electricity" (Bell), the roots of the video call go back more than a century. Furthermore, the technology has been introduced several times, without much success. When the American Telephone and Telegraph Company (AT&T) introduced their "picturephone" at the 1964 New York World's Fair, for example, they touted it as a "new way of communicating" that would "displace today's means of communication" (Lipartito 50). Instead of making its way into businesses, let alone households, across the country, the fate of the picturephone suffered from a lack of "early adopters," it was cost prohibitive, and those who owned a picturephone could only use it to communicate with others who also owned one. To call the picturephone a failure, however, is too simple. As Kenneth Lipartito urges readers to consider, the "failure" of the picturephone makes room for other information technology, such as the personal computer and the internet, to "enact the same rhetoric" (79). These technologies, he says, "promote the idea that technology can be liberating by allowing us to transcend space and simulate personal contacts and connections with virtual ones" (79). Indeed, transcending space and simulating personal connections via video calls is now commonplace. Now, during the COVID-19 pandemic, more than ever, families—not just businesses and their employees—are fully embracing the use of video-calling technologies as part of our everyday routines.

When we consider how the rapidly changing landscape of new media technology continually influences our lives and the ways we communicate, we also think about other earlier technologies that might have had a similar impact on households as the now ubiquitous video call. What first comes to mind is the telephone, as it enabled instantaneous communication with geographically distant family members from within the comfort of the home. We also think further back to the telegraph, the first electrical telecommunications system that provided more rapid communication between distant locations, although this technology would have been less accessible and certainly uncommon in individual homes. The seed of the video call can, however, be traced back to the telegraph, for it was a technology that initiated the near-synchronous bridging of space and "marked the decisive separation of 'transportation' and 'communication'" (Carey 164). Thanks to the telegraph, a coded message could be sent far more quickly than a written missive, as electric currents travelling through wires as opposed to a physical object travelling via a messenger. The telegraph would thus have been an improvement on the postal service, as letters would have taken hours, days, or weeks to be physically transported from one location to another. However, senders would have needed to rely on telegraph offices as the locations in which to send and receive messages rather than from the comfort of their own kitchens and living rooms. Telegraphs were also, by their nature, impersonal; they would not have allowed a child to hear their grandparent's voice, for example, as they would have with a telephone, or to see a live image, as they now do with the video call.

Although they have revolutionized communications across considerable distance, technologies like the telegraph, the telephone, and now the smartphone are not without drawbacks. The telegraph, when introduced, would have required both the ability to travel to a telegraph office and the economic means to pay the significant costs for the transmission of messages: These factors "kept the telegraph from being the utopia of universal contact" (Durham Peters, *Speaking into the Air* 139). The telephone was much more affordable, and "one reason phones have become so indispensable for communicating is that the cost keeps dropping to make calls" (Zagorsky). Yet even with the increasing level of access and decreasing costs associated with new media communications technologies, connectivity is still far from universal.

Smartphones come with purchasing costs and monthly or data-use fees. Beyond the economic limitations or challenges that accompany the initial purchase of hardware and ongoing costs of data transfer, the new media devices themselves, as objects that mediate communication between the people on either end, are subject to the span of the technology life cycle and, more specifically, to a product life cycle (Tassey 1797). To improve the communication experience, avoid potential miscommunication, and even prevent being cut off from communication entirely, individuals and families are required to continually upgrade their computing devices and their data plans to ensure constant access and connection. In fact, "the proliferation of household media devices has raised pressures on parents to create optimal conditions in which these gadgets are appropriated in the domestic space" (Lim, "Through the Tablet Glass" 22). Now that our family relies on devices for video calls with extended family, we need to maintain our equipment and make sure to always have data remaining on our mobile plans. Furthermore, Oli regularly expresses his interest in possessing his own computing hardware, or at least securing our family's devices for his own use. Although we are not planning to purchase him his own device in the short term, we do sometimes wonder when that will change and how much his peers' expectations regarding direct communication with him may influence our decision.

In addition to potentially prohibitive cost factors, communication mediated through a computing device is affected by a lack of emotional connection, which is more easily established and facilitated during in-person shared experiences. Even though the frequency of communication between our family and our extended family has increased substantially since we began making regular video calls, we do not actually get to share physical space with one another: "We can't feel the mood in the room through our screens. We can't hug or offer a reassuring hand on a shoulder. We can't even make eye contact, the foundation of emotional connection" (Leszcz 7). The camera on a computer or mobile device is not in the same exact space as the screen on which we see the person or people with whom we are communicating, so if we are looking into the camera to present our eyes to their screen, we cannot also be looking directly at our screen to see the other's eyes. Conversely, when both parties are looking directly at the screen, neither is looking directly into the camera.

These limitations aside, video calls have facilitated family bonding for us, enabling our son Oli to interact with his grandparents in some form on a regular basis. These virtual visits, which tide us over between our in-person visits, have enriched Oli's relationship with his grandparents. In their study on when and why parents involve young children in video-call communication, Joanne Tarasuik and Jordy Kaufman found that engaging with video communication between in-person visits "reduced or even eliminated the need to re-establish rapport at each physical meeting" (94). We can certainly see that ourselves in the case of Oli and his grandparents: Whereas he used to be quite shy and quiet at the beginning of each in-person visit with his grandparents, needing some time to warm up to them again, now it takes mere seconds before he becomes his silly, boisterous self around them. This may be, in part, because he has become comfortable being that silly, boisterous self during video calls as well. In their study, Tarasuik and Kaufman note that their respondents felt video call communication was "more suitable," "more engaging and enjoyable," and "always lasted much longer" than telephone communication (95). Respondents felt their "children could act in their normal manner during video communication ... as it was quite natural and similar to how they would behave during a physical visit" (95), and relatives of these children also reported being content to observe them at play rather than seeking a more in-depth conversation. That being said, the study did find that these interactions become more in-depth as children's communication skills improved (96). We have also observed this in Oli's video communications with his relatives: As his language skills were beginning to develop, Oli was content to play, babble here and there in the smartphone's general direction, and perhaps show off the occasional toy to his grandparents. Now, as his vocabulary and conversation skills are advancing at a rapid pace, he is able to sit down and hold a conversation, albeit a relatively brief one, before being distracted by something else.

What was for Andrew a far-fetched fantasy he saw on *The Jetsons* over thirty years ago is now a reality for our own son, at least in most respects; in fact, he "may consider such a life [a life without screen media] incomprehensible" (Tarasuik and Kaufman 100). The possibility, however, that he may not experience the longing for connection with relatives that was more commonplace before the digital communications revolution we are currently living in will quite possibly be a disbenefit for Oli. Missing someone like a grandparent and wishing to communicate and spend time with them is instrumental to developing a strong emotional bond; now that Oli can video call grandma or grandpa whenever he likes, he may never know what it means to miss them while they are still living.

Video-calling technology has changed the space of our home. What was before a private space—a refuge from the outside world, into which we could invite people on our terms—is now open for visitors whenever a computer or mobile device is near at hand and a video call comes in. The boundary between our home and the outside world has been "not just altered, but eroded" by digital technologies (Cundy 22). Media such as a video call is "not simply the *medium* by which we interact and communicate with others but more literally a *place*"; in other words, digital communications technology has created a world in which "place is less a stable notion than an affective, circulating, and evolving series of encounters" (Rickert 44). The virtual space of a smartphone screen has become one of the places in which we interact with our loved ones. What worries us as parents is that Oli will grow up in a world where a virtual place, such as the video call, comes to replace a physical place, such as a playground, a park, or a relative's home. Oli has easily adjusted to seeing his relatives over a video call, which is convenient and even necessary in the moment due to the COVID-19 pandemic, but we hope that he continues to be able to adjust to leaving the video call aside and appreciate and enjoy seeing people in person and sharing experiences in physical spaces. We do not intend to prohibit Oli's use of new media, but ideally we wish to strike a balance so that he can responsibly engage with digital media while continuing to have physical experiences, enjoy face-to-face interaction with friends and family, and appreciate and share physical space, which will affect his relationships and interactions into adolescence and adulthood.

Time Travelling

There are relatively few photographs of Andrew from his childhood and only slightly more from Angela's. Andrew was born in 1983, and although his parents did have a film camera, in order to produce photos they needed to invest in film, first, and then, once the film spool was used up, to pay for production of the prints. Angela, born only five years later than Andrew, certainly has a larger collection of printed photos from her childhood than Andrew does, but the amount is nowhere near the mass of digital images, not to mention digital videos and audio recordings, that we have already accumulated from Oli's first two and a half years of life.

After Andrew's paternal grandfather passed away in November 2019, he received a package from his aunt: It contained a large box full of photos that his grandfather and grandmother had collected from Andrew's childhood. He had never seen most of these photos, as his grandparents had taken them during visits to Winnipeg from their home in Toronto, or they had received the prints in the mail from Andrew's parents. After receiving this box of treasures, Andrew's brother and his family joined our family to look through the time capsule. We were taken back in time to the 1980s and 1990s as we sorted through baby photos, toddler photos, and even photos from the brothers' first days of public school. Similarly, even though Angela has had access to her parents' collection of photos from her childhood since she was young, her grandparents had also gathered a collection of their own photos, which they gave to us when we got engaged. We learned that they had created a personalized photo book, including handwritten captions on the photos, for each of their grandchildren, and they have begun the tradition of passing them along as we each start a family of our own. Looking at these carefully curated physical photo books, we can remember the grandparents who thoughtfully gathered these memories and cherished them. We can also enjoy the nostalgic feelings inspired from being transported back to our childhoods while simultaneously looking forward to experiencing—and documenting— our own son's childhood.

By contrast, Oli already has a huge digital archive. We dare not estimate its size because the number of digital photos of this young person numbers in the many thousands, complemented by many hundreds of videos and dozens of audio recordings. From the first day of Oli's life in St. Boniface Hospital, documentation of his childhood has never ceased. Initially, we were motivated to document everything so we could relive happy moments for all of our lives. Additionally, all of his early visitors wanted to take photos of him, and many wanted pictures of themselves with him in their arms to document their first meeting. It is no surprise that Oli has become something of a social media star to our circle of family and friends, as Angela has posted many photos of him to her Instagram and Facebook accounts, as do his grandparents. Due to the nature of social media and digital storage, Oli will possibly never lose access, even for short periods of time, to his childhood images. He will be able to access images on our family's computing devices whenever he likes. By transporting himself back in time on a regular basis, viewing images of himself from weeks, days, and even years past, he is undoubtedly softening any possible future effects of time travelling through photo albums as we have experienced.

Viewing his digital memories may also have a significant impact on the development of his own memories, and this is especially true when Oli views images and videos too soon after an event. Immediate playback of events on digital devices does in fact shape children's memories, as Julia Cho discovers and writes in her *New York Times* article. Cho spoke with Daniel Schacter, a psychology professor at Harvard, who describes viewing a photo or video as "reactivating an experience" and notes that this process "can even change the original memory" (qtd. in Cho). Elizabeth Loftus, a cognitive psychologist and expert on human memory, expands on this and differentiates between the first-person perspective of experience—"You see others while you act"—and the third-person perspective of watching—"You learn something about how others see you" (qtd. in Cho). Our memories from our own childhoods were preserved in photographs and the odd audio or video recording, and at the time, these mediums did not generally allow for immediate playback. We got to "linger in the experience for a while, from our own perspective, not the camera's" (Cho). We may wish for Oli to be able to "linger" in his experience, but with the immediacy and accessibility of digital media, combined with his increasing tech-savviness, this possibility is becoming more and more remote. Furthermore, as "autobiographical memory plays an important role in personal identity" (Gopnik 144), we need to consider how Oli's identity is affected by the role digital media plays in shaping or even altering his autobiographical memory. Perhaps at Oli's current age this is less of an immediate concern, as Alison Gopnik states that children around two years old may recognize themselves in a mirror or video, but "they don't seem to understand how this self is related to their past and future selves" (145). However, this will eventually be something that we will want to be aware and perhaps even wary of. It also is something that we should be aware of for ourselves; playing back these videos and looking through photos will also change the memory of our children's childhoods for us as parents. Things we may have forgotten or remembered differently are brought back to the front of our minds and perhaps even reshaped by looking back through Oli's digital archive. Initially, as we have noted, reliving special moments throughout our lives is exactly what motivated us to document Oli's childhood. In fact, the very act of documenting these moments has the potential to detract from our real-time experience of them, and reliving them, whether immediately or later in life, unavoidably shapes and reshapes our memories.

Despite our concerns about how it may affect his memories, we do allow Oli to view photos and videos of himself, although we do generally take precautions to allow some time to lapse between the event itself and the viewing of it on a screen. When we enrolled him in Little Kickers FC, a soccer league for one-and-a-half-year-olds, we took countless photos and videos of him and Andrew on the field or in the community centre doing soccer drills. We would show Oli the videos, and they became some of his favourites to view, occupying him on many a bus ride to and from daycare. Each week when we arrived at the soccer venue, he was thrilled to know that we were amassing more videos and photos for his collection, and sometimes it felt as though he was performing for the camera.

More recently, Oli has discovered how to access his digital archive himself by using one of our family devices: the iPad Mini. On this device, he can easily touch the screen to enter different applications, including counting, matching, and sorting games we have installed for him and entertainment programs, such as Netflix and Disney+, although he is often drawn straight to the "Photos" app. Once in this app, Oli can browse his whole life in photos and videos that are housed on the cloud, and he seems to recognize himself; one of his early sentences was "Oli is in there," which he would exclaim as he browsed the app. Furthermore, Oli can manipulate the iPad Mini in order to take photos of himself, "selfies," so after he has been playing with the tablet for a period of time we are likely to discover that he has taken a handful, if not dozens, of pictures of himself. He is hardly the only toddler taking selfies,[1] and although they do not realize it, these young children are taking part in developing their sense of self and curating their own digital collections while participating in a process of self-disembodiment by putting images of themselves into a medium.

Oli is continually in contact with his digital archive. Either on his own or with our assistance, he reviews the first two-and-a-half years of his life and continues to document himself. What does this continual retrospection and image production mean for how Oli sees himself and for how he understands his reality? It is difficult to assess whether Oli knows that when he sees himself in photos and videos that he is seeing an earlier moment in time, captured and immortalized by a camera, or that these images are in fact an aspect of himself that exist outside of his body, an externalization of the subject. This recognition is likely to take place at the fourth level of self-awareness, permanence, as outlined by Philippe Rochat: One identifies the self "beyond the here and now of mirror experience" and a "permanent self is expressed: an entity that is represented as invariant over time and appearance changes" (722). Rochat describes the process of identifying the self in videos and photos as the "Me-But-Not-Me dilemma" (727). Children understand that the person they see in the mirror or the screen looks like them, but they still do not understand that it *is* them. Rochat further notes that viewing videos of themselves can help children to "slowly bypass the Me-But-Not-Me dilemma" and suggests that this recognition happens not prior to the child being approximately three years old (727). By this measure, it is unlikely that Oli yet recognizes his "permanent self" as the one he sees on the screen, but this recognition is fast approaching.

Just as it is difficult to know what stage Oli has reached in Rochat's five levels of self-awareness—likely moving from level three, identi-fication, to level four, permanence; certainly not yet level five, self-consciousness or "meta" self-awareness[2]—it is also difficult to evaluate whether he is likely to suffer from Marshall McLuhan's "narcissus narcosis"—"a syndrome whereby [an individual] remains as unaware of the psychic and social effects of [their] new technology as a fish of the water it swims in. As a result, precisely at the point where a new media-induced environment becomes all pervasive and transmogrifies our sensory balance, it also becomes invisible" (237). Reflecting on McLuhan's concept alongside the Greek myth of Narcissus falling in love with his own reflection, Henry Jenkins notes that "the reflection is an interesting metaphor for thinking about media as at once part of us and yet also apart from us" (45). Digital images and videos are at once a part of Oli's identity, but they are also apart from him; they are a reflection of his past, memories from his childhood that are separate from his current self, but they will also undoubtedly shape his sense of self as he grows up in the digital age. As parents, it is our responsibility to help guide Oli to find the proper balance between the virtual and real worlds and to help him learn how to engage in both appropriately.

Although McLuhan's narcissus narcosis obviously harkens back to the Narcissus myth—as does our common understanding of what it means to be narcissistic—a social-developmental perspective differentiates between narcissism and self-esteem. Narcissism has at its core an "inflated sense of one's importance and deservingness," whereas "self-esteem is defined as a sense of one's worth as a person" (Brummelman and Sedikides 83). Eddie Brummelman and his colleagues have suggested in multiple articles that parental overvaluation causes narcissism, whereas parental warmth fosters high self-esteem (Brummelman and Thomaes; Brummelman and Sedikides). Since we allow Oli to access and manipulate his digital archive, we must take care to ensure that his perception of himself veers away from narcissism, or an elevated sense of superiority and entitlement, and instead stays within the realm of positive self-esteem. We must ensure that viewing himself on a screen does not encourage him to develop "unrealistically positive views of [himself] (*illusion*), strive for superiority (*superiority*), and oscillate between hubris and shame (*fragility*)" (Brummelman and Sedikides 84). Rather, by sharing in his engagement with his digital archive, we can indicate appreciation for him and his abilities and encourage him to develop "positive but realistic views of [himself] (*realism*), strive for self-improvement (*growth*), and feel intrinsically worthy, even in the face of setbacks (*robustness*)" (Brummelman and Sedikides 84). Since viewing his digital memories will necessarily shape Oli's memory, and thus his sense of self, as he grows, it is our job as parents to help guide that development.

As one example, Oli loves riding his glider bicycle down what we call "the mountain"—a small hill sloping from the parking lot of our neighbourhood high school down to its athletic track. At first, Oli loved pulling up his feet as he rode down the hill, and we often took videos of him doing so. He began to feel overly confident, watching these videos play back and seeing what he was capable of. One day, he was riding down the hill as Angela was taking a video, and he began to lose control of his bike. He managed to right himself, but it rattled him, and when we watched the video together a few days later, he remembered his near fall. The next time we went out to "the mountain," Oli announced that he was going to "go down more careful" this time. Viewing his minor setback on video reinforced that while he is capable of riding his bike down the hill without his feet on the ground, he should try to be more careful. He remained confident in his abilities but also showed room for growth and maturity.

As Eddie Brummelman and Sanders Thomaes suggest, "children construct their self-concept based on the social relationships they have, the feedback they receive, the social comparisons they make, and the cultural values they endorse" (1769). In other words, social experiences influence how children view themselves (1769). If we consider this in relation to the concerns at hand, we can begin to attempt to understand how Oli uses digital media as a lens to help him construe his social experiences and how this will affect his later view of himself. Brummelman and Thomaes conclude their article with a reference to psychologist Lev Vygotsky's insight that "we become ourselves through others" (1770). What does it mean for Oli that one of the others through whom he becomes himself is himself, reflected back to him through a screen? What happens when Oli learns to evaluate himself through his own eyes as though he were seeing through the eyes of others? Beyond potentially changing his memory, our use of digital technology is also shaping the way that Oli learns to understand and view himself as a self, in the present and into the future.

Although it is important to consider how viewing photos and videos of himself affects Oli's sense of self, it is also interesting to wonder what he sees and understands when we show him photos (either digital or printed) of other people. We have one photograph of Andrew's late sister Katherine, for instance, who passed away at the age of six in 1996. We received this photo in the package from Andrew's aunt after his grandfather's death and have hung the frame on our basement wall. We have shown this photo to Oli and explained that it is a picture of his aunt who passed away many years ago. Oli, however, sees another person (though disembodied) and might not understand that the photo is taking us all back in time. Even though we are referring here to a photo of someone who has in fact passed away, Durham Peters suggests that "all mediated communication is in a sense communication with the dead, insofar as media can store 'phantasms of the living' for playback after bodily death" (*Speaking into the Air* 142). Even if Katherine were still alive, this photo would represent an aspect of her that faded like a trace the moment it was taken. Additionally, because he is so used to seeing other family members on the screen—in digital photos, videos, and in real-time video calls—it may be difficult for Oli to understand that he will never have the chance to meet this aunt in real life, even though he sees pictures of our other siblings and knows that he can also see them, hug them, and interact with them in person.

Oli's photos and videos will speak to him, and to us, from the past in the years to come. In a way, he will experience what Kate Eichhorn refers to as "the end of forgetting." An effect of growing up in the digital age, the "end of forgetting" signals the loss of the freedom to destroy or escape the past, which Eichhorn sees as an essential part of growing up. "The real crisis of the digital age is not the disappearance of childhood," Eichhorn writes, "but the spectre of the childhood that can never be forgotten" (12). Oli's digital collections will certainly present him with a narrative of his childhood that has been curated: by his parents, by his younger self, and perhaps most significantly by the software which houses his digital photographs. Though he is not writing about childhood specifically, Durham Peters notes that "an effect of modern media, again, is the externalization of the fragile and flickering stuff of subjectivity and memory into a permanent form that can be played back at will. The supposed ease of transfer was paid for with ghostliness" (*Speaking into the Air* 164). The sights and sounds of his younger self which Oli will see and hear when he revisits his digital photo and video archive later in life will be a ghostly or spectral version of his more mature self.[3] What he remembers about his past, how he relives those memories and experiences, and how the past will shape the formation of his identity will undeniably be influenced by the presence of his digital archive.

Growing Up Digital

When reflecting on what it means to be a parent within a culture of near-ubiquitous new media usage and expectations, we relate to what Sun Sun Lim refers to as "the practice of 'transcendent parenting' which goes beyond traditional, physical concepts of parenting, to incorporate virtual and online parenting and how these all intersect" ("Through the Tablet Glass" 21). Changes in the new media landscape are placing more demands on parents today. Not only must we monitor and direct our son's media consumption and exposure, we are also expected to engage with media as part of our parenting role. Indeed, Lim suggests that the "always-on and always-on-hand mobile media" devices, which surround us "have come to play a central role" in what it means to be a family (*Transcendent Parenting* 2). Similarly, Rachael Levy notes that information and communications technology (ICT) "has become ingrained into family life and has a bearing on the ways in which physical spaces are created in the home as well as reconfiguring the 'time-spaces' of the family, in terms of activity" (151). Technology, then, will not only influence the development of Oli's identity as he grows up in the digital age but will also influence our identities as parents and have a significant role in shaping the dynamics of our family.

As parents of a toddler, we are in the first phase of "transcendent parenting," wherein our son is becoming familiar with mobile media— such as the iPhones we use to FaceTime his grandparents and the iPad Mini he uses to play games, watch shows, and access and curate his digital archive. We have also used mobile media applications to monitor his development and activity, specifically the Wonder Weeks app Angela used to track Oli's mental and physical development during the first twenty months of his life and the HiMama app she now uses to receive daily updates, photos, videos, and supplies requests from his daycare. We have and will continue to use mobile media extensively in our parenting, to communicate with Oli as he moves through the city, to communicate with his teachers, and to communicate with the parents of his friends.

According to Lim, transcendent parenting has three core principles. First, technology can be used to transcend the physical distance between parents and their children. We currently use mobile media primarily to transcend the distance between our family and our extended family and to develop Oli's digital archive, but we can anticipate the moment in time when mobile media will increasingly fulfill the function of connecting us across space with Oli, as it has begun to with the use of the HiMama app for his daycare. Second, mobile media can be used by parents to transcend the online and offline environments their children move through, for instance by attempting to monitor internet usage through applications designed to track just that or, once Oli is independent enough to move through the city on his own, to follow his physical location using another purpose-built application. And third, parents transcend time by being constantly engaged in active parenting, whether their child is with them physically or not, as mobile media connect parent and child timelessly (Lim, *Transcendent Parenting* 3-5), placing parenting duties "on an endless loop" ("Through the Tablet Glass" 27). There are certainly benefits to having the ability to be in continual communication, but transcendent parenting is not necessarily a positive thing, for it will subject both parent and child to increased communication burden and possible outside monitoring (Hemelryk Donald 397). "In this mobile-infused climate," Lim writes, "each stage of the child's life introduces fresh communication and media access opportunities but also presents new challenges for parents" ("Through the Tablet Glass" 25). As Oli grows up digital, we need to be prepared to meet these challenges and learn how to use technology in the best way that works for us.

Technological interventions already influence our son's identity and how he identifies others. Oli recognizes an aspect of himself as existing in a new media technology, just as he sees grandpa's face or grandma's face in the same machine. Both he and others are disembodied in these machines, yet Oli is becoming more aware of the difference between prerecorded videos of himself at an earlier moment in time, fixed and unalterable, and the mirror image he sees during a live video call, while taking a "selfie," or when using an Instagram filter. His evolving interaction with digital communications and collections will certainly influence him in a multitude of manners, as he continues to connect to others using technology and as he retrospectively accesses the accumulating mass of digital data documenting his life. The ever-changing and ever-present media landscape challenges us, as parents, to moderate the ambient environment to the best of our abilities and knowledge so that Oli does not depend solely on machine-mediated communication and that his digital archive does not completely replace a physical one.

Undoubtedly, Oliver will have a different childhood than either of his parents. Space and geographical distance will not be as much of a barrier for him as it was for us. He will be able to communicate easily

with his out-of-town family through video calls, which will considerably bind the space between them and enable them to meet
regularly in online spaces. Oli will also travel in time through his
digital archive, reflecting on how he looked and sounded when he
was younger. These opportunities will come with their own sets of
challenges, however. How space-binding and time-binding technologies influence Oli's identity will depend largely on how we as
parents choose to respond to the opportunities they create and to how
Oli chooses to live and engage with the technologies he encounters. It
will also be up to Oli, as he grows up digital, to learn to navigate the
physical and virtual spaces of his life. He will need to make decisions
regarding where and how to establish boundaries in the virtual world
as well as when and how to revert back to living and communicating
face-to-face in physical spaces.

Endnotes

1. Toddler selfies have received quite a bit of attention from news
   outlets, such as *The Atlantic, Global News,* and *Time* (Fetters;
   Flaccus; Drexler).

2. It is important here to note that Rochat does not suggest that
   children reach level five of self-awareness, which happens from
   birth to age four or five, and remain there throughout adulthood: "As adults, we are continually oscillating in our levels of
   awareness.... In fact, each of these oscillating states of self-
   awareness can be construed as constant transition between the 5
   levels emerging early in life" (728).

3. Will Oli recognize the sound of his young voice as belonging to
   him, as he now recognizes an image of himself in the iPad Mini?
   Even when as adults we hear our own voices on recordings, it can
   be difficult to recognize them as our own. The combination of
   image and sound in video recordings offers undeniable proof that
   the sounds one hears are coming from the body projecting them.
   The sound Oli might hear when he revisits his video archive in
   several years will be a ghostly version of his more mature voice; his
   recorded voice will speak to him from the past, verifiable by its
   association with his own but younger image that might be just as
   unrecognizable to him.

Works Cited

Bell, Alexander Graham. "Editorial and Articles on the Possibility of Seeing by Electricity." *Library of Congress*. 10 Apr. 1891, www.loc.gov/resource/magbell.37600601/?st=text. Accessed 15 May 2022.

Brummelman, Eddie, and Constantine Sedikides. "Raising Children with High Self-Esteem (But Not Narcissism)." *Child Development Perspectives*, vol. 14, no. 2, 2020, pp. 83-89.

Brummelman, Eddie, and Sanders Thomaes. "How Children Construct Views of Themselves: A Social-Developmental Perspective." *Child Development*, vol. 88, no. 6, 2017, pp. 1763-73.

Carey, James W. *Communication as Culture: Essays on Media and Society*. Routledge, 2009.

Cho, Julia. "Is the Immediate Playback of Events Changing Children's Memories?" *New York Times*, 25 Apr. 2019, www.nytimes.com/2019/04/25/well/family/video-altering-memory.html. Accessed 15 May 2022.

Cundy, Linda. "Attachment, Self-experience, and Communication Technology: Love in the Age of the Internet." *Love in the Age of the Internet: Attachment in the Digital Era*, edited by Linda Cundy, Taylor & Francis Group, 2014, pp. 1-29.

Durham Peters, John. *Speaking into the Air: A History of the Idea of Communication*. The University of Chicago Press, 1999.

Durham Peters, John. *The Marvelous Clouds: Toward a Philosophy of Elemental Media*. The University of Chicago Press, 2015.

Drexler, Peggy. "The Millennials Are All Right." *Time*, 1 Feb. 2014, time.com/3465/the-millennial-kids-are-alright/. Accessed 15 May 2022.

Eichhorn, Kate. *The End of Forgetting: Growing Up with Social Media*. Harvard University Press, 2019.

Fetters, Ashley. "Toddlers Are Delighted with Themselves." *The Atlantic*, 11 Feb. 2020, www.theatlantic.com/family/archive/2020/02/why-toddlers-love-taking-selfies/606355/. Accessed 15 May 2022.

Flaccus, Gillian. "Toddlers Love Selfies: Parenting in an iPhone Age." *Global News*, 28 Jan. 2014, globalnews.ca/news/1111516/toddlers-love-selfies-parenting-in-an-iphone-age/. Accessed 15 May 2022.

Gopnik, Alison. *The Philosophical Baby: What Children's Minds Tell Us About Truth, Love, and the Meaning of Life.* Farrar, Straus, and Giroux, 2009.

Hemelryk Donald, Stephanie. "Review Essay: Transcendent Parenting: Raising Children in the Digital Age." *Journal of Children and Media*, vol. 14, no. 3, 2020, pp. 396-99.

Jenkins, Henry. "Enhanced Memory: 'The Entire History of You.'" *Through the Black Mirror: Deconstructing the Side Effects of the Digital Age*, edited by Terrence McSweeney and Stuart Joy, Palgrave Macmillan, 2019, pp. 43-54.

Leszcz, Benjamin. "The Missing Touch: The Agony and Ecstasy of Endless Screen Time." *The Globe and Mail*, 18 Apr. 2020, www.theglobeandmail.com/opinion/article-the-missing-touch-the-agony-and-ecstasy-of-endless-screen-time/. Accessed 15 May 2022.

Levy, Rachel. "Young Children, Digital Technology, and Interaction with Text." *Deconstructing Digital Natives: Young People, Technology, and the New Literacies*, edited by Michael Thomas, Routledge, 2011, pp. 151-66.

Lim, Sun Sun. *Transcendent Parenting: Raising Children in the Digital Age.* Oxford University Press, 2020.

Lim, Sun Sun. "Through the Tablet Glass: Transcendent Parenting in an Era of Mobile Media and Cloud Computing." *Journal of Children and Media*, vol. 10, no. 1, 2016, pp. 21-29.

Lipartito, Kenneth. "Picturephone and the Information Age: The Social Meaning of Failure." *Technology and Culture*, vol. 44, no. 1, 2003, pp. 50-81.

McLuhan, Marshall. *Essential McLuhan.* Edited by Eric McLuhan and Frank Zingrone. Routledge, 1995.

Rickert, Thomas. *Ambient Rhetoric: The Attunements of Rhetorical Being.* University of Pittsburgh Press, 2013.

Roberts, Ivy. "'Edison's Telephonoscope': The Visual Telephone and the Satire of Electric Light Mania." *Early Popular Visual Culture*, vol. 15, no. 1, 2017, pp. 1-25.

Rochat, Philippe. "Five Levels of Self-Awareness As They Unfold Early in Life." *Consciousness and Cognition*, vol. 12, 2003, pp. 717-31.

Tarasuik, Joanne, and Jordy Kaufman. "When and Why Parents Involve Young Children in Video Communication." *Journal of Children and Media*, vol. 11, no. 1, 2017, pp. 88-106.

Tassey, Gregory. "Technology Life Cycles." *Encyclopedia of Creativity, Invention, Innovation and Entrepreneurship*, edited by Elias G. Carayannis, Springer, 2013, pp. 1797-1807.

Zagorsky, Jay L. "Rise and Fall of the Landline: 143 Years of Telephone Becoming More Accessible—and Smart." *The Conversation*, 14 Mar. 2019, theconversation.com/rise-and-fall-of-the-landline-143-years-of-telephones-becoming-more-accessible-and-smart-113295. Accessed 15 May 2022.

Section III
Enabling: Digital/Physical Nexus

Chapter 8

Crossed Wires: Mothering/ Death/Adult Children

Elaine Kahn

S ome days, I feel I have only a slightly better understanding of mothering than I do of the internet, having grown up with both almost simultaneously. My twin daughters miraculously showed up when both their parents were not quite twenty-six, and we all had to learn about computers and the wired world, which have moved into the house in increasing degrees of sophistication over our lifetimes. I'd gotten my driver's license a week after my sixteenth birthday and, in 1984, my word processor brought us into the incipient home computer world fairly early, but I had no more interest in understanding how my car works than I did in understanding computer and internet technology. I have vague memories of being taught in high school about cathode tubes in televisions and the transition to transistors—yes, I'm that old, and, no, it didn't stick.

What follows is a slice of "technobiography"—a useful term I came across only recently and described as "a powerful tool to examine how communication technologies are appropriated and play a role in changing experiences across the lifespan" (Fernandez-Ardevol 9).[1]

Fragmentation

Less than a year before COVID-19 isolated us all, my husband died, leaving me alone. Clearing out a drawer, I came across the basic battery-powered radio Larry had insisted we have for emergencies. Many of the spare batteries were dead.

There is such a tendency after a death to worry and, these days,[2] to become apocalyptic in every thought. Let me dial it down. I have only a cell phone. I misplace it, the same way I misplace my glasses, the technology that lets me see. There is no longer someone here to help me find either. We had given up our landline during a temporary relocation out of state for a few years, and I deemed it too old fashioned, let alone too expensive, to have one installed now. "Dial it down" entered English in full force only after dials became obsolete.

Both of my daughters are married, and each has two children. Rachel lives a mile away, in the same New Jersey town as I do; Sara is in upper New England. They would describe us as a "close family." Years before I became a mother, I accepted for myself both "Ms." and the understanding that "girl" is not a respectful term for an adult female—"girls' night out" has never been part of my vocabulary. I make an exception for my daughters. I will never stop being a mother to those girls. Almost every Friday night of their lives, their father and I blessed them for Shabbat, a Jewish tradition so deeply ingrained in me by now that I have carried it on alone. In our COVID-19 world, it is the tether that reminds me what day it is. When we cannot be together, I bless the girls over the phone. Vocally. So we hear each other's voices once a week. In the intervening days, unless we are physically together, we mainly text and email and Zoom, although during the pandemic, they Zoom so much at work that there is usually no Zoom energy left for me. We therefore are in touch much more than we would be if all we had were phone calls, but it is a far less sensuous experience. And somehow less particular: We tap those same buttons to communicate with everyone, and it all sounds the same. Although the vocabulary changes: I don't sign off as "Mummy" to anyone else.

Whether due to age or physiology or both, I find that communication by email or text takes more energy than the ebb and flow of a phone call. And I still prefer, I still need, to hear my children's voices, more than they feel the need to hear mine. It helps put the illusion of touch back into the communication. Touch is part of the reason I still send greeting cards and write the occasional letter on actual paper with a fountain pen, for the feel of the paper and the flow of ink. I ask for pretty stamps when I go to the post office and buy a bunch—I'm not sure my girls own any.

Cleanup

We're all still pretty raw from Larry's death, and no matter how many emojis proliferate online, there is less nuance in texting and email than in a phone call, and misunderstandings take longer, even if sometimes only a little longer, to fix. I know I am feeling hurt more often when no hurt is intended; usually, I can't even bring myself to mention it to them.

The meatloaf, for example. The girls' cousin Charles, my nephew in Toronto, discovered online their late grandmother's meatloaf recipe, which had run twice in the *Toronto Star*. He posted it on Facebook, and my girls replied to his post with great excitement and the expressed desire to try the recipe. Which they could have tried at any point in the past several decades had they ever bothered to look through the family recipe book and found my printed paper copy, as told to me by their grandmother long ago.

I don't remember often asking my own mother's advice, and my girls need mine even less because they can Google. As Marshall McLuhan wrote: "The human family now exists under conditions of a global village. We live in a single constricted space resonant with tribal drums" (392). My tribe doesn't drum, but it also doesn't call. I miss hearing the phone ring. My grandchildren don't even understand what I mean when I say that. Out of all the possible notifications my smartphone can provide, the only sound I keep on all the time is for the phone. It took repeated tries and many months for me to understand that they would hear this information as nonsense because, for them, the phone is not telephonic.

I am desperate to keep up with uses of the internet in order not to fall irreparably behind my family and lose ways to communicate with them and to mother/grandmother. This seems to amuse them. As Joshua Meyrowitz writes:

> New patterns of access to information through electronic media bypass traditional channels and gatekeepers and undermine the pyramids of status that were once supported by print. Parents, teachers, doctors, corporation presidents, political leaders, and experts of all kinds have been losing the controlling elements that supported their traditional status in a print society. The status of many of these roles is therefore declining. (163)

I am worried that I will hit a tech wall beyond which I am unwilling to pass by learning anything more. For my late grandmother, that was the tape recorder, as much as she wanted to get her story down on tape. And even though she loved music, I think she got stuck at radio. I never saw her operate the record player to which she had access. My mother in Toronto can't and won't handle cell phones or computers. The physical border between our two countries has been COVID-19-closed for months, and I can't help care for her via technology without an intermediary, whether her part-time caregiver or my sister when they're together.

I think her life would be fuller if she would at least schedule times with her children and grandchildren on some platform, allowing us to see each other, but she says she is fine without it and that it makes her happy just to hear my voice on the phone every night. This frustrates me because right now I want all of it. I want to be able to communicate with my girls in all possible ways, and I don't want to fall behind the world either: "Dwelling in the past, the elderly person ceases to be a contemporary of his or her own history" (Vincent 250).

Needing distraction and companionship, almost the first thing I did after shiva[3] for my husband ended was call my cable company to negotiate a broadcast and streaming selection tailored to me, and then I learned how to use it. I still listen to terrestrial radio[4] rather than podcasts, but I recently signed up for a Twitter account. I often wonder where I will draw my own tech or communications line. Maybe streaming printed 3D food. Except it might be a fun way to send my family cookies.

The lightbulb moment for my gut understanding of McLuhan's extensions of (hu)man clicked on when I couldn't get the kids to understand why I desperately want someone to invent an affordable extension cellphone. It is normal for them to have their mobile phones in or by their hands all the time—besides, they also have landlines:

Writing in the 1960s, Marshall McLuhan described the media as "technological extensions of man"; in the 2010s it had become more obvious than ever that technologies like the smartphone are not merely extensions but technological prosthetics, enhancements of our own capacities, which, by virtue of being constantly attached to us or present on our bodies, become a part of us. (Wu 339).

I have grandchildren who can't even grasp the concept of an extension phone. Those extension phones, with one in almost every room, made telephone technology convenient, accessible, and invisible the way cell phones do now. I have bedtime fears that are probably not even on the radar of those who remain connected 24/7, with no sense of times of day that are too early or too late for one's phone to tremble. "When my phone/Trembles/After midnight/I never think/of good news," writes Nikki Giovanni,

I always look
For a way to hold
Myself
Together

Being a '60s person
I know
You have to be
Strong. (104)

And what will I do if I fall, and the mobile isn't right beside me or bounces away or shatters? In old movies, in ads, and in stories, the fallen person drags themselves to the place where the phone sits, pulls on the phone cord until the device drops to the floor, and then if still conscious, dials for help. If the phone's base unit and receiver remain separated for more than a minute or two, which could mean the person is dead, the phone emits a busy signal, and someone will eventually notice they can't connect or get through and will call someone for help or come to investigate. I feel too young for one of those wired alert bracelets. If I can't get to my single unextended cell phone, what will happen when I've fallen and I can't get up? (An earworm ad for the ages).

A few years ago, I finally learned how to text, and the girls and I typically contact each other multiple times a day by text or email, but there is an underlying ground rule that a day in which I don't hear from them—surely by now we should say "see from them"—is not a day in which something is wrong at their end; it just means they're busy. Children, after all, "are not a medicine or a vaccine which stamps out loneliness or isolation, but...people, subject to the same weaknesses as friends and lovers" (Irena Klepfisz qtd. in Kramarae 91).

This Does Not Compute

In the hospital during the last week of my husband's life, I saw that doctors and nurses still relied on phone calls when they needed to reach someone urgently. The girls, their husbands, and I did too—more than once we would ask each other whether a particular moment of crisis merited a call to someone or merely a text. I think I had my laptop with me in hospital too, as I prefer it for email and information. Nothing about those days is very clear yet, except some of the worst bits. The laptop is how I checked out the hospices, not that we ended up needing them.

Close family in Toronto got phone calls telling them they should get to New Jersey as quickly as possible. When I told my husband they were on their way, he did not look happy; some telegraphed meanings haven't changed. On what ended up being his last night, Sara asked me what his favourite songs were, and she streamed them by his bed.

I have never been as grateful for the internet as I was that week. So much texting, so many heart (and broken-heart) emojis sent back and forth, especially among the girls and me. I constantly checked in to see how the other two were doing, especially emotionally. Whichever one of us was at the hospital sent updates on Larry's condition or asked when she could be spelled off for a few hours. We even texted back and forth between whoever was in his room and whoever was taking a break in the waiting room or cafeteria. A wiry river of information and communication flowed in more than one direction. And, as much as I tried to take care of my children, what I remember more is how hard they worked to take care of me.

And then they took care of getting out word of the death, via email and social media. A deluge of hundreds of messages came back even before the funeral two days later, and that's when the girls and I switched to different channels: They were consoled by the swift unceasing flow and replied to many messages immediately, whereas I was simply swamped.

I waited to reply to most messages until I got the printed thank-you-for-your-kind-thoughts from-the-family-of cards from the funeral home. I made my girls sit for a couple of hours deciding with me who would answer whom and in which medium—an exercise I only recently realized was almost pointless for them (they each took only a few cards, having already contacted online most of those they wanted to answer) and certainly painful. It took me months to write out my "thank you" notes, and even the stamps were chosen with care to reflect a couple of my husband's infinite interests. For me to feel most comforted, I needed to stick with old tech.

Since then, I have thought (and, because I need them, overthought) how often to text, email, phone, or visit Rachel and Sara, as I did not want to put extra pressure onto their grieving. We worked out the details of the gravestone mainly via email.

Since childhood, I think, our girls have split up shared responsibilities or obligations in "twin-y" ways known only to them. Since their father died, Sara has spent more time than Rachel on the phone with me, often simply to check up. My guess is that it's their trade-off for Rachel living in the same town as I do. After tropical storm Isaias knocked out power in New Jersey in August 2020, Rachel's was restored two days before mine, so she fed me and gave me fridge and freezer space for my food.

I felt protected by Larry every time I turned on the emergency radio.

It used to bother me terribly when, in my presence, he said "my daughter" or "my grandchild" instead of "our." I always used the plural, and the pain of his death is present, though in lessening measure, each time I go singular. Those last two sentences are likely more properly placed in a personal journal than here, but I don't keep a journal. My girls and others suggested it to me as a way to get relief in the immediate aftermath of our bereavement. I'm sure they meant a keyed-in journal, not the soft and giving medium of pen and paper, the ink held by the page. I didn't listen because I didn't realize that, living alone with no one else here to bear witness and remember, if I didn't write it all down myself, my life would be dead ended.

Endnotes

1. "Technobiography" as a term dates back to 2001, but I first came across it in Fernández-Ardèvol, Sawchuk, and Grenier's *Maintaining Connections*.

2. I am writing in the United States in the fall of 2020 during the COVID-19 pandemic and mere weeks before the November elections.

3. In traditional Judaism, shiva is the first seven days of mourning

after a funeral and the gathering together during that time by family and friends at the home of the immediate family of the deceased.

4. I first heard the term "terrestrial radio" in a presentation by Nick Altman at the virtual Media Ecology Association conference in June 2020.

Works Cited

Fernández-Ardèvol, Mireia, and Kim Sawchuk and Line Grenier. "Maintaining Connections: Octo- and Nonagenarians on Digital 'Use and Non-Use.'" *Nordicom Review* vol. 38, no. 1, 2017, pp. 39-51.

Giovanni, Nikki. *Chasing Utopia: A Hybrid.* HarperCollins, 2013.

McLuhan, Marshall. *The Book of Probes.* Edited by Eric McLuhan, William Kuhns, and Mo Cohen. Gingko, 2003.

Meyrowitz, Joshua. *No Sense of Place: The Impact of Electronic Media on Social Behavior.* Oxford University, 1985.

Vincent, Gérard. "The Body and the Enigma of Sex." *Riddles of Identity in Modern Times.* Vol. 5 in *A History of Private Life*, edited by Antoine Prost and Gérard Vincent and translated by Arthur Goldhammer, The Belknap Press of Harvard University Press, 1991.

Wu, Tim. *The Attention Merchants: The Epic Scramble to Get Inside Our Heads.* Knopf, 2016.

Chapter 9

Bionic Parenting: On the Enabling Possibilities and Practices for Parenting with Digital New Media

Robyn Flisfeder and Matthew Flisfeder

As parents of a young child with type 1 diabetes (T1D), we have seen firsthand some of the more advantageous aspects of new digital and social media for parents and children. Diabetes Canada explains that T1D "is a disease in which the pancreas does not produce any insulin [which] is an important hormone that helps your body to control the level of glucose (sugar) in your blood." As a result, insulin must be taken through either having subcutaneous injections from pens or syringes several times a day or by pushing buttons on an insulin pump that is inserted under the skin and worn on the body. People with T1D are not immunocompromised, and they are considered to be healthy, providing they are not suffering from complications. But T1D is a chronic illness that permeates all aspects of living, and the work to manage it is often done behind the scenes. Although, as rhetoric and diabetes scholar Jeffrey A. Bennett points out, "The visual trope of the child is represented repeatedly in diabetes history" (173), it is important to note that T1D is no longer considered to be a juvenile disorder, as it can occur at any age. But unlike adults, children cannot take care of themselves independently.

Keeping children safe and healthy can be challenging at the best of times, but the stakes get even higher when parenting a young child with T1D, as the parents become responsible for taking over the relentless, around-the-clock job of the human pancreas: Life and death decisions about T1D management have to be made all day, every day. It is often seen as walking on a tightrope, as we aim for the target range for blood glucose numbers—what the online T1D community calls "unicorns"—that will decrease the risk for harmful long-term complications associated with sustained high blood glucose levels. On the flip side, vigilance is needed at all times, as low blood glucose levels represent an immediate and acute threat that can lead to seizures, coma, and even death when missed or not treated promptly. The ever-present task of balancing blood glucose levels is so great that it is often seen as taking care of an invisible family member because T1D is not a visible disease or disability, but it is always there and in need of care (Dreeckmeier). The particular circumstances of our parenting, therefore, provide an alternative lens through which we perceive and experience the role of new media and the internet in our home, as it has become an essential part of the living and lifestyle of our family. Given the proliferation of digital and algorithmic new media, screens, and devices in the home, as well as concerns about their influence and the possibly deleterious effects of biometric technologies on children and families, we ask the question: What are some of the more enabling dimensions and future potentials of these technologies for T1D families?

Drawing from our own personal narrative, we examine some of the positive aspects of new digital media and communications technologies and biotechnologies as well as the essential role that they play in raising a child with T1D. Seemingly ordinary devices, such as cell phones for text messaging and tablets for entertainment, have proven to be immensely valuable in raising a child with T1D. The various pages, groups, and organizations on social media have given us access to new information about T1D from around the world as well as a sense of community and camaraderie through the sharing of personal stories of trials and triumphs; they have empowered us to believe that our daughter will not be held back from anything because of her diagnosis. In material terms, the devices and practices for monitoring blood glucose and administering insulin have also improved dramatically since the discovery of insulin by Dr. Banting in 1921, but they remain somewhat cumbersome, require vigilance, and are susceptible to human error. Looking forwards, we are optimistic about the new developments on the horizon that use algorithmic new media and cloud-based technologies, or even potential biotechnologies and biohypermedia, to create a liberating functional cure, which will remove and alleviate the risks, variables, and dangers from ongoing and daily life and death decisions. We read our narrative against proliferating scholarly discourses about new, posthumanist, and biopolitical ethics to rethink the future of human and societal possibilities as well as parenting practices; the future, as we claim in our conclusion, is bionic.

T1D Parenting, the Internet, and the Essential Role of Digital Distraction

In what feels like a parallel universe, our lives changed dramatically when our daughter was diagnosed with T1D in 2013 at the very young age of fifteen months. After displaying unfamiliar signs of illness, we took her to a paediatrician in our new neighbourhood for medical assessment. She was quickly diagnosed with an ear infection, and our concerns were quelled; as new parents, we trusted the doctor and filled her prescription for antibiotics. However, her health continued to decline, and we went back to the paediatrician's office a couple more times until a different doctor told us to go to the local ER. It was there that we got the life-changing news: Our daughter was in the life-threatening state of diabetic ketoacidosis (DKA), which meant she had T1D, and there was no cure. We were then taken by ambulance to the ICU at the Hospital for Sick Children in Toronto. In retrospect, we cannot help but regret the fact that we decided to put our full trust in the medical doctor without seeking answers from "Doctor Google." Since then, it has been a harsh reminder to trust our intuition as parents and to Google symptoms when we are worried about something, even when an expert says otherwise, because we know our child best. We know we will not always get the right answers online, and sometimes you can get downright crazy answers on the internet, but it can also arm us with information that we can bring to the doctor's attention to open up a dialogue and to get tests to rule out possibilities, even if they seem rare and unlikely.

With the T1D diagnosis, screen time became an unexpectedly

essential part of our lives. Having T1D meant our daughter would need to take insulin via subcutaneous injections into her limbs and torso (needles!), and we would have to check her blood glucose levels by pricking her fingers and drawing blood (pokes!). Mustering up the courage to give our precious and beautiful, fifteen-month-old insulin injections with syringes and finger pokes to draw blood was terrifying. The very thought of it felt wrong, recalling for Robyn a horrible scene from Toni Morrison's *Tar Baby,* in which a child was pricked with pins. However, the fear of performing those vital medical tasks quickly faded for us when we saw that our daughter barely flinched from her injections and pokes thanks to the loud and vibrant YouTube videos which we used to keep her focus off of what was happening and that is when we learned the art of digital distraction. Although the sharp needles and lancets continued to be scary for a while, we quickly recognized that each insulin injection and finger poke was an act of love; without the injections, she would have died. For some parents, avoiding screens entirely is an option, but it was not for us. Using devices of digital distraction became an essential part of our T1D management with a toddler.

Giving needles to chubby, little limbs and drawing blood from tiny, little fingers are the things of nightmares for most people, and those activities definitely seemed like the scariest part of this new ordeal, until we learned that insulin cannot simply be injected once a day like many medications and do its job independently; rather, we would be required to take on the role of the human pancreas. Akin to the second shift, we now had an additional mental load: monitoring our daughter's blood glucose levels all day and night; watching for signs of low blood glucose and finding ways to coax her to ingest sugar and food at those times; carefully calculating insulin doses for the day and her meals; planning and noting her carbohydrate consumption; and assessing the impact of her physical activities, among many other factors, such as illness, on her blood glucose levels. We were to do all of this primarily on our own without the immediate guidance of medical professionals, but we could always call members of our diabetes team for support and answers to general questions or the paediatric endocrinologist on call at the hospital if we had urgent concerns. Everything we once took for granted—such as eating a meal, going for a walk, and sleeping soundly through the night—had changed.

Mealtimes for most parents can be a complicated affair, as toddlers and young children are notoriously picky and inconsistent eaters, and grazing can be the preferred mode of operation. It is not uncommon these days for parents to let children of all ages use such devices as tablets, cell phones, or computers to watch shows on Netflix or YouTube to help them eat their meals. However, the Canadian Paediatric Society discourages parents from bringing digital devices to the table during mealtimes. For us, there was little choice. Like other toddlers, our daughter had her own agenda at mealtime, which is, in fact, developmentally normal. We are often told by dieticians that children can regulate their own eating and that they will not starve themselves. It is the parents' duty, they say, to offer a variety of healthy options. However, people with diabetes need to eat at least enough carbohydrates to ensure they can take, at the bare minimum, a half unit of insulin without their blood glucose levels dropping too low. When you have a sixteen-pound, breastfeeding, and picky-eating toddler, this gets a bit more challenging. To ensure our daughter was eating the required amount of carbs at her meals and snacks, which took place every two hours, it was again digital distraction to the rescue, as we ate our meals to the sweet sounds of Netflix shows, such as *The Wiggles* and *Max and Ruby*.

In the early days, our main goal as parents was to keep our daughter safe because toddlers cannot tell their parents when they are feeling low. We tested her blood glucose levels using the suggested device, a FreeStyle Lite glucometer, by sitting her down with a YouTube video, pricking her finger with a sharp lancet, drawing blood, and reading the number derived from the blood sample. This process requires washed hands, a clean space to work, compliance from the child, and time. Since this process was cumbersome and painful for her fingertips, rather than checking her every minute of every day, we had to watch her behaviour closely and read her signals to figure out if her blood glucose levels were in a safe range—cue the hovering parent! Low blood glucose, or hypoglycemia, for children (and adults) include mild symptoms, such as hunger, shaking, weakness, sweating, irritability, and drowsiness, whereas more dangerous symptoms include the inability to eat due to lethargy, seizures, and passing out. Conversations throughout the day went as follows: "Matt, she's looking a bit sleepy. Do you think she's low or just tired?" "Robyn, she is not listening to me. Do you think she's just working on her autonomy, or is she having a low?" Once we got used to life with T1D, we started looking into continuous glucose monitoring (CGMs) devices, such as the Dexcom, but the ones available were costly, bulky (worn on the body), painful to insert, and required the use of a transmitter that needed to be nearby at all times. We were hesitant to make a change at that point, but thanks to social media, we found out that a smaller, less painful and costly CGM called the FreeStyle Libre was being used in Europe and the Middle East already. We crossed our fingers and hoped that it would be approved in Canada sometime in the near future. Until then, we would have to continue hovering and using our devices of digital distraction to keep our daughter healthy and safe.

Given the particular demands of raising a child with T1D, we could not afford to be scared or overly skeptical of technology and new media. The public rhetorics of diabetes management, in fact, often contrast with those of biotech, hypermedia, and screens. As Bennet explains: "The history of scientific advancement is frequently shadowed by the fears and anxieties accompanying new technologies. Inventions meant to better the human experience are regularly punctuated by misgivings about cultural changes in the present and the implications of those developments for the future" (188). Although the issue of screens in the home has divided parents for some time, we see the very question of using screens or not as a somewhat privileged one. Like many first-time parents, we read a lot of often conflicting and problematic pieces of information about parenting and screen time from different online sources, such as posts from the Facebook groups for moms *Pink and Blue Toronto* and articles from *Today's Parent*. Overwhelmed with information and recommendations from experts and pseudoexperts alike, we decided to use our own best judgment as much as possible and to follow our child's cues and attend to her needs in the best way we saw fit. When it came to watching online YouTube videos and using children's apps in the first year, we found that our daughter was simply not interested in them, but we were not fundamentally opposed to screens. However, choosing to follow the rules shared by the Canadian Paediatric Society and limiting screen time based on their recommendations can determine whether or not you are considered to be a good and responsible parent in the eyes of others. Parents, especially mothers, who do not put rigid limits on screen time are seen as lazy, selfish, or even negligent. It is an especially controversial topic on social media, which has led to the experience of mommy shaming for many, whereas those shamed for their choices often see the parents posting antiscreen sentiments on social media as self-righteous and virtue signalling. As parents of a child with a chronic illness, we quickly learned that such surface-level dichotomies did not capture the unique and challenging circumstances of our parenting.

From Information and Resources to Empowerment: The T1D Online Community

After our weekend of diabetes bootcamp at Sick Kids Hospital in Toronto in 2013, we left with an abundance of information about T1D management, including a handful of photocopied leaflets, a book called *When a Child Has Diabetes*, and several new medical skills, not to mention an overwhelming number of new worries. Thankfully, there are amazing resources for T1D families and individuals in Canada that can be accessed through the healthcare system. Every three months, we were seen by a medical team—including endocrinologists, diabetes educators, dieticians, social workers, and nurses—at a diabetes education centre in a nearby community hospital. Our appointments lasted hours as our daughter got a physical check-up, and we worked together to come up with T1D management plans, set goals, and discuss issues, among other things. They also gave us some entertaining resources for families and children, such as a low-budget DVD called *Pajama Party* by children's singer Mary Lambert, an illustrated Disney book about Coco, a monkey who has diabetes, and some more leaflets. After moving to Winnipeg in 2016, our new diabetes team gave us a well-organized binder full of more information and documents, and we continue to see them every three months. Even though we had drawers filled with information about T1D and a knowledgeable team of professionals to turn to for advice, we were always on the lookout for more resources about parenting children with T1D, specifically. So, as we do for everything else, we googled!

From research about causes, treatments, and cures to managing daily life and enhancing wellbeing for people with T1D and their caregivers, the online world has proven to be a treasure trove of resources, revolutionizing and democratizing access to information for families today. That being said, there can be a lot of misinformation and pseudoscience online about T1D—notably websites that promote miraculous cures and treatments that involve extreme diets and medicinal supplements from what Dr. Jen Gunter calls the "wellness industrial complex" (CBC News). However, legitimate organizations, such as the JDRF and Diabetes Canada, have filled in the gaps for us with their interactive and user-friendly websites, which provide extensive information to the T1D community. Their mission is to make the "invisible disease more visible" through research, advocacy, education, and programs (Diabetes Canada). Likewise, JDRF—which is no longer referred to as the Juvenile Diabetes Research Foundation, since many people are diagnosed later in life and the majority of people living with T1D are actually adults—is also committed to funding research studies for cures, treatments, and prevention. The JDRF website also provides ample information and promotes opportunities to get involved in research, clinical trials, and fundraising. These websites are informative and helpful, but they did not necessarily give us the sense of community for which we were searching.

In the early days of raising our daughter postdiagnosis, typical online parenting spats over feeding, sleep, and screens began to feel so petty, and concerns over buying the most ethical and current baby gear felt overly luxurious. Although we had amazing friends and baby groups to celebrate and commiserate with in the real world, the social isolation we felt due to life with T1D was challenging. Desperately searching for some camaraderie and shared understanding, we found some Facebook groups and pages for parents of children with T1D that were not great, but they gave us at least a sense that we were not alone. Unfortunately, there was a lot of competition and shaming, as parents judged each other's choices for T1D management, since it is not really a one-size-fits-all type of situation. It was when we found the nonprofit organization Beyond Type 1 that the internet went from providing helpful and informative resources to becoming an integral part of our lives. Founded by teen popstar Nick Jonas, who was diagnosed with T1D at age thirteen, Beyond Type 1, as the name suggests, is basically a new social movement working towards a change in perspective about living with chronic illness; the mission is about breaking down boundaries and overcoming obstacles so that people with T1D can live life to the fullest. The various Beyond Type 1 platforms—such as the app, Facebook page, and Instagram account—have been incredible online spaces of information, support, and inspiration over the years. Reading through the posts and connecting with others on the app definitely gives us a sense of community based on common struggles, but we prefer reading through the stories posted on the Beyond Type 1 Facebook and Instagram platforms, as they give us strength and hope as well as feelings of empowerment.

Recognizing the social-emotional aspects of T1D and the benefit of people seeing themselves represented and thriving in the world, the Beyond Type 1 contributors report on the latest T1D connections in pop culture. We draw strength from the profiles of celebrities, athletes, public figures, and everyday people with T1D who are living beyond their T1D diagnosis and shooting for the stars. These stories are uplifting and inspiring for us, as they reinforce the fact that our daughter is not a prisoner of her chronic illness. Recently, a story was published about *The Babysitter's Club* (2020), a children's show on Netflix that has a T1D character and storyline; it is a series based on the original books by Ann M. Martin. Since then, we have enjoyed watching *The Babysitter's Club* series many, many times over with our daughter. She identifies with the strong and capable but also super stylish character named Stacey, who has T1D. It is amazing how seeing herself represented on the screen gives our daughter a sense of pride about having T1D. Likewise, the show depicts Stacey's parents' approach to her T1D diagnosis and how they chose to protect her by urging her to hide it from the world. This storyline was confusing to our daughter, and it led to some deep conversations about stigma and shame around chronic illness. *The Babysitter's Club* has also given us as parents an opportunity to think about how we will approach T1D management as our daughter becomes a teenager. Since T1D is not simply an individual diagnosis but an invisible illness that impacts greatly upon all caregivers and members of the family, the Beyond Type 1 posts are beneficial for all members of the family.

Many stories shared on the Beyond Type 1 Facebook and Instagram feeds are written from the perspective of parents and caregivers, and their narratives encourage us to take care of ourselves, as individuals, in the face of the relentless demands of T1D, which rob us of sleep and give us anxiety. Being part of the Beyond Type 1 community online is a daily reminder that we are not alone at all; rather, we are part of something much bigger: a vibrant and strong global community, spanning 150 countries, with over two million members (Beyond Type 1). This virtual world has helped us navigate the challenges of parenting a child with T1D, and it has empowered us to envision a bright future that is not limited by a diagnosis. It has also introduced us to many of the new digital lifelines that have changed our lives for the better and have the potential to emancipate those with T1D as well as their parents and caregivers from the burdens associated with managing an all-consuming, chronic illness.

New Digital Lifelines for Parenting T1D

Communication plays a central role in the management of T1D, but instant communication is essential as blood glucose levels can fluctuate from moment to moment, and young children need assistance monitoring themselves when they are not at home with their parents. Instant communication via text messages has been our lifeline since our daughter, who is now ten years old, started school. Even as we sit side by side on our computers to write this chapter, the alarming flurry of sound notifications from incoming text messages disrupts our focus. "Ding, ding, ding": It is our daughter's camp counsellor texting us to say that her blood glucose is 4.9 mmol/L with a trend arrow going across, indicating a lower but stable level, according to her FreeStyle Libre glucose monitoring system. Although her counsellor seems worried, we know that is a good number, and today would be considered a good day because our daughter's blood glucose numbers are in the target range for her age. But that range between 4 and 8 mmol/L before meals is like a tightrope with little room for error and great potential for danger when the blood glucose drops. We are "chasing unicorns" as they say in the online T1D community, which is a beautiful image, but keeping blood glucose numbers in range is actually quite messy behind the scenes. At this point, we have already text messaged back and forth with the counsellor for several hours. Physical activity lowers the blood glucose and our daughter has already had to have rounds of sugar in the form of gummies and juice to prevent her blood glucose levels from dropping too far down while she swims, plays sports, and runs around outside with her new friends. It is only noon.

Many parents do not have to worry about sending their children to daycare, school, or day camp; they pack a lunch and a backpack, give them a kiss, and then send them on their way. For parents of young children with T1D, everything becomes more complicated. Prior to the start of day camp or school, we meet with the administration and staff as well as a public health nurse. We go over low blood sugar protocols, emergency procedures involving calling EMS, practice blood glucose testing, and swap cell phone numbers for daily text messaging. We bring in a bin of T1D supplies, including low-blood glucose treatments, such as gummies, fruit leathers, juice boxes, and cake icing as well as glucometer for finger checks if the reading from the Libre seems off. We also include emergency supplies in the event that our daughter's blood sugar is very low and she cannot ingest sugar orally because she is too lethargic or has passed out. This includes the glucagon nasal powder Baqsimi, which we learned about on Beyond Type 1, and can be administered like a nasal spray to an unconscious individual while calling 911. Basically, we do not travel lightly; spontaneity and living off the grid are luxuries we cannot afford. Everything in our life revolves around ongoing communication and planning ahead.

T1D management is multifaceted; on a medical level, it involves not only injecting insulin, counting carbohydrates, and monitoring blood glucose levels but also finding patterns and attempting to predict how different foods, activities, emotions, illnesses, weather changes, and everything else will impact blood glucose. At summer camp, our daughter will have much more vigorous physical activity than she has had in previous months being home during COVID-19 quarantine. Even though we lowered her insulin dose for camp time and sent extra snacks to increase her carbohydrate consumption, we will need to make some changes to our plan. Even prior to the pandemic, like most children, the number of physical activities fluctuated during different times of the year, between the more sedentary winter months and the more active summer months. We plan for these changes by adjusting her insulin doses and carbohydrate intake. Like all children going to summer day camp, our daughter will experience various emotions, such as excitement for what is ahead and possibly nerves when meeting new people. Many people are surprised to learn that these sensations have an impact on blood glucose levels. In people with a working pancreas, blood glucose is regulated automatically by the secretion of hormones, such as insulin and glucagon. However, in people with T1D, the duties of the pancreas are carried out externally, and we can only use our knowledge and devices to make the most educated guesses as to how it will play out.

There have been significant technological advancements since our daughter's initial diagnosis in 2013, and they have given our family a new level of freedom. It took a few years, but the FreeStyle Libre Flash Glucose Monitoring System, which is considered to be a CGM, arrived on the Canadian diabetes tech scene in 2017, just in time for our daughter to start grade one. Even though it was expensive, setting us back about two hundred dollars a month because it was not going to be covered by our insurance plan, we were first in line to get it. The Libre system includes a slim and discreet sensor that is inserted (with minimal pain) into the arm to measure and store glucose levels from the interstitial fluid. A handheld flash reader, or a cell phone with the LibreLink app, is then used to scan the sensor and then display a blood glucose reading and a trend arrow to show where the blood glucose levels are heading. The trend arrow provides us with important information because it lets us plan ahead. Before the Libre, we would have to guess which way her blood glucose levels were going to go after taking a reading, but now we can anticipate what interventions will be needed before she goes too high or low. Moving beyond traditional glucometers, which simply record all of the individual readings, the Libre stores the previous eight hours of data and makes sense of it for the user through graphs that show daily patterns and calculates average blood glucose levels for previous weeks. It also calculates the potential A1C, which is a measure of average blood glucose levels, and allows the user to know how they are doing rather than waiting to do bloodwork in a lab. The information can be easily uploaded onto a computer and then sent to the medical team when necessary. Using devices such as these helps to alleviate a lot of the guesswork involved in diabetes management, which at times can be cognitively taxing and subject to human error.

Managing the technical aspects of T1D involves a lot of math and decoding of patterns that can be simplified using digital media. As Bennett explains:

Attempting to achieve the normative ideals of health has become inextricably linked to innovations that combat material disease. The line between human and machine has been dissolved by an integration of the agent who performs diabetes management and their body, which is the scene of treatment. The body of the patient has been melded with technologies that keep them alive, and that communion is the site of medical knowledge. This expertise is not confined to the space of the clinic, but must be continually reenacted by people with diabetes. (180)

Diabetes planning and parenting can, itself, seem somewhat algorithmic at times if we understand digital algorithms as programs used for pattern recognition in sets of data used to solve complex problems based on data variables and established protocols. Right now, we are witnessing the transition from metaphorical management algorithms to actual algorithmic media through JDRF's Artificial Pancreas Program; the aim is to fully automate the process of insulin injection and blood glucose management to give users (and their caregivers) the ultimate freedom from the burdens and anxieties of T1D. On a basic level, closed-loop systems allow insulin pumps (which deliver insulin through a small catheter that is inserted into the body with the push of a button) and CGMs to communicate with each other while integrating advances in algorithms to control blood glucose better and using cloud technologies for data storage. Unlike skeptics of new media, as parents of a child with T1D, we are excited about the more enabling and liberating potentials of such advancements. Our material position and ideological perspective give us an alternative view towards some of the contemporary debates in the digital humanities and in communication and media studies about posthumanist futures, digital surveillance (or dataveillance), and the ethical dimensions of what some refer to as biopolitical capitalism.

Struggling with Biopower

Biopolitics is a term that originates in the work of the French social theorist Michel Foucault, who is known for arguing that modern power has taken on a more productive, rather than merely repressive, veneer. Power, he argues, produces bodies, in contrast to forms of authority that regulate through the wielding of violence. Biopower, therefore, concerns discourses and practices designed to produce certain kinds of sanctioned life. Foucault's writing on biopower, as well as his conception of panopticism, is commonly cited in studies on technological surveillance, especially social media forms of data-veillance, and speaks to common fears about the role of new media in monitoring and facilitating mechanisms of power and control that are tied to our everyday communications and interactions online. Such fears are augmented the more we increasingly wear our communications devices on our bodies—in the form of smartphones, tablets, and other forms of mobile new media—that combined with GPS and data aggregation software create the conditions for our deeper integration into the grid. Our over acute sensibilities about the possibilities for techno-surveillance and control can also be measured in the context of what the media theorist Claire Birchall calls "shareveillance." Because media users participate in their own surveillance by freely sharing information on social media and other new media and digital platforms, it may appear for many as though such platforms and cloud technologies serve merely as systems for our control. But viewed through the lens of T1D management and parenting, we are perhaps able to perceive differently the more enabling qualities of biotechnologies and what Tiziana Terranova refers to as "biohypermedia."

Over the past two decades, online and digital networks have shifted from using heavier devices, such as desktop and laptop computers, towards smaller, portable, and mobile devices. This, according to Terranova (citing Giorgio Griziotti), has created "a new social and technical landscape" organized "around 'apps' and 'clouds' which directly 'intervene in how we feel, perceive, and understand the world'" (395). Terranova explains that biohypermedia "identifies the ever more intimate relation between bodies and devices which is part of the diffusion of smartphones, tablet computers, and ubiquitous computation" (395). In her writing on biohypermedia, she draws on the work of the design and media theorist Benjamin Bratton, whose notion of "the stack" describes the multilayered infrastructures of emergent new mediated societies, the most common metaphor for which is the "smart city." The stack explains the emergence of com-putation as a global infrastructure (Bratton 14). It is in many ways facilitated by cloud computing. The metaphor of the cloud is here used to describe the massive data processing and storage centres, usually owned by large corporations, used to link together apps and platforms to individual devices. The stack, therefore, according to Bratton, is "not the grid but an accumulation of grids," some of which operate by communicating with one another using nonhuman digital languages or binary coding.

Since platforms now make up the technological infrastructure of global society (Williams and Srnicek 357), it is important to weigh the benefits of the technology against their setting in digital or platform capitalism. We should not confuse the drawbacks of new media as inherent to the technology. The context of capitalist structures of accumulation and exploitation should be distinguished from the enabling dimensions of new media that we experience. Although platforms "are what make possible particular sets of actions, relationships, and power," as the authors of the *Manifesto for an Accelerationist Politics*, Alex Williams and Nick Srnicek, explain, "much of the current global platform is biased towards capitalist social relations" (357). However, this, they say, "is not an inevitable necessity" (357). Platforms—which guide production, finance, logistics, and consumption—can certainly be reprogrammed towards much more equitable ends. This after all becomes a necessary framework for thinking when it comes to modern medical needs and diabetes in particular, where, as Bennett notes, to separate people from technology is quite literally an invitation to demise (179). For him, the risk and anxiety that sometimes come from our experiences with technology is "not explicitly attached to technology, but the capitalistic impulses that keep such technology out of reach of scores of people" (181). This is still a view that contrasts with much of the discourse on biopolitics and biopower.

On the one hand, it is certainly the case that mobile digital and social media have the potential to increase practices of surveillance and control, both in the interests of regulating the productive forms of power (something that is certainly concerning to contemporary parenting contexts) and as integrated into the medical maintenance of the body. This is especially true in the case of T1D management, which increasingly relies on these devices. On the other hand, the fact that such technology makes life liveable and eases some of the difficulties of T1D management forces us to question whether the problem here is one of technology reducing us to bare life or whether the flawed aspects of new media and biometric technologies are a matter of the economic and governance structures of platform and neoliberal capitalism.

Bionic Parenting: Towards a Cyborg Future?

The context of parenting a child with T1D helps us to see many of the positive and enabling aspects of advances in digital media, social media, cloud computing, and algorithmic technologies and bio-technologies. As we have shown, the anxieties of parenting a child with T1D have the potential to be relieved by such innovations, as we continue to care for our daughter's physiological needs as an extension of her pancreas from outside of her own body. We recognize that people still have anxieties about giving "themselves over to the machines unreflexively, not acting with discernible personal agency" (Bennett 191), but a complete, bionic integration of the body and technology, in which the machine operates autonomously, is still in the early stages of conceptualization and research. Current bio-technologies still require monitoring and inputs from users accounting for mealtime carbs, accepting recommendations from devices for correcting and adjusting blood glucose numbers, and calibrating blood glucose sensors daily. As Bennett notes, "The closed-loop system demands a more activated patient, not one prone to apathy or neglect" (193). Human agency remains an integral part of managing T1D, even with some of the advances in new media that we have described. The bionic cyborg body reflects a context of care that is social rather than merely individual, as we use traditional modes of communication as well as new digital media and social media to take care of our daughter, including the following: in-person and phone meetings with the members of our diabetes medical team; corresponding on a daily basis with the principal, teachers, and office staff from our daughter's school as well as camp counsellors via text and email; and participating with the T1D online community through social media. Thus, managing T1D is still very much a human, social, and care-centric affair, and that includes the input from parents caring for children with diabetes. For parents of children with T1D, having such auto-nomous technologies as stage six of JDRF's Artificial Pancreas Project, the Fully Automated Multi-Hormone Closed Loop system (JDRF), as well as Sernova's implanted cell pouch would be a dream come true. We hope for new media to truly become an extension of our humanity, as Marshall McLuhan might have put it. Paradoxically, this can only be done through an integration with technology as a cyborg (Bennett 194).

The cyborg—a bionic human whose body is augmented by technology—is one of the most common literary metaphors drawn from popular culture, science fiction, and cyberpunk cinema. It is often used to reconcile ourselves towards the integration of technology and biology. The cyborg figures for posthumanist thinkers, such as Donna Haraway, as a nonessentialist representation of the ties between nature and culture (or nature-culture). When we consider the fact that media, medicine, and biotechnologies have all in one way or another been integrated into our regular lives, we come to see that the notion of a natural body is much more of a myth than the fictional cyborg itself. The cyborg metaphor is also useful in dispelling liberal notions of a fully autonomous individual, capable of functioning independently without the help of others. The bionic human is a social body—one that is still reliant on the care of the family and the community. It is against liberal notions of pure individuality and the natural organic body that the cyborg metaphor responds, since it helps to demonstrate that we thrive more fully when we live in societies of mutual care and assistance. But we should also acknowledge that the anxieties people seem to feel about a more integrated media system pertains to the social and political contexts of new media rather than the technologies themselves. Our experience has undoubtedly led us to see the emancipatory potential of new media for parents of children with T1D, as well as individuals with T1D caring for themselves. Since T1D is one of many chronic illnesses, we imagine a bionic future will be beneficial to vast and diverse populations around the globe.

Works Cited

Bennett, Jeffrey A. *Managing Diabetes: The Cultural Politics of Disease.* New York University Press, 2019.

Birchall, Claire. *Shareveillance: The Dangers of Openly Sharing and Covertly Collecting Data.* University of Minnesota Press, 2017.

Bratton, Benjamin. *The Stack: Sovereignty and Software.* MIT Press, 2015.

CBC News. "One Doctor's Fight Against the 'Wellness Industrial Complex.'" *Front Burner*, 30 Sept. 2019, www.cbc.ca/radio/frontburner/one-doctor-s-fight-against-the-wellness-industrial-complex-1.5302187. Accessed 18 May 2022.

Daneman, Denis, Marcia Frank, and Kusiel Perlman. *When a Child Has Diabetes*. 3rd Ed. Toronto, ON: Key Porter Books, 2010.

Diabetes Canada. "Our History." *Diabetes Canada*, www.diabetes.ca/about-diabetes-canada/our-history. Accessed 18 May 2022.

Dreeckmeir, Michellè. 2018. "The Invisible Family Member." *Beyond Type 1*, beyondtype1.org/invisible-family-member/. Accessed 18 May 2022.

Foucault, Michel. *The History of Sexuality, Volume 1*. Translated by Robert Hurley, Vintage Books, 1990.

Foucault, Michel. *The Birth of Biopolitics: Lectures at the College de France, 1978-1979*. Translated by Graham Burchell, Picador, 2008.

Haraway, Donna. *Simians, Cyborgs, and Women: The Reinvention of Nature*. Routledge, 1991.

Terranova, Tiziana. "Red Stack Attack!" *#Accelerate: The Accelerationist Reader*, edited by Robin MacKay and Armen Avanessian, Urbanomic, 2017.

Williams, Alex, and Nick Srnicek. "#Accelerate: Manifesto for an Accelerationist Politics." *#Accelerate: The Accelerationist Reader*, edited by Robin MacKay and Armen Avanessian, Urbanomic, 2017.

Chapter 10

Enabled by the Internet: A Multicultural Mother and Daughter in Japan

Suzanne Kamata

Introduction

Much has been written about the negative impact of the internet on contemporary youth and on family relationships (Beard; Škařupová, Ólafsson, and Blinka; Navarro, Yubero, and Larranga). For example, research has indicated that internet access is responsible for a decline in our ability to concentrate, that peering at small screens can lead to poor eyesight, and that our children might be cyberbullied under our own roofs. However, as an English-speaking American mother in Japan of a biracial daughter who is deaf, has cerebral palsy, and therefore uses a wheelchair for mobility, the internet has been an overwhelmingly positive addition to our lives. Having internet access has allowed me, as a Western mother in Japan, to communicate with other parents of children with disabilities who have similar cultural values (Weatherill). It has also allowed me easy access to information about my daughter's disabilities and various therapies and treatments. Furthermore, it has enabled me to write, edit, and publish essays, articles, and books about mothering a child with disabilities in other countries, such as the United States (US). Internet access has also transformed my daughter's life. Although in the past children with disabilities were often overprotected and lacked autonomy (Iwakuma and Nussbaum; Nishikawa, Sundbom and Hägglöf), such developments as email, web cameras, and social networks have allowed my daughter to communicate with others, meet new people, and develop friendships despite her lack of mobility. Additionally, the internet has enabled better communication between my daughter and me and among the other members of our multilingual, multicultural family. In this chapter, I expand upon the positive impact of the internet on myself, as the mother of a child with disabilities, and on my daughter with disabilities.

Privacy, Autonomy, and Overprotective Parents

In Japan, parents tend to be especially protective of daughters in comparison to Westerners (Iwakuma and Nussbaum 203). Typically, young women live with their parents until marriage. From conversations with my students, I have learned that many Japanese parents insist that their daughters attend universities close to home and impose curfews into adulthood. Not surprisingly, this protectiveness is even more pronounced among parents of daughters with disabilities. As many young disabled women need some degree of caretaking, such as assistance with communication, using money, going to the bathroom, or transportation, their autonomy and privacy are often compromised. In Japan, mothers tend to be the primary caretakers for disabled children living at home (Eijiri and Matsuzawa 239). A recent study found that Japanese women with disabilities would rather not receive care support from those closest to them (Kawaguchi 52). As one woman interviewed responded, "I'm opposed to the connecting of affection with care support provision" (Kawaguchi 52). Although hiring a home helper would seem to be a solution to this dilemma, Japan suffers from a severe labour shortage (Bookman 2).

Furthermore, people with disabilities in Japan have been expected to remain as dependents of the household head. For a daughter with a disability, marriage has long been assumed to be out of the question (Stevens 115; Kawaguchi 52). This is partly because prospective suitors and their families might worry that the disability is genetic and could be passed down to future generations (Stevens 115). Some Japanese women with disabilities are rejected as marriage partners because of an inability to do housework (Kawaguchi 54). Because marriage is seen to be an indicator of adulthood in Japan, unmarried disabled women dependent upon their parents are, in effect, eternal children.

In addition to an infantilization of people with disabilities, other negative attitudes can become barriers to personal freedom in Japan. In the past, at least, family members with disabilities in Japan were sometimes hidden or were encouraged to hide their disabilities (Nakamura 77; Stevens 36). Miwako Watanabe writes, "Of Western nations, the United States is generally considered the most advanced in terms of social welfare and human rights" (14). In the US, an individualistic society, a disability is not considered as much of a "social obstacle" (Watanabe 14) as it is in Japan. In contrast, collectivist communities, such as Japan, tend to put a greater value on "duty, conformity and self-sacrifice" (Zaromatidis et al. 1194). As Watanabe argues, "These values lead to considering a family with a member who has a disability as a threat to that family's social standing" (15).

Towards a Better Future for Individuals with Disabilities in Japan

Attitudes are slowly changing. In recent years, disability activists and lobbyists in Japan have been influenced by initiatives and legislation in other countries, such as the UN International Year of Disabled Persons in 1981, which mandated "full participation and equality" and recognized that "social attitudes were a major barrier" to this goal (United Nations). Other major influential legislations include the Americans with Disabilities Act in 1990 and the UN Convention for the Rights of Persons with Disabilities in 2006, which led to the creation in Japan of the Barrier Free Transportation Law in 2000 and the Law for the Elimination of Discrimination Against Persons with Disabilities in 2013 (Bookman 13). Another significant event, the International Forum on Independent Living, which allowed thirteen hundred disability activists in Japan, the US, the Philippines, South Korea, and the United Kingdom to discuss accessibility issues was held in Tokyo from November 2 to 4, 1998, in various internet chatrooms. Just as the 1964 Summer Olympics in Tokyo spurred changes in policy regarding persons with disabilities, so has the 2020 Tokyo Summer Olympics (which actually took place in 2021 due to the COVID-19 pandemic). Thanks to the latter, hotels have sought to make their accommodations more accessible, sign language apps have been developed, and ramps and elevators have been installed. Other improvements include lower ticket stands at train stations for wheelchair users, the availability of white boards at train stations for nonverbal communication, and additional Braille tiles on the pavement.

In anticipation of an influx of foreign visitors with disabilities to Japan, several non-Japanese residents of Japan have launched initiatives. Canadian-born Josh Grisdale, a wheelchair user who works in ICT in Tokyo and has taken Japanese citizenship, started a website called *Accessible Japan*. In addition to English-language articles about the accessibility of various tourist sites, there is a chat room for online information exchange. Grisdale has also authored an electronic guidebook, *Accessible Japan's Tokyo (2020): All You Need to Know about Traveling to Tokyo with a Disability*. Another foreign-born resident, Michael Gillan Peckitt, PhD, a university instructor in Kobe from the United Kingdom, maintains the blog *Barrier Free Japan*, featuring articles about disability from Japanese media translated into English. Mark Bookman, PhD, an American who completed research on the history of disability in Japan in Tokyo, proposes developing an app to help visitors readily understand which buildings and other facilities are accessible and to whom.

Just as important as changes in infrastructure are changes in attitude towards persons with disabilities. Television, movies, manga, anime, and other forms of popular entertainment have a strong effect on public perception of individuals—in this case, young women—with disabilities. Before the 1990s people with disabilities were largely absent from both Japanese society and television, as well as other forms of entertainment, due to stigma and shame, but they have since become much more visible (Stibbe 23). The boom in Japanese television dramas with a disability theme began with the 1993 *Hitotsu no yane no shita* (*Under One Roof*), reprised in 1997, which features a young woman with paraplegia who uses a wheelchair. Other dramas include *Hoshi no kinka* (*Star Coins*) in 1995, *Shin hoshi no kinka* (*New Star Coins*) in 2001, as well as *Kimi no te ga sasayaiteiru* (*Your Hands are Whispering*) in 1997, which features female characters who are deaf. However, as Arran Stibbe points out, "In all the dramas, the tendency is to portray disabled characters as isolated victims of circumstance, having little contact with other disabled people and no contact with political empowerment groups" (25). In one drama, the main character is stifled by a lack of accessibility: "When Meiko, the deaf protagonist of *Kimi no te ga sasayaiteiru*, has an important package to deliver, the train suddenly stops and she looks at the loudspeaker in frustration that she cannot hear the announcement. When she arrives at the station, she stares at a telephone she cannot use" (Stibbe 25). Of course, this being the 1990s, Meiko does not have a smartphone; the characters do not yet have access to the internet.

Internet access enables young women with disabilities to develop relationships and pursue interests without a caregiver's help or interference. This allows for greater independence and privacy. In the case of deaf and hard of hearing (DHH) individuals, intelligible communication through lipreading and speech production can be difficult (McGuire 6). Also, DHH people raised and educated among hearing people who do not use sign language sometimes find it difficult to form close relationships with hearing peers and family members (McGuire 7). However, texting apps can help to level the field. Furthermore, Azy Barak and Yael Sadovsky have shown that interactions in cyberspace allow deaf and hearing-impaired adolescents to conceal their disability, if they so desire, which may give them a sense of equality and security (1811). This could apply to individuals with other disabilities as well. Additionally, Stephanie Bannon et al.. found that internet use helped adolescents with additional support needs to develop "identity, competence and a sense of connectedness and belonging within a social network" which are key to positive self-esteem (504).

In multicultural families, communication among members with cultural and linguistic diversity can be complicated by disability (Bridges 62). However, the internet has provided access to a plethora of apps, such as Facebook, Twitter, LINE, and Google Translate, which can ease such communication. The emergence of emojis has also enhanced online communication among both deaf and hearing users (Okuyama). Additionally, individuals who are deaf or hearing impaired can now easily converse via webcam. Clearly, the internet has had a positive effect on many individuals with disabilities and their families.

Accessing Support in the Early Days of the Internet in Japan

When I first came to Japan from the United States in 1988, there was no internet. For my first few years in this country, I communicated with my American friends and family via airmail letters and expensive, occasional, long-distance phone calls. This was in the days before Amazon, and although there was a small selection of books in English at two or three local bookstores, most of these books were Japanese novels in translation or novelizations of popular films. Although it was possible to order books from abroad, postal rates were high, and it often took a long time for them to arrive in Japan.

My Japanese husband and I connected to the World Wide Web around 1999, the year that our twins were born fourteen weeks prematurely. This was fortunate because I needed access to information, and I was not highly literate in Japanese. Having internet access allowed me to search for books related to topics that were suddenly of interest: twins, prematurity, and disability. It also allowed me to find articles and other sources of information online.

I was especially in need of emotional support after learning that our daughter was deaf and had cerebral palsy. Although I believe North American hospitals often point new mothers in the direction of counsellors and support groups, I was not given any such guidance in Japan. Later, when I had the opportunity to meet Japanese mothers of children with disabilities at the School for the Deaf, which my daughter attended, I discovered that Americans and Japanese have different cultural attitudes towards disabilities (Watanabe). For example, Japanese people tend to go out of their way to avoid causing trouble, whereas Americans believe that necessary change can be effected through gathering signatures, staging protests, and launching hashtag campaigns on Twitter. In other words, Americans tend to adhere to the homily "The squeaky wheel gets the grease." I also discovered that disability was stigmatized more in rural Japan than in my native country (Watanabe). One mother worried out loud that her hearing daughter's marriage prospects might be dimmed by having a deaf sibling. I found this attitude difficult to relate to; the Japanese mothers, in turn, found my ideas and my dreams for my daughter's future (e.g., college, marriage, and foreign travel) to be strange and overly idealistic.

What might have been a lonely time was made better by my having access to the internet. As Pamela Weatherill notes, "On-line communities provide a virtual third space that is similar to geographical community spaces inhabited by mothers at home" (174). Not only could I communicate almost immediately with friends and family who understood my cultural background, but I also could connect with other likeminded mothers of children with disabilities, including Western women married to Japanese men living in Japan. I started a blog, *Gaijin Mama*, in which I shared my experiences as an expat mother of a daughter who was deaf and had cerebral palsy. I found other blogs on similar topics. Gradually, my blog attracted more and more visitors, some who became regular commenters and offered much needed support. Some of them were even in cross-cultural relationships like me. Although I was the only foreign mother of a disabled biracial child in my town, the internet enabled me to make friends with other members of this niche group.

When I began blogging, my children were small, and my posts were mostly focused on my experiences as a mother. As my children grew and became more articulate, I began to see the importance of respecting their privacy (Kwan; Moore; Wimmer). Now if I write about them, I only do so with permission, after carefully discussing the topic and the intended audience. If possible, I allow them to read what I have written before sharing it.

Sharing Experiences as a Writer and Mother

Until the birth of my children, I was a full-time English teacher. However, I made the decision to stay home with them while they were small. I could not send my medically fragile twins to daycare without risking their lives, and I wanted to spend as much time as possible with them so that they would acquire English.

I decided to work as a freelance writer at home, something that would have been difficult without the internet. Whereas before I had mailed queries with self-addressed stamped envelopes to magazines across the ocean, by this time, it was possible to connect with editors by email. For myself, as for many women around the world, the internet enabled me to pursue a flexible career while staying at home.

During naps, after bedtime, and later when my twins were in

preschool, I managed to write poetry, short stories, newspaper and magazine articles, a novel, and edit two anthologies with contributors from around the globe: *Call Me Okaasan: Adventures in Multicultural Mothering* and *Love You to Pieces: Creative Writers on Raising a Child with Special Needs*. I also became the fiction editor of *Literary Mama*, an online journal, working with editors in Michigan, California, and many other states in the US. None of this would have been easy—and may not even have been possible—without the internet.

Unplugged, Uninformed, and Lonely in Early Childhood

While my husband and I used the internet for a variety of things—including online games (my husband), shopping, email, blogging (me), and information retrieval—we did not allow our twins access until they were in late elementary school. Neither my husband, a physical education teacher, nor I, a writer and teacher, had grown up playing video games. As we were aware of the dangers of excessive internet use (Beard; Škařupová, Ólafsson and Blinka; Navarro, Yubero, and Larranga), we wanted our twins to stay away from screens as much as possible. My husband encouraged our children to exercise and play sports, preferably out of doors. I tried to engage them in artistic activities, such as finger painting and drawing, and made sure that they had plenty of books. However, once they started school, they encountered kids with game devices and cellphones. My son's baseball team communicated via an online group chat, so without a cellphone, he was often left out of the loop concerning meeting times and changes in schedule. Likewise, my daughter was excluded from online communication among her fellow students at the school for the deaf because she did not have her own device.

My daughter attended the local School for the Deaf, where she learned to read and write in Japanese and to sign in Japanese sign language (JSL) from preschool throughout high school. Throughout her school years, there were fewer than fifty students, totally, enrolled. Many parents, especially those who live far away, try to mainstream their children in schools closer to home. This may be partly because JSL "holds a minority status in schools and more generally in society" and "has yet to be recognized as a national language" (McGuire 2).

Therefore, although there were several children of the same age in my daughter's class when she was in preschool, the numbers had thinned out considerably by junior high. There were only three students in my daughter's cohort; the other two were boys. In the years above and below, there were three girls each, who bonded easily because they studied together. Due to having multiple disabilities, my daughter was mostly taught one on one. Except for lunchtime, she had few chances to socialize with other girls close to her own age.

Outside of school, the older girls sometimes spent time together. They all lived nearby each other in the same city. Their mothers were close in age and socioeconomic status. They had all been born and raised in the same conservative Japanese town and did not speak English. As one might expect, they had become friends and were accustomed to arranging meetups for their daughters. Although I could speak Japanese, I was a foreigner—an outsider.

When my children were small, I was concerned about racial isolation (Chang) and typically took them to playdates with other biracial and bicultural children to foster pride in and comfort with their biracial status. It was also an opportunity for me to socialize with other foreign women married to Japanese men who were raising bicultural children. However, although my daughter had the chance to meet other girls—and boys—with similar ethnic backgrounds, it was difficult for her to form close relationships with them due to language issues (McGuire 7). It was also difficult for her to develop friendships with other deaf girls at her school. It was not possible for my daughter to meet up with the other girls on her own; she uses a wheelchair, and although there are some accessible buses, she had never taken one by herself. To get to the bus stop nearest our house entailed going up a steep incline. The bus stop itself was just a sign stabbed into the dirt with a waiting area precariously close to traffic. Due to my daughter's lack of mobility—and her lack of a social network—she was mostly dependent upon me, her mother and primary caretaker, for companionship and entertainment, as is often the case (Eijiri and Matsuzawa 239). Although she now tells me that she has no memory of being lonely as a child, at the time, I was desperate for her to have a friend.

Enabled by Cellphones in Adolescence

Although American school kids have been lugging around laptops for quite some time, Japan, despite its futuristic image, has remained surprisingly low tech. Although as early as 2009, 97 per cent of elementary and secondary school classrooms in the US were equipped with computers, the same could be said of only 35 per cent of Japanese classrooms in 2011 (Kusano et al. 31). Likewise, as of September 2019, 50.4 per cent of Japanese people between the ages of thirteen and sixty-nine used computers, and 70 per cent between the ages of thirteen and fifty-nine used smartphones (Statistics Bureau of Japan), whereas in the US, as of June 2019, 74 per cent of adults owned a laptop or desktop computer and 89 per cent of adults between the ages of eighteen and sixty-four owned smartphones (Pew). Many Japanese families have only one computer for all members to use. Many Japanese parents and children are also wary of sharing personal information online. As in other countries, cyberbullying is a serious problem. One recent celebrity suicide—that of Hana Kimura, who appeared on the popular Japanese reality TV show *Terrace House*—has been attributed to nasty commentators on Twitter (Hanaway).

Nevertheless, tablets and other devices are increasingly used in schools, including those for the disabled. My daughter received a tablet through school for educational purposes. She learned how to use the internet for practical purposes both on our home computer and at school. Among other things, she learned how to send and receive emails, search for information, order goods from online vendors, such as Amazon, and download games and apps. At school, students are taught about the dangers of sharing personal information on the internet. As parents, we installed software blocking potentially obscene materials from appearing on our children's device screens.

Once my daughter had her own cellphone with internet connectivity, she was no longer dependent upon me for her social life; finally, she was able to engage in group chats on the popular Japanese app LINE with her school friends. She expanded her network to include other graduates of the School for the Deaf. Although there were—and continue to be—occasional misunderstandings in these online communications, my daughter developed a greater sense of belonging. She was also able, for the first time, to propose and organize social gatherings. She invited friends to our house for afternoons of snacks and cosplay or to meet up at the nearby mall. Whereas the other girls had previously not included her because she used a wheelchair and they were uncertain about her mobility, they began spending time together outside of school.

Another cellphone application that my daughter learned to use was for drawing pictures. Since early childhood, she has been a fan of manga and anime, starting with *Sailor Moon* and moving on to *Naruto* and *Tokyo Ghoul*, among others. She has also drawn her own manga characters and stories. She often shares her artwork with friends via the internet. Furthermore, although she is forthcoming about her disabilities, she has managed to connect with nondisabled manga and anime fans across Japan and in other countries, enabling her to develop her "identity, competence and a sense of connectedness and belonging within a social network" (Bannon et al. 504), which are important for self-esteem.

Communication Via Apps within a Multicultural Family

The members of my family use three different languages in varying degrees. My Japanese husband was raised in a monolingual family and grew up speaking only Japanese with his parents, sister, and extended family. Like most Japanese people, he began studying English in junior high school, continuing throughout high school. (At university, he chose German as his required foreign language.) His English ability was good enough for him to teach English at a cram school while he was a university student, and it is our main language of communication as a couple.

I was born and raised in the US in a monolingual family. I began to study Japanese at the age of twenty-two, when I first arrived in Japan to work as an assistant language teacher (ALT) in public schools. Although I am now a fluent speaker of Japanese, my literacy level is low. (In 1990, I passed level three of the Japanese-Language Proficiency Test, but I have not taken the test since then.) When our children were born, we decided to speak only English at home, following the minority language at home strategy. However, once our son entered a Japanese kindergarten and became more fluent in Japanese, our communication with him evolved into the one parent–one language mode. Thus, my husband and son speak to each other in Japanese, whereas my son and I communicate with each other solely in English.

Communication with our daughter was more complicated. As I have written in detail elsewhere (Kamata), my husband and I were urged to use only Japanese and JSL with our daughter. I learned JSL alongside her when I accompanied her to early intervention sessions at the School for the Deaf. However, by the time she was in sixth grade of elementary school, her level of written Japanese was far beyond my own. She had mastered many kanji, ultimately achieving level five (mastery of around 1006 kanji) on the national Kanji Proficiency Test, whereas I still hover at around a second-grade reading level (around 240 kanji). Thus, my main form of communication with my daughter at home is JSL accompanied by spoken Japanese (on my part). My daughter is, for the most part, nonverbal. Her preferred method of communication is JSL, followed by written Japanese. As her father and brother have not learned JSL, she communicates with them mostly via written Japanese. In a pinch, she might draw a picture to make her point. She knows only a few words and phrases in English, as she was not enrolled in English classes at school.

In multilingual, multicultural families like ours, communication can be complicated (Bridges). As one might expect, it is difficult for all the members of my immediate family to communicate on an equal basis at the dinner table. Someone is always called upon by someone else to translate something. This leads to impatience, misunderstandings, and hurt feelings at being excluded. Using the internet, however, our communications are often more inclusive. We have created a family chat group using LINE. This app has a translation function, so if I, for example, enter a message in English, it will be translated into Japanese and appear in both languages. In addition to expressing herself in Japanese, my daughter is adept at using emojis to convey her feelings as do other Japanese deaf and hearing users (Okuyama). We also use the LINE webcam feature to communicate via JSL.

The internet has also proved useful for my daughter on trips to the US. As no one in my extended family knows more than a few signs of JSL and no one can read or write in Japanese, direct communication between my daughter and her American relatives is difficult. Early on, she relied heavily upon me for translation. More recently, thanks to applications, such as Google Translate, she has been able to communicate with non-Japanese/non-JSL users. She uses her device to type what she wants to convey to another in Japanese and then immediately translates it into English using the app, and vice versa. This enables her to have private conversations without parental intervention.

Apps, Access, and Approaching Independence

After my daughter graduated from high school, she decided that she would like to try living in a supported environment in Kyoto. Although the historic city is about two hours by car from our home, I wanted to encourage her desire for independence. After all, I had travelled halfway around the world from the US to make my home in Japan. So although some people in Japan have wondered why we, her parents, allow her to live so far away, her father and I are excited that she can develop further independence.

She has now lived in Kyoto for three years. We continue to keep in touch and communicate via the LINE app and through video chats in JSL. On her own, using the internet, she has successfully located someone to fix a punctured wheelchair tire, searched for recipes, found a maker of kimonos adapted to wheelchair users, and researched tourist sites and events. She also keeps up with current events via her smartphone.

In the summer of 2019, she was shocked and saddened by the deadly fire set by an arsonist at the venerated Kyoto Anime Studio. We had seen one of their productions at the movie theatre together—*Koe no Katachi* (*A Silent Voice*), a story about a relationship between a deaf girl and a bullied hearing boy. My daughter expressed her desire to pay her respects to the dead anime creators and lay flowers at the shrine, which had been erected temporarily near the site of the fire. She investigated the details via her smartphone, and we took the train to the site.

When we arrived on that hot summer day, several reporters from various Japanese newspapers were on the beat. They were expected to file stories related to the tragic fire daily. There were few other visitors, and we were no doubt conspicuous—a foreign mother and a young biracial woman in a wheelchair. They were eager to interview us. Although I have often written about my daughter (and am doing so here), I know that she can share her thoughts on her own. As she was twenty years old, and therefore a legal adult in Japan, I encouraged her to speak to the reporters, with an understanding that her words would appear in the newspaper. Using their respective smartphones, one of the reporters interviewed my daughter. She managed to convey both her sadness and the empowerment of seeing a young deaf woman represented in a popular anime movie. I was proud of her, yet I knew that other young deaf Japanese women living in another era, without the internet, might have gone unheard (Nakamura). However, thanks to modern technology, she has been able to exercise her independence and connect with the world.

Conclusion

To a certain extent, everyone in my family is dependent upon the internet. Perhaps some of us are even addicted. I personally spend far too much time checking my Twitter and Facebook feeds, and I know that my daughter sometimes stays up too late texting friends. Despite its drawbacks, however, the internet is a boon to multicultural, multiabled families such as my own. It has enabled me to keep in touch in real time with family far away, and it has allowed my daughter a degree of autonomy that would not have been possible thirty years ago. I expect that thanks to online programs and apps, communication between speakers of different languages, as well as between disabled and nondisabled people, will only continue to improve. Long live the internet!

Works Cited

Bannon, Stephanie, et al. "The Positive Role of Internet Use for Young People with Additional Support Needs: Identity and Connectedness." *Computers in Human Behavior*, vol. 53, 2015, pp. 504-14

Barak, Azy, and Yael Sadovsky "Internet Use and Personal Empowerment of Hearing-Impaired Adolescents." *Computers in Human*

Behavior, vol. 24, no. 5, 2008, pp. 1802-15.

Beard, Keith. W. "Working with Adolescents Addicted to the Internet." *Internet Addiction: A Handbook and Guide to Evaluation and Treatment*, edited by Kimberly. S. Young and Cristiano Nabuco de Abreu, John Wiley & Sons, 2011, pp. 173-189.

Bookman, Mark. "Politics and Prosthetics: 150 Years of Disability in Japan." 2000. University of Pennsylvania, Unpublished dissertation.

Bridges, Sheila J. "Multicultural Issues in Augmentative and Alternative Communication and Language: Research to Practice." *Topics in Language Disorders*, vol. 24, no. 1, January-March 2004, pp. 62-75.

Chang, Sharon H. *Raising Mixed Race: Multiracial Asian Children in a Post-Racial World*. Routledge, 2016.

Eijiri, Keiko, and Akemi Matsuzawa. "Factors Associated with Employment of Mothers Caring for Children with Intellectual Disabilities." *International Journal of Developmental Disabilities*, vol. 65, no. 4, 2019, pp. 239-47.

Grisdale, Josh. *Accessible Japan's Tokyo: All You Need to Know about Traveling to Tokyo with a Disability*. Self-published. 2020.

Hanaway, Tom. "'Terrace House' Season Canceled Following Death of Hana Kimura." *Japan Times*, 27 May 2020, www.japantimes.co.jp/culture/2020/05/27/entertainment-news/terrace-house-canceled-hana-kimura-suicide/. Accessed 19 May 2022.

Iwakuma, Miho, and Jon F. Nussbaum. "Intercultural Views of People with Disabilities in Asia and Africa." *Handbook of Communication and People with Disabilities: Research and Application*, edited by Dawn O. Braithwaite and Teresa L. Thompson, Lawrence Erlbaum Associates, 2000, pp. 196-210.

Kamata, Suzanne "An American Mother Raising a Deaf Daughter in Small-Town Japan." *Intercultural Families and Schooling in Japan: Experiences, Issues, and Challenges*, edited by Melodie Lorie Cook and Louise George Kittaka, Candlin and Mynard, 2020, pp. 197-217

Kawaguchi, Naoko. "Difficulties Disabled Women in Japan Face with Regard to Love, Marriage, and Reproduction." *Ars Vivendi Journal*, vol. 11, 2019, pp. 48-60.

Kusano, Kodai, et al. "The Effects of ICT Environment on Teachers' Attitudes and Technology Integration in Japan and the U.S." *Journal of Information Technology Education*, vol. 12, 2013, pp. 29-43.

Kwan, Amanda. "Mommy Bloggers Suffer Privacy Conflicts on Facebook." NBC News, 14 Aug. 2020. www.nbcnews.com/id/wbna38697298. Accessed 19 May 2022.

McGuire, Jennifer M. "Who Am I with Others?: Selfhood and *Shuwa* Among Mainstream Educated Deaf and Hard-of-Hearing Japanese Youth." *Contemporary Japan*, vol. 32, no. 2, 2020, pp. 197-217.

Moore, Faith. "Children of Mommy Bloggers Starting to Realize They're the Subject of Blogs... and They're Not Happy." *PJ Media*, 15 Jan. 2019, pjmedia.com/news-and-politics/faith-moore/2019/01/15/children-of-mommy-bloggers-starting-to-realize-theyre-the-subject-of-blogs-and-theyre-not-happy-n63114. Accessed 19 May 2022.

Nakamura, Karen. *Deaf in Japan: Signing and the Politics of Identity.* Cornell University Press, 2006.

Navarro, Raul, Santiago Yubero, and Elisa Larranaga, editors. *Cyberbullying Across the Globe: Gender, Family and Mental Health.* Springer International Publishing, 2016.

Nishikawa, Saori, Elisabet Sundbom, and Bruno Hägglöf "Influence of Perceived Parental Rearing on Adolescent Self-Concept and Internalizing and Externalizing Problems in Japan." *Journal of Child and Family Studies,* vol. 19, 2010, pp. 57-66.

Okuyama, Yoshiko. "Japanese Deaf Adolescents' Textisms."*IJCBPL*, vol. 4, no. 2, 2014, pp. 20-32.

Peckitt, Michael Gillan. *Barrier Free Japan.* barrierfreejapan.com. Accessed 19 May 2022.

Pew Research Center. "Internet and Technology. " *Pew*, 12 June 2019, www.pewresearch.org/internet/fact-sheet/mobile/. Accessed 19 May 2022.

Škařupová, Kateřina, Kjartan Ólafsson, and Lukas Blinka. "The Effect of Smartphone Use on Trends in European Adolescents' Excessive Internet Use." *Behaviour & Information Technology*, vol. 35, no. 1, 2015, pp. 1-7.

Statistics Bureau of Japan. *Statistical Handbook of Japan 2020*, www.stat.go.jp/english/data/handbook/index.html. Accessed 19 May 2022.

Stevens, Carolyn S. *Disability in Japan*. Routledge, 2013.

Stibbe, Arran. "Disability, Gender and Power in Japanese Television Drama." *Japan Forum*, vol. 16, no. 1, 2004, pp. 21-36.

United Nations. *The International Year of Disabled Persons 1981*, UN, 2022, www.un.org/development/desa/disabilities/the-international-year-of-disabled-persons-1981.html. Accessed 19 May 2022.

Watanabe, Miwako. "A Cross-Cultural Comparison of Attitudes Towards Persons with Disabilities: College Students in Japan and the United States." 2002. University of Hawaii, Unpublished master thesis.

Weatherill, Pamela. "Mothers at Home, Online." *Stay-at-Home Mothers: Dialogues and Debates*, edited by Elizabeth Reid Boyd and Gayle Letherby, Demeter Press, 2014, pp. 173-186.

Wimmer, Kurt. "A Child's Right to Online Privacy." *Pogo Was Right*, 1 Jan. 2013, www.pogowasright.org/mommy-bloggers-a-childs-right-to-online-privacy/. Accessed 19 May 2022.

Zaromatidis, Katherine, et al. "A Cross-Cultural Comparison of Attitudes toward Persons with Disabilities: Greeks and Greek-Americans." *Psychological Reports*, vol. 84, no. 3_suppl, June 1999, pp. 1189-96.

Chapter 11

Discourses, Practices, and Paradoxes of Natural Parenting in the Digital Age

Florence Pasche Guignard

Natural parenting is a particular approach to parenting, which combines elements of attachment parenting (see Bowlby; Sears) with a strong environmentalist mindset and relevant ecofriendly practices. This chapter explores the impact of internet use and technology on mothers who engage in natural parenting and some of the paradoxes associated with it. Three case studies in natural parenting will be analyzed in relation to internet use by mothers: babywearing and breastfeeding, fertility awareness, and maternal entrepreneurship. These examples were chosen because they are some of the most prominent practices in the natural parenting movement and because they also increasingly rely on digital and connected technologies. In other words, these selected cases illustrate one of the paradoxes of natural parenting: an emphasis on nature and sustainability coupled with a high reliance on internet use and technology.

Past research has already highlighted the "paradox of natural mothering" (Bobel, *The Paradox*; Bobel, *Resisting*). This paradox consists in approaching some parenting practices as natural while insisting that these practices are a mother's (or a family's) conscious choice—free from constraints and often resisting cultural, social, and medical norms, especially technocratic ones (for instance, through homebirth or a preference for holistic and alternative systems of healing; see Davis-Floyd). Most of these studies were published in the early 2000s and before the rise of social media and the increased digitalization of our daily lives, including in the domain of parenting.

Since Chris Bobel's pioneering research, the internet and digital media have become the main source of information for parents. For example, mothers (and in some cases their partners) use them to learn babywearing, solve breastfeeding issues, track their menstrual cycle for procreative or contraceptive purposes, or engage in maternal entrepreneurship. If the rise of digital media has brought mothers and families more opportunities to learn, to connect, to form communities of shared values, and to participate in home-based business economies, it has also brought about some challenges and new paradoxes in natural parenting. As the three case studies in this chapter will demonstrate, the promotion, dissemination, and implementation of lifestyles choices and practices presented as natural and that are, in many ways, "techno-skeptic" in fact rely heavily on technology and high-tech devices. In natural parenting milieux, mothers use such devices and the internet for themselves or to benefit their children but rarely with them. The case studies will also show how recent evolutions in technology (connected devices, Internet of Things, and algorithms) affect mothers and their families, especially in fields related to reproduction (femtech) and motherhood.

Natural Moms

The three case studies presented below were taken from a larger study conducted between 2012 and 2017, with most interviews conducted in 2013 (including those quoted in this chapter, with pseudonyms given to my informants). This chapter builds on results already published elsewhere[1] and includes more recent observations of developing trends in the francophone contexts of natural parenting. The participants in the original research were from francophone countries (Belgium, Canada, France, and Switzerland); all of them were members of natural parenting online communities. Although members of these online communities share a strong environmentalist commitment and similar practices, the extent of their engagement with such practices varies among them. For example, although most will endorse homebirth as an option, not all were homebirthers. Indeed, homebirth with the assistance of a professional midwife is easier to access in

Switzerland and Quebec than it is in France, where a lack of liberal midwives makes it more difficult to give birth at home (Ingar 20-21; see also Fedele and Pasche Guignard) and where there remains a strong criticism against homebirth in general by mainstream obstetricians (Nisand), amplified by mainstream and online media.

Most participants in these online forums call themselves "mamans nature," which might be translated as "natural moms." With few exceptions, they formed heterocentred nuclear families, and although some expressed being in line with feminist ideals of equity and equality, questioning such family norms was not a major concern for them. The heteronormative model of the family, though not necessarily involving marriage, remains prevalent in the francophone contexts considered in this research, and natural parenting discourses neither challenged nor particularly reinforced such cultural norms. From my observation of and participation in the specific online spaces of natural parenting during the research and over time, I noticed that few parents in same-sex couples participate in them, although they are not completely absent. A few "mamans nature" identified openly as lesbians online, for instance in the signature appearing at the end of each one of their posted messages: Their identity as lesbian mothers was not the central focus of their online participation. Rather, like other participants, they engaged online with practical issues (e.g. types and brands of washable diaper to use and recommended readings on natural parenting). Although I also participated in online conversations with mothers who wrote that they were in same-sex couples and practicing natural parenting, all of the participants who agreed to participate in recorded semistructured interviews stated that they were in traditional and stable monogamous relationships, with the exception of one mother, who was in the process of separating from her (male hetero-sexual) partner.

This absence or invisibility of parents in same-sex relationships in the online spaces of natural parenting studied in this research can easily be explained by two factors. First, parents identifying as LGBTQ+ have carved out their own online safe spaces where they discuss issues specific to their own communities in relation to parenting and where the internet also plays a major role, especially for accessing information and advice (e.g., about fertility treatments, surrogacy, or other options that may not be available legally to same-sex couples in

France, Switzerland, Belgium, and other francophone contexts considered here). Although such dedicated spaces were beyond the scope of the present study, reading such forums showed that natural parenting and ecofriendly practices were not central to discussions that instead involved such issues as legal struggles regarding adoption or homophobic remarks from the doctors and teachers of their children. LGBTQ+ parents might well have participated in several sections of the forum, but there was no significant evidence of an overlapping of both types of identities, conversations, and communities in online spaces for parents.

Additionally, a critical perspective in motherhood studies must also point out that some discourses of natural parenting have a potential to reinforce the association of the natural with the idea of natural law, which is understood by some conservative groups as heteronormative and as excluding forms of families that do not conform to traditional norms and values. However, such understandings of "the natural" as the absence of any medical intervention (such as IVF, donor eggs or sperm, or surrogacy) or sociolegal arrangements (such as adoption or open relationships) in creating a family remained extremely rare in the discourses of my francophone informants, most of whom tended to have liberal views regarding family structures and laws in general (e.g., supporting legal same-sex marriage and access to adoption). Their focus on nature was on the environment rather than on any notions linked to sexual morality and religiously informed ethics of reproduction. As I discuss elsewhere in more detail, most of my francophone informants identified as non-religious, agnostics, or atheists (Pasche Guignard, "Back Home" 190). Most mothers in natural parenting simply uphold a heteronormative ideal of the family without questioning it, as this corresponds to their gender identity and heterosexual orientation. This behaviour should not be misread as their actively promoting agendas of so-called natural family values as might be the case in North American, anglophone contexts, where some strands of natural parenting remain associated with conservatism (especially religious conservatism). In the conversations I had with these mothers, most indicated that their political engagement remained low. Furthermore, political debates were extremely rare on their forums that focused on more practical issues, materiality, embodiment, and experiences. Their practices and experiences position these mothers as marginal, in their specific contexts, although they otherwise fit in many of the other cultural norms, including being in stable, monogamous, and heterosexual relationships as they became mothers.

At a more general level, the natural moms engage in such online communities because they are looking for spaces where they can freely express themselves about their lives, their relationship to their children, their partners, and other social or medical actors. They also consider that online forums and blogs—more so than friends, relatives, or healthcare professionals—provide safe spaces for authentic expressions of the practices and challenges of natural parenting. Furthermore, the mothers I interviewed reported that the actors of the mainstream medical field either had limited knowledge of natural parenting, were unfavourable to related practices (such as homebirth or unconventional diets, like veganism), or could not understand some of their concerns and answer their questions (for instance on vaccination and other medical procedures). In short, the natural moms I interviewed tend to feel that mainstream healthcare practitioners lack empathy and a real understanding of the questions and issues they are confronted with.

Mainstream francophone media tend to portray practitioners of natural parenting negatively and to caricature them as "fanatics," who religiously adopt any and all practices related to natural parenting (Pasche Guignard, "Back Home" 191-96; Fedele and Pasche Guignard, 140-141). My ethnographic research reveals a more nuanced picture, where natural parenting is not a rigid list of mandatory practices but rather a cluster of options and reasoned choices, which require flexibility and agile solutions. In fact, most parents must adapt not only to a number of constraints, especially their budget, but also to their family members, friends, and other caregivers. The use of washable diapers provides one such example, as they are emblematic objects of "green moms" and "sustainable motherhood" (Takeshita 118): Most parents who use washable diapers do not use them exclusively. When they travel or visit friends, most also use disposable diapers, although they purchase these from small, chemical-free brands. Likewise, most natural moms do not impose washable diapers on other caregivers, such as daycare workers or grandparents.

A New Paradox in Natural Parenting

Following Bobel's work, I highlight a new paradox in natural parenting. Many discourses in natural parenting encourage a critical attitude towards some aspects of contemporary technology while relying heavily on technology in approaching, disseminating, and implementing natural parenting. For example, online discourses in the natural parenting community not only promote breastfeeding as healthy but also value it as natural. However, the use of connected breastpumps, fridges, and freezers—that is, devices that all involve advanced technology—to store human milk is common among natural moms. Although there is no outright rejection of technology in general in the discourses of the natural parenting movement, there is, however, a widespread suspicion and even some degree of distrust especially towards conventional agriculture, food production, and medical and pharmaceutical industries (Katz Rothman; Odent). The natural parenting movement typically resists medical tests and procedures that it considers invasive or unnecessary (e.g., episiotomy).

Despite largely cautious attitudes, the case studies discussed below show that digital technologies now play a major role in natural parenting, including in the transmission of forms of knowledge regarded as alternative to the norm, which raises important questions. For example, how does natural parenting interact with new internet technologies and resolve the apparent paradox? In families where technological interventions are not embraced with blind enthusiasm, how is the use of such digital tools approached? Could there also be a potential for creativity and empowerment for mothers who engage in natural parenting via technology? Is the "ordinary Internet, the web in [the] social practices and relationships" (Martin and Dagiral) of natural moms different from that of most people? Do they engage with such technologies in a different way, which might strengthen natural parenting discourses and practices rather than undermine them?

To explore these questions, this chapter uses three case studies that each represents a distinct attitude towards internet-based technologies. The first one focuses on the pedagogic potential of internet-based technologies to learn "techniques of the body" involving the parent and the child that are typical of natural parenting, such as breastfeeding and babywearing (see Mauss 79, for a mention of carrying babies as a "technique of infancy"). The second case study focuses on communities of mothers in relation to enhanced body literacy through practices of digital fertility awareness to achieve or avoid pregnancy. The third case study relates to commercial and entrepreneurial uses of the Internet by natural moms who themselves run a business related to natural parenting.

First Case Study: Learning Babywearing and Breastfeeding from a Screen

Babywearing and breastfeeding are both key components of natural parenting that draw from attachment parenting while also being valued as natural and regarded as effective bonding practices between parent and baby. Both also typically involve digitalization and learning from a screen rather than, or in addition to, from scratch (Pasche Guignard, "Mediated Babywearing" 29-32). Carrying a baby with a cloth wrap efficiently and safely is an example of an embodied technique that is not instinctive but must be learned. For many parents engaged in natural parenting, this learning is typically achieved through online tutorial videos (e.g. on YouTube), in which experienced mothers (and sometimes fathers) demonstrate the various techniques of babywearing (baby in front, on the back, on the hip, etc.; see also Russell for an analysis of babywearing in the age of the internet). Online communities are a privileged space for mothers to share not only practical advice but also their experience and feelings in a context where babywearing is still marginal in comparison with the more traditional "distal" practices of parenting in francophone countries (see Keller 25, for definitions of "distal" and "proximal" parenting techniques). For example, participants in these online communities share the negative comments that their relatives and friends make about their choice to engage in babywearing and other unconventional practices of natural parenting (e.g. bedsharing and extended breast-feeding).

Another example of the internet as a source of information for natural parenting is breastfeeding. National breastfeeding rates and median duration varied depending on the contexts of my informants. For instance, according to a 2012 study, the breastfeeding initiation rate was 74 per cent in France, dropping to 22.5 per cent at six months (including human milk and formula hybrid modes of feeding; see

Salanave et al. 475), whereas it was above 90 per cent (at birth) in the other francophone contexts surveyed (for a more detailed discussion see Pasche Guignard, "Discours"; also see Wagner et al.). The mothers I interviewed were often the first among their close relatives (e.g., their own mothers and, sometimes, grandmothers) to breastfeed, as opposed to using formula, which remains the statistical and cultural norm in their contexts, at least past the first few weeks after birth. These mothers found information on breastfeeding and support through various online forums, such as Facebook groups. These groups generally identify as probreastfeeding and, as such, are not places for debating breastfeeding versus formula. Participants in such online groups are assumed to be committed to breastfeeding or, at least, well-disposed towards it. Such online groups are not platforms to promote breast-feeding but spaces where participants show support and empathy, which is apparent through friendly messages and digital symbols members use, such as emoticons or gifs.

Lupton and others have shown that information on pregnancy, childbirth, and postpartum, are highly valued sources of information—especially when they are shared online (Lupton, "The Use and Value" 171). Digital spaces seem to be perceived as both atemporal (i.e., they are always available and searchable) and immediate (i.e., one can get an answer to a specific question in seconds), which makes them highly attractive. When a mother seeks a practical solution to an urgent problem, what she needs is immediately available, contrary to lactation consultants who visit mothers at home or at the hospital. Adding to this particular maternal perception of time afforded by online spaces is "tickers,"[2] another highly popular feature of natural parenting forums. Tickers allow participants to automatically keep track and display information on their profile, giving a sense of instantaneity to using these websites. For instance, some users will display in their signature messages such as "I have been breastfeeding for twenty-three months and four days," thus marking this person as someone with experience that others may want to turn to request advice online.

The Case of Fanny and Julien

Illustrating the process of learning to breastfeed online is the case of Fanny and Julien, a Swiss couple who lived in South America when I interviewed them. Fanny and Julien had two babies who were both born at home and breastfed. Although the birth of her first child at home went well, Fanny had difficulties when starting to breastfeed for the first time. She herself had not been breastfed, so she could not turn to her mother (in Switzerland) for advice; moreover, the nearest La Leche League (LLL[3]) association that could offer support was a six-hour drive away. In short, Fanny felt isolated and had considered not breastfeeding at all, although this would have been quite uncommon for a mother engaged in natural parenting. When I asked her what made her change her mind, Fanny explained:

> Well... I told myself that I would try. And it did not go well, not at all... But I do not know [why I persisted]. I would say an instinct... an animal instinct coming from I don't know where.... I tried, and it did not go well, and I had no support because my mother had no experience at all. There is no lactation consultant [in her area]. And then I was at home. I had chosen to not go to the hospital, so I was a little bit alone... I remember spending two months and a half crying every time. And then, well, I really do not know why... why I kept on breastfeeding, but this sounded logical. Yes, we watched videos of latching, with my husband who would press on pause every second and who was trying to correct the position [laughs].

During the same interview, Julien[4] also mentioned the important role of online videos, as both parents were learning about breastfeeding. Julien reported that they "watched quite many of these videos together" and that he would try to "position the baby differently" for latching. He emphasized feeling that he was "not a great help" and that his greatest support towards Fanny was that he was "in favour" of her breastfeeding. He also stated that, in contrast to him, in Switzerland, some fathers "are against this" ("ils sont contre ça") and even oppose their wife's breastfeeding in public spaces, in his opinion. In the South American country where they had chosen to live, this was rather common, he noted.

Although most of the francophone parents I interviewed had found information on natural parenting through the internet, this case study illustrates that such online information is all the more important to couples—like Fanny and Julien—who live outside of their home country and are unable to access information in their first language.

Such online information is also important to parents whose natural parenting practices are regarded as marginal or are criticized by their relatives or mainstream healthcare practitioners. In other words, parents who feel isolated or marginalized are even more likely to look for information on natural parenting specifically in digital form, such as online resources and advice.

That said, this process of online learning does not mean that mothers do not also participate in in-person groups and meetings with their babies. For example, Fanny attended LLL meetings and later launched a local mothers' group with in-person meetings in her area to support other mothers and share experiences. More than in anglophone contexts, where, at the time of this study, more printed material and resources were available, this ideal of sharing experiences and not just professionally sanctioned expertise was especially strong in franco-phone contexts and remains so. Through blogs and discussion forums, mothers (and sometimes couples) can share their experience of natural parenting, the challenges they face, and how their practices are perceived by society in general. As Catherine de Pierrepont suggests in her analysis of online forums on postpartum sexuality, "Testimony can be associated with the transmission of popular or expert knowledge" (my translation, 117). This is also the case in the digital expressions of natural parenting: Personal accounts encourage and comfort other people who encounter similar difficulties or who doubt the outcomes of their parenting choices and their environmentalist commitment. Furthermore, these digital expressions also disseminate practical and embodied knowledge, such as breastfeeding and babywearing.

Second Case Study: Fertility Awareness

Fertility awareness can be defined as the monitoring of one's menstrual cycle through self-observation of bodily symptoms, such as basal body temperature, cervical mucus, and the position and shape of the cervix. Fertility awareness is mainly used to determine whether somebody is fertile at any given time. Although there are exceptions to this general consideration,[5] most people who engage in fertility awareness are cisgender heterosexual women who are in relationships with cisgender heterosexual men. Since ovulation and the start of the infertile phase of the cycle can be confirmed two days after a spike in basal body temperature, fertility awareness typically consists of taking temperature at regular intervals, preferably every morning. During the potentially fertile phase of the cycle, couples who do not wish a pregnancy will abstain from penetrative sex or use barrier contraceptive methods.

Fertility awareness practices and methods are diverse (Pasche Guignard, "Digital Tools") and are sometimes lumped together with such terms as "natural contraception" or "natural family planning." Yet the term "natural" is problematic (Hargot 24-25) and misleading, since fertility awareness is a cultural phenomenon and also an increasingly a technological and digital one as well. The term "natural" is first used as a marketing tool, and it is rejected by those who teach and promote the method known as "symptothermie" in French ("the symptothermal method"; see also Wettstein and Bourgeois 6). The questioning and distrust of hormonal contraception—and therefore an interest in other contraceptive methods, such as fertility awareness— is partly tied to the highly mediated "pill scare" scandals in France, which were a "major controversy [that] arose around third- and fourth-generation pills in late 2012 and early 2013" (Bajos et al. 1; see also Debusquat). Yet for many natural moms, concerns about the pill include broader issues around women's bodily autonomy and sexuality, obstetrical violence, and, most importantly, what it means to become a mother for the first time. For example, many of my interviewees explained that the project of pregnancy, and the prospect of becoming a mother for the first time, is what motivated them to stop taking hormonal contraceptives. Some of them also explained that when they did stop taking these, they were "feeling alive again," "finding [themselves] again," or "reconnecting to [their] body and sexuality." After the birth of their first child, these mothers often considered that the mainstream (hormonal) contraceptive options available to them were disconnected from their journey towards an ecofriendlier lifestyle. A few opted for a copper- and hormone-free intrauterine device, although this was not a suitable option for all. For others, fertility awareness-based methods thus became the long-term, preferred option.

Social scientists rarely have investigated fertility awareness practices and even less so with a focus on their recent and ongoing digitalization. Thus, in this section, I consider how using computing technology can affect the lives of mothers in natural parenting families. In particular, fertility awareness is a prime example of what I see as the paradox of advocating natural or ecofriendly practices while relying heavily on high-tech devices and the internet to implement them.

Although fertility awareness is not new, its increasing digitalization in the last decade has made it more accessible, though not more popular. In their article on "domesticated health tools," focusing on the example of the home pregnancy test, Janet Childerhose and Margaret MacDonald note that women use (or are subjected to) medical technologies "in conjunction with other technologies, particularly social media, to new ends: to maintain familial and social ties, and to create new connections and communities with other women and couples" (4). Social media and specialized websites dedicated to fertility awareness and tracking of the menstrual cycle provide a space where methods, practices, and experiences can be taught and discussed with peers and experts. Some of these online communities also feature apps, through which users share data about their menstrual cycle. For example, Kindara, one of the most popular fertility tracking apps, has a built-in community feature, where users can share their menstrual charts, comment on them, and answer one another's questions. The profiles do not mention the user's sex or gender identity as a category, but this can be indicated in the description or through tags. Most users are cisgender women in heterosexual relationships who chart their cycles in order to conceive or to avoid pregnancy. The few members who identify as trans, queer, or nonbinary tend to explicitly describe their gender identity when they post and share their cycles to the Kindara community.

As already noted by Sarah Fox and Daniel A. Epstein in their study of designs of digital menstrual tracking, such digital spaces and their corresponding apps "often make heteronormative assumptions about people tracking their menstruation and reinforce binary conceptions of gender" (740). Gender-neutral language is rarely used, and feminine aesthetics are prominent because apps developers market such digital tools to cisgender heterosexual women who use fertility awareness for cognitive, procreative, or contraceptive purposes. Digital fertility awareness as practiced in natural parenting thus also highlights dynamics in cisgender heterosexual parental couples. Indeed, one of the key requirements of fertility awareness is to first clarify one's intentions about a pregnancy: Does the woman want to achieve or avoid pregnancy? Does she accept whatever comes her way or "what Nature sends her" in terms of pregnancy? Likewise, it is important to consider the perspective of the partner. Does he wish to become a father? Is he eager to negotiate with and assist his partner? Technologies of fertility monitoring are therefore inscribed in the heteroconjugal sphere, in which the maternal and parental project is most often approached in terms of pregnancy—whether or not it is desired, intended, planned, accepted, or rejected.

Users of fertility awareness methods increasingly rely on apps to store and explore data. In particular, it seems that embodied and maternal knowledge about the body is transferred to technology and algorithms. Whether the purpose of fertility awareness is cognitive, procreative, or contraceptive, these practices participate in a process of the "quantified self" (Lupton, *The Quantified Self*). This is not new, since women have monitored their menstrual cycles for centuries. What is new is that such practices of the embodied and female quantified self are now partly digital. Since there are few sociological studies on fertility awareness, it is difficult to assess the impact of its digitalization on couples and on family dynamics. What can be said is that in those mostly heterosexual couples, the female partner remains largely in charge of it. It is she who collects, monitors, and interprets data on fertile or infertile phases. The hands-on, day-to-day involvement of their partners is poorly documented but arguably low. Another key issue mentioned by several mothers is that hormonal contraception had a negative impact on their libido and, thus, on their partnered sexual life. Additionally, it would be interesting to investigate, for example, whether a father is more involved in the fertility monitoring process than a man who never had children. That said, for many of my interviewees, using the internet to access information about fertility awareness and share with others was perceived as empowering.

Third Case Study: Maternal Entrepreneurship

For some mothers in the natural parenting movement, the internet is not only a source of information and a platform for communication but also a tool to launch and run a business, as this last case study will show. Although the figure of the stay-at-home mother was central in earlier implementations of natural mothering (Bobel, *The Paradox*, 115-119), the work-from-home mother and businesswoman has now emerged. Staying home and homemaking are no longer sufficient: Beyond the "green angel in the house" (Redela 195), an increasing number of natural moms have become "mompreneurs," who design, market, and sell products and services related to a natural-family lifestyle for which they often serve as evangelists. Starting a business, though, is by no means a guarantee for success. For a typical natural mompreneur, however, "subscribing to capitalist ideals of 'success' is not central to her existence" (Redela 197). The two examples discussed below illustrate this entrepreneurial and commercial use of the internet by mothers in natural parenting, with a focus on the seller's side rather than on the consumer's. The first example is Vanessa's business of babywearing wraps, and the second example is Johanne's online haberdashery.

Vanessa's Babywearing Business

Originally from France, Vanessa lived for several years in the United States after getting her university degree. There, in 2009, she gave birth to her daughter, at home. That same year, she moved to francophone Switzerland with her partner. Like many parents in my study, Vanessa had discovered natural parenting through the internet, in her early thirties. I recruited Vanessa for an interview through the natural-mothering section of an online forum on pregnancy and childbirth called *Doctissimo*,[6] where she had been a regular contributor.

Vanessa started babywearing with the birth of her daughter and was so passionate about it that she became a babywearing instructor. After earning her certification through training offered by one of the leading brands of babywearing wraps, she became a sales representative for this brand. At the time, babywearing products were not broadly available in mainstream baby-gear stores, and by the early 2010s, Vanessa became the only official importer for this brand in Switzerland. She was selling these products through a website she created herself, making a small profit on each sale. She also used the website to advertise her services for private and collective babywearing workshops. Several other mothers who had expertise in particular practices of natural parenting told me in the interviews that they used digital tools and social media to launch their small business. In addition to babywearing, the other examples from my study included birth and postpartum doula services, baby massage workshops, courses on essential oils and alternative healing practices, courses or coaching on fertility awareness, as well as the example examined below in more details.

Johanne's Online Haberdashery

Another mompreneur relying heavily on internet use is Johanne, a Swiss mother of a three-year-old and a one-year-old who, was deeply engaged in natural family living when I interviewed her.[7] Like many mothers in the natural parenting movement, Johanne endorsed the idea that a mother is responsible not only for the wellbeing of all members of her family but also for the consequences of their consumption on the environment. She also insisted that ecofriendly practices requiring more planning and domestic work had to result from personal conviction and highlighted several times that the lifestyle choices she had made were hers and were never imposed by her husband or anybody else. For example, when Johanne mentioned her need to buy an up-to-date computer, she reported that she had to convince herself rather than her relatives and friends who were also committed to environmentalism. Regarding this forthcoming purchase of a new computer, she stated, "If we need a new computer, even if we have an old one which still works, but too slowly, then we will buy a new computer." In this case, she further reasoned that although problematic in terms of consumption, purchasing a brand new, updated device would allow her not only to continue her part-time academic work but also to raise awareness on environmentalist issues and to work towards the launch her ecofriendly business.

In her own words, Johanne practiced a sustainable approach to parenting that was "engaged, but not rigid." Within the limits of this family's budget, they preferred buying food that was seasonal, local, and organic. The house they rented had a garden where she grew vegetables. She also purchased organic produce directly from a farm nearby. However, she stated that she would not refrain from purchasing imported goods, such as avocados for instance, if these were organic and fair-trade products. Johanne emphasized that her environmentalism was not "aggressive, sectarian or whatever" but "sustainable" while her family also engaged in voluntary simplicity and minimized consumption due to their reduced income at the time.

Coming back to maternal entrepreneurship, Johanne also mentioned that she started to develop her skills in sewing with the help of books and online tutorials. Without any immediate opportunity in the academic job market, she decided to set up an online store selling eco-friendly haberdashery supplies, such as kits to sew zero-waste products (i.e., reusable makeup remover and menstrual pads) or other items that she used for herself or her children. Managing this online store left her with more time to be with her children than if she had found a full-time job in academia. Besides, this activity supplemented her family's income, which was much appreciated given that her husband was also a precariously employed academic researcher.

Johanne's example also illustrates that internet-based businesses involve fewer financial risks, investment, and upfront expenses for mompreneurs, compared to traditional (i.e., not internet-based) businesses. Furthermore, for mompreneurs in general, social networks are key to developing contacts with other mothers and to the sale of products and services, many of which are in line with their values and "self-identification as environmentally friendly, smart, and caring mothers" (Takeshita 118). The type of products sold online by Johanne and her own practical implementation of environmentalism in the domestic sphere show such an alignment of values, manifested through internet use.

Concluding Remarks on the New Paradox of Natural Parenting in the Digital Age

This chapter has explored some ways in which the internet—especially social media—has influenced mothers who engage in natural parenting, but many questions remain. One of these is how children use digital technologies connected to the internet in natural parenting families. This topic indeed emerged as a concern among some of the parents who had school-aged children in my study. Remarkably, even these parents of older children did not use the internet with them in any collaborative way (e.g., to play online games together or to communicate on a daily basis). Rather, most uses that the natural moms pointed out related to activities done to benefit their children (e.g., searching for information about babywearing or breastfeeding) or their family in general (e.g., finding recipes or tutorials for making ecofriendly cleaning supplies) while enhancing their environmentalist engagement through minimal or ethical consumption. Those who had babies and toddlers were more concerned about their own use and consumption of social media as well as about the effects of digital technology on society in general. Although my study was not quantitative, approximately one-third of my interviewees were either themselves in professions directly related to the internet (e.g., a webmaster, a computer engineer or technician, an IT specialist, or a social media manager) or were married to a partner in such industries. Most declared that they had no television set at home, but all were avid users of social media and the internet in general. I also recruited them for my study online through information and communication technologies, which greatly facilitated this transnational research.

Some mothers were cautious about letting their children, especially the youngest ones, access internet technology without parental supervision. One of my informants said that she was upset with her in-laws because they had given iPads as Christmas gifts to their grandchildren. She and her husband did not want to purchase or own such devices; they did not want the additional burden of monitoring their use. Moreover, she was also bothered by the electronic device in itself, as a material object. She considered herself a responsible consumer, engaged in ethical trade (Dubuisson-Quellier), just like Johanne and her family (discussed in the previous section). Like other participants in my study, she hoped to lead by example and to encourage her children to follow in her footsteps. Neither herself nor her five- and seven-year-old children felt a need to acquire such objects, which are produced, according to her, under conditions that did not reflect her and her family's values in terms of sustainability. Other parents emphasized similar issues about cheap, low-quality toys and plastic gadgets that would be used for a limited time before being tossed away. An aggravating issue with electronic devices was that these would be even harder to recycle. For natural mothers who are implementing an environmental ethos in their daily consumption choices and parenting practice the soon-to-be obsolete electronic devices, and especially those that connect to the internet, are unacceptable waste. Yet in other areas of their life as women and mothers, these active participants on natural parenting online forums relied on such devices, for instance to monitor their fertility.

Reconsidering previously published materials (see Pasche Guignard in the works cited) from a more encompassing and matricentric perspective on natural parenting for this chapter in *Parenting/Internet/ Kids* has confirmed some observations and raised new questions. Discourses of natural parenting often emphasize resisting some cultural, social, and medical norms, with a focus on how nature opposes technocracy. The norm of the heteronormative nuclear family as the primary site of implementation of natural parenting remains, however, practically unchallenged. Yet in the francophone contexts included in this study, natural parenting did not feature moral discourses on forms of family. Most of the various understandings of "the natural" in my informants' discourses centred on nature, the environment, and environmental ethics rather than on morality about family forms. This certainly was not the case at the time this research was conducted, but we might ask if public debates in francophone contexts will slowly be evolving to include discussions of LGBTQ+ issues in parenting, including in relation to using various technologies (including medical ones as well as communication and information technologies to create specific online spaces).

Natural parenting is not immune to the fact that so many activities in our daily lives now rely on the internet to be implemented. Rather than an outright rejection of all technology, the most prevailing attitude of the parents I interviewed was characterized by suspicion and selectivity: They embrace some aspects of the internet, the devices, and the technologies that it requires because these extend or enhance practices that they regard and value as natural, sustainable, or ecofriendly, such as breastfeeding or fertility awareness. They used the internet not only as a primary source of information but harnessed its transformative potential to foster their lifestyle choices and the dissemination of specific practices and worldviews. With the impact of the measures taken during the COVID-19 pandemic, we may ask if these attitudes towards their own and their children's use of technology will shift in the future. As technology and internet use have become even more unavoidable (such as for online education, shopping, contact tracing, etc.)—and sometimes even compulsory (digital certificates)— have discourses of natural parenting brought more pressure on the natural moms than on other parents who may not have held the same reservations about internet use and its effects on the individual and society as a whole? In any case, these parents will continue to use the internet to form usually benevolent online communities of likeminded parents organized around practices that often remain marginalized in their own cultural contexts or around shared values, including the strong environmentalist ethos that characterizes the discourses of natural parenting.

Endnotes

1. These publications include: Pasche Guignard, "Back Home" and "The In/Visibility," for further contextualization, definition and considerations on the discourses and worldviews of natural parenting in general; Pasche Guignard, "Mediated Babywearing," for an analysis of "mediated babywearing as aesthetic orthodoxy" and a case of practical spirituality for mothers and parents in the age of media and the internet; Pasche Guignard, "Nurturing the Sustainable Family," for an analysis of ethical consumption and voluntary simplicity in relation to natural parenting; Pasche Guignard, "Discours," for a discussion of breastfeeding and natural parenting; Pasche Guignard, "Digital Tools" and "High Tech Mediations" for a focus on fertility awareness; Fedele and Pasche Guignard, "Pushing from the Margins," for a critical and comparative discussion focused on homebirth and natural childbirth from the perspective of natural parenting; finally, see Pasche Guignard, "Material, Maternal, Embodied, and Digital," for a discussion of research methods including cyberethnography.

2. A ticker is a banner with the signature of a forum's user, displayed automatically at the end of each message posted, with personalized animations or images. One of its key features is the countdown. For instance, a banner referring to a future event (birth) could be "Due date in two months, one week and three days." Referring to a past event, it could read: "I started trying to get pregnant five months and ten days ago." On most parenting forums, tickers are easy and quick to create and customize.

3. As found on their website, La Leche League International's mission statement is "to help mothers worldwide to breastfeed through mother-to-mother support, encouragement, information, and

education, and to promote a better understanding of breastfeeding as an important element in the healthy development of the baby and mother." For a critical and comparative perspective on attachment parenting and intensive motherhood in the UK and France, see Faircloth. Despite some overlaps, the environmentalist ethos guiding the decisions of the French mothers in my study was more important than what Charlotte Faircloth observed in attachment parenting circles.

4. The case of Julien contrasts with that of most fathers in the natural parenting movement. Most of the time, in heterosexual couples, mothers rather than fathers are the most engaged in this process of online learning. Likewise, mostly doulas, midwifes, or lactation consultants provide mothers with in-person help and support regarding breastfeeding issues. Husbands and (male) partners are rarely regarded as knowledgeable or even as interested in learning natural parenting practices from online sources.

5. For instance, lesbian women may use fertility awareness to increase their chance of a successful insemination. Moreover, not all women menstruate and not all who menstruate identify as women. The few existing studies on fertility awareness from a nonmedical perspective (such as Hargot) typically ignore the situations and specific issues of non-heterosexual couples and non-cisgender people. Others clearly acknowledge their focus on ovulation monitoring and reproductive heterosex (Wilkinson, Roberts, and Mort).

6. *Doctissimo* is one of the most important francophone websites for medical communication to the public: www.doctissimo.fr/

7. A more detailed analysis of this case study can be found in Pasche Guignard, "Nurturing," 61-63.

Works Cited

Bajos, Nathalie, et al. "The French Pill Scare: Towards a New Contraceptive Model?" *Population and Societies*, vol. 511, no. 5, 2014, pp. 1-4.

Bobel, Chris. "Resisting, But Not Too Much: Interrogating the Paradox of Natural Mothering." *Maternal Theory. Essential Readings*, edited by Andrea O'Reilly. Demeter Press, 2007, pp. 782-91.

Bobel, Chris. *The Paradox of Natural Mothering.* Temple University Press, 2002.

Bowlby, John. *A Secure Base: Clinical Applications of Attachment Theory.* 1988. Routledge, 2005.

Childerhose, Janet E., and Margaret E. MacDonald. "Health Consumption as Work: The Home Pregnancy Test as a Domesticated Health Tool." *Social Science & Medicine,* vol. 86, 2013, pp. 1-8.

Davis-Floyd, Robbie. "The Technocratic, Humanistic, and Holistic Paradigms of Childbirth." *International Journal of Gynecology and Obstetrics,* vol. 75, 2001, pp. S5-S23.

Debusquat, Sabrina. *J'arrête la pilule.* Les Liens qui Libèrent, 2017.

Dubuisson-Quellier, Sophie. *La consommation engagée.* Presses de Sciences Po, 2009.

Faircloth, Charlotte. *Militant Lactivism? Attachment Parenting and Intensive Motherhood in the UK and France.* Berghahn Books, 2013.

Fedele, Anna, and Florence Pasche Guignard. "Pushing from the Margins: 'Natural Childbirth' in Holistic Spiritualities and Natural Parenting in France and Portugal." *Sacred Inception: Reclaiming the Spirituality of Birth in the Modern World,* edited by Marianne Delaporte and Martin Morag. Lexington Press, 2018, pp. 131-49.

Fox, Sarah, and Daniel A. Epstein. "Monitoring Menses: Design-Based Investigations of Menstrual Tracking Applications." *The Palgrave Handbook of Critical Menstruation Studies,* edited by Chris Bobel et al., Palgrave MacMillan, 2020, pp. 733-50.

Hargot, Thérèse. *Pour une libération sexuelle véritable. Vivre les méthodes naturelles de régulation des naissances.* Editions François-Xavier de Guibert, 2010.

Ingar, Cynthia. "Birth in France: The *Maisons de Naissance* Experimental Project and the Horizon of Homebirth." *Midwifery Today,* vol. 132, 2019, pp. 20-25.

Katz Rothman, Barbara. *A Bun in the Oven: How the Food and Birth Movements Resist Industrialization.* New York University Press, 2016.

Keller, Heidi, et al. "The Bio-Culture of Parenting: Evidence from Five Cultural Communities." *Parenting,* vol. 4, no 1, 2004, pp. 25-50.

La Leche League International. "All About La Leche League." *La Leche*, 2020, www.llli.org/about/ Accessed 19 May 2022.

Lupton, Deborah. *The Quantified Self : A Sociology of Self-Tracking*. Polity Press, 2016.

Lupton, Deborah. "The Use and Value of Digital Media for Information about Pregnancy and Early Motherhood: A Focus Group Study." *BMC Pregnancy and Childbirth*, vol. 16, no 1, 2016, p. 171.

Martin, Olivier, and Eric Dagiral, editors. *L'ordinaire d'internet. Le web dans nos pratiques et relations sociales*. Armand Colin, 2016.

Mauss, Marcel. "Techniques of the Body." *Economy and Society*, vol. 2, no 1, 1973, pp. 70-88.

Nisand, Israel. "Accouchement à domicile: qu'en pensent les obstétriciens ?" *Le Figaro, Actualité Santé*, 9 Sept. 2016, sante.lefigaro.fr/actualite/2016/09/09/25376-accouchement-domicile-quen-pensent-obstetriciens. Accessed 19 May 2022.

Odent, Michel. *Le fermier et l'accoucheur*. Editions de Médicis, 2004.

Pasche Guignard, Florence. "Back Home and Back to Nature? Natural Parenting and Religion in Francophone Contexts." *Open Theology*, vol. 6, no. 1, 2020, pp. 175-201.

Pasche Guignard, Florence. "Digital Tools for Fertility Awareness: Family Planning, Religion, and Feminine Embodiment." *The Routledge Handbook to Religion, Medicine and Health*, edited by Dorothea Lüddeckens et al., Routledge, 2021, pp. 293-307.

Pasche Guignard, Florence. "Discours, représentations, pratiques et modes de transmission des savoirs et des idées sur l'allaitement dans les milieux francophones du parentage naturel." *Allaiter. Histoire(s) et cultures d'une pratique*, edited by Yasmina Foehr-Janssens and Daniela Solfaroli Camillocci. Brepols, 2022, in press.

Pasche Guignard, Florence. "High Tech Mediations, Low Tech Lifestyles: The Paradox of Natural Parenting in the Digital Age." *Religion and Media: The Global View*, edited by Stewart M. Hoover and Nabil Echchaibi, De Gruyter, 2021, p. 41-62.

Pasche Guignard, Florence. "The In/Visibility of Mothering against the Norm in Francophone Contexts: Private and Public Discourses in the Mediation of 'Natural Parenting.'" *Canadian Journal of Communication*, vol. 40, no 1, 2015, pp. 105-24.

Pasche Guignard, Florence. "Material, Maternal, Embodied, and Digital: Objects and Practices in Natural Parenting." *Digital Humanities and Material Religion: An Introduction*, edited by Emily Clark and Rachel McBride Lindsey, De Gruyter, 2022, pp. 137-158.

Pasche Guignard, Florence. "Mediated Babywearing as Aesthetic Orthodoxy." *Practical Spiritualities in a Media Age*, edited by Curtis Coats and Monica Emerich. Bloomsbury, 2015, pp. 17-34 and 210-212.

Pasche Guignard, Florence. "Nurturing the Sustainable Family: Natural Parenting and Environmentalist Foodways in Francophone Contexts." *Mothers and Food: Negotiating Foodways from Maternal Perspectives*, edited by Florence Pasche Guignard and Tanya M. Cassidy, Demeter Press, 2016, pp. 55-69.

Pierrepont, Catherine de. "La sexualité post-partum dans les fora internet. " *Civilisations : Revue internationale d'anthropologie et de sciences humaines*, vol. 59, no 1, 2010, pp. 109-27.

Redela, Pamela Morgan. "Eco-Momma: The Green Angel in the House." *Stay-at-Home Mothers. Dialogues and Debates*, edited by Elizabeth Reid Boyd and Gayle Letherby, Demeter Press, 2014, pp. 195-201.

Russell, Nancy Ukai. "Babywearing in the Age of the Internet." *Journal of Family Issues*, vol. 36, no. 9, 2015, pp. 1130-53.

Salanave, Benoît et al. "Taux d'allaitement maternel à la maternite´ et au premier mois de l'enfant. Résultats de l'étude Épifane, France, 2012." *Bulletin épidémiologique hebdomadaire*, vol. 27, 2014, pp. 450-57.

Sears, William, and Martha Sears. *The Baby Book : Everything You Need to Know about Your Baby—From Birth to Age Two*. 2nd edition. Little Brown and Company, 2003.

Takeshita, Chikako. "Eco-Diapers: The American Discourse of Sustainable Motherhood." *Mothering in the Age of Neoliberalism*, edited by Melinda Vandenbeld Giles, Demeter Press, 2014, pp. 117-31.

Wagner, Sandra et al. "Durée de l'allaitement en France selon les caractéristiques des parents et de la naissance: Résultats de l'étude longitudinale française Elfe, 2011." *Bulletin épidémiologique hebdomadaire*, vol. 29, 2015, pp. 522-32.

Wettstein, R. Harri, and Christine Bourgeois. *Sympto Therm Basic. Pour que sexe et fertilité se lient d'amitié.* SymptoTherm cop., 2006.

Wilkinson, Joann, Celia Roberts, and Maggie Mort. "Ovulation Monitoring and Reproductive Heterosex: Living the Conceptive Imperative?" *Culture, Health & Sexuality*, vol. 17, no 4, 2015, p. 454-69.

Section IV

Regulating Domestic Use and Surveillance: Who Is in Charge?

Chapter 12

Mothering/Cyberbullying/ Kids

Lisa H. Rosen and Linda J. Rubin

Charlie was enthusiastic about entering the 6th grade at Middlebury
Middle School. After the first few weeks of school, however, his peers
began verbally ridiculing him on a regular basis during lunch and
recess... His parents had given him a new smartphone at the
beginning of the school year to use in case of an emergency, but it
soon became a receptor of hurtful e-mails from many of his peers. At
first, Charlie ignored the taunting and hurtful e-mails, but the
situation became unbearable and his mother could see the obvious
distress he was experiencing.

—Hani Morgan 147

Cyberbullying is a growing concern for parents, mothers, and
children. Stories like Charlie's are becoming increasingly
common as the proliferation of computers and smartphones
enables children to inflict harm on their peers from anywhere and at
any time. We begin this chapter by defining cyberbullying, highlighting
common forms of this behaviour, and providing prevalence estimates.
Next, we discuss how cyberbullying relates to adjustment outcomes
and focus on the bully, the victim, and the parents—especially the
mothers. Although cyberbullying affects families and parents, our
research focuses on mothers in the role of emotional caregivers. We
conclude with a discussion of family-level risk and protective factors for

both cyberbullying and cybervictimization, and we pay attention to the role mothers can play in both deterring their children from cyberbullying and supporting children who are victims of cyberbullying. Throughout this chapter, we interweave quotes from mothers and children to share the lived experiences of some families as they reflect on and react to the complex and frequently painful dynamics of cyberbullying.

Although we highlight the role mothers can play in peer dynamics in this chapter, it is critical to note that parenting is just one element within a constellation of influences that extend beyond the family to include peers, teachers, as well as larger societal forces (Espelage and Swearer). Although historically mothers have often been blamed for the struggles of their children, it is important to recognize that these interrelated social factors extend well beyond the role of a mother. Mother-blaming creates a heavy and unwarranted burden for mothers in their efforts to help their children navigate the complexities of their social worlds, both online and offline (Jackson and Mannix). Moreover, children often go to great lengths to hide experiences of both cyberbullying perpetration and victimization from caregivers. We urge readers to interpret these associations between mothering and peer dynamics with caution, especially as mothers are not solely responsible for resolving digital environmental pressures and ultimately require the support of agencies and schools to help those involved in cyberbullying.

Defining Cyberbullying

The definition of cyberbullying mirrors that of traditional bullying; however, rather than occurring face to face, the aggressive conduct unfolds over digital channels. Marilyn Campbell and Shari Bauman define cyberbullying as "intentional harmful behavior carried out by a group or individuals, repeated over time, using modern digital technology to aggress against a victim who is unable to defend him/ herself" (3). As evident in the definition of cyberbullying, which parallels the definition of traditional bullying, there are three essential criteria: the behaviour is intentional, repetitive in nature, and characterized by an imbalance of power that favours the bully.

Although the key distinction between traditional and cyberbullying is the means through which the behaviour occurs, aggression via digital media differs in important ways from face-to-face bullying. Sonja Perren and colleagues note that the repetitive nature and the power imbalance inherent in bullying can take different forms through digital channels (284-85). For instance, when cyberbullies share embarrassing content online, the implications can be repetitive in nature for the victim, as the material remains available to a wide audience to access and share long after the initial upload. Similarly, for traditional bullying, the bully usually has greater physical power or social power in the form of popularity; however, in the case of cyberbullying, the bully's power may originate from other sources afforded by digital media. Cyberbullies may have the power advantage because they possess more advanced technological skills, elect to conceal their identity, and behave in a manner that makes their victims feel unable to escape. These differences between traditional and cyberbullying have led some scholars to refer to cyberbullying as an "opportunistic offense, since it results in harm without physical inter-action, requires little planning, and reduces the threat of being caught" (Tokunaga 279). Consequently, bullies may feel less inhibited as they do not have to face their victim directly and believe anonymity will enable them to avoid reprimand.

Children and their mothers often recognize that cyberbullying can be an "opportunistic offense." Adolescents are sophisticated enough to realize that perceived anonymity can drive more aggressive conduct online. In a focus group conducted by Nikita Midamba and Megan Moreno, one male adolescent recounted the following: "Yeah, there is less accountability I guess. So, it's actually weird, it makes people seem more confident. People you who [sic] would not actually say something like that would suddenly say something because they are behind the computer or behind the phone" (112). Similarly, mothers acknowledge that children exhibit less restraint in their online conduct. As is the case for adolescents, mothers recognize that cyberbullies can have a lasting effect and quickly reach a large audience as evident in the following quotes from mothers participating in a focus group conducted by Claire Monks and colleagues. In line with the argument articulated by researchers, one mother in the focus group reported: "On the Internet it [the bullying] needn't be again and again because it is still there and the impact will go on and on" (44). Mothers also pointed to the potential for cyberbullying content to be widely disseminated: "It can be very upsetting because not only do the person they're aiming it at see it but everyone on their friends list can see it" (44). Children and mothers also highlighted the omnipresence of cyberbullying. As one mother suggested, "Bullying [occurred] when they were coming into school or in the playground or at lunchtime, but now you've got them 24/7 you can ring that kid at goodness knows what time of the night or ... they turn their computer on ... and there it is" (44). Thus, children and mothers seem to recognize that although cyberbullying often overlaps with traditional forms of bullying, this type of peer harassment is unique in many ways given the ubiquity of technology and the perpetual background noise it generates.

Common Forms and Prevalence of Cyberbullying

Cyberbullying can take many different forms. Oftentimes, cyberbullying behaviours resemble relational aggression, such as online exclusion or spreading rumours. However, cyberbullying can sometimes also include threats of physical aggression levied online (Underwood and Rosen). Rebecca Dredge and colleagues interviewed adolescents who had negative experiences on social networking sites (SNS; e.g., Twitter, Facebook), and over 60 per cent indicated that they had mean messages or threats posted to their SNS and that they had received malicious emails or messages via SNS. Adolescents indicated that it was also common for cyberbullies to share humiliating images, try to tarnish victims' reputations, and exclude or ostracize others on SNS. Less commonly, cyberbullies establish a SNS page pretending to be the victim and post content deliberately intended to injure the victim emotionally.

Estimates of the prevalence of cyberbullying vary from study to study. Differences in prevalence rates may stem largely from differences in study methodology and sample characteristics (Campbell and Bauman). For instance, some researchers rely on global questions to assess whether adolescents have ever cyberbullied others or experienced cyberbullying, whereas other researchers ask about specific behaviours, which may yield higher prevalence estimates because respondents might not fully understand cyberbullying or may fail to think of certain exemplars of cyberbullying when responding to global questions. Some scholars suggest that 20 to 40 per cent of youth have been victims of cyberbullying (Tokunaga). However, a recent study by the Pew Research Center found that 59 per cent of American adolescents reported being victim to at least one form of cyberbullying (Anderson). Online name calling and rumour spreading were among the most common cyberbullying offenses. Greater time online is associated with a higher probability of experiencing cyberbullying; 45 per cent of adolescents reported that they are almost always online, and 67 per cent of these youth report cybervictimization. The survey by the Pew Research Center also asked for adolescents' perceptions of how their parents address cyberbullying. Of those surveyed, 59% of adolescents believed that their parents were doing a good job addressing cyberbullying. In contrast, only 42 per cent thought teachers were doing a good job addressing cyberbullying.

Fewer studies have examined parental perceptions of cyberbullying prevalence. The Pew Research Center also surveyed parents and found that 59 per cent worried that their adolescent would experience cyberbullying. Interestingly, the vast majority (90 per cent) of parents were confident in their ability to teach their children to be good digital citizens (Anderson). However, Francine Dehue and colleagues found that parents may inaccurately assess whether their child is involved in cyberbullying as either a perpetrator or victim. Parents tend to underestimate their children's involvement in cyberbullying, and this may reflect a lack of knowledge of the time adolescents spend online as well as their online conduct (Barlett and Fennel). It may also be reasonable to consider the possibility that parents do not want to believe that their own child would be involved in cyberbullying. Parents may also be overwhelmed with other responsibilities, particularly in a pandemic or postpandemic world. Even bystanders and educators who have knowledge of bullying often ignore incidents (Stein).

Consequences for Bullies, Victims, and Their Mothers and Families

Researchers are beginning to document that negative consequences accrue for both perpetrators and victims of cyberbullying. Those who perpetrate cyberbullying experience higher levels of internalizing problems, such as depression and anxiety. Engaging in cyberbullying is also associated with externalizing problems, such as aggression, rule breaking, and substance use (Campbell and Bauman; Nixon). Even more negative adjustment outcomes are associated with cyberbullying victimization. Some scholars postulate that cyberbullying victimization results in more severe adjustment problems than traditional forms of victimization (Huston et al.; Nixon). As adolescents are almost constantly digitally connected, cybervictimization can occur outside of school hours at any time, which may contribute to victims never feeling safe. In addition, online platforms can lead to a wide audience witnessing the bullying and allow the perpetrator to remain anonymous, which can be profoundly distressing to the victim. Victims of cyberbullying report feelings of anger, sadness, and hopelessness (Nixon). The painful effects are glaringly apparent in the statement of one adolescent victim: "It [cyberbullying] makes me hurt both physically and mentally. It scares me and takes away all my confidence. It makes me feel sick and worthless" (qtd. in Hinduja and Patchin, "Identification, Prevention, and Response" 2). Correspondingly, empirical studies overwhelmingly indicate that cybervictimization is associated with internalizing problems (e.g., depression, low self-concept, anxiety, somatic complaints) as well as externalizing problems (e.g., aggression, rule-breaking). Furthermore, experiencing cybervictimization predicts academic difficulties, school avoidance, and a myriad of other problems, including sleep difficulties (Banks et al.; Nixon).

Though not as well researched, mothers also suffer when their children are involved in cyberbullying. Suniya Luthar and Lucia Ciciolla suggest that mothers are particularly affected by their children given the centrality of the maternal role to their identities. In their thought provoking article, "Who Mothers Mommy: Factors that Contribute to Mothers' Well-Being," Luthar and Ciciolla begin by highlighting a quotation from Rich's *Of Woman Born: Motherhood as Experience and Institution*: "My children cause me the most exquisite suffering of which I have any experience. It is the suffering of ambivalence: the murderous alternation between bitter resentment and raw-edged nerves, and blissful gratification and tenderness" (1812). As children can profoundly affect their mothers, greater attention is needed to understand how mothers navigate the trials of motherhood, including the recent challenges brought on by the rapid proliferation of technology (Luthar).

Mothers of victims of cyberbullying may suffer because of their children's experiences. Luthar and Ciciolla hypothesize that for mothers "to some degree, the contagion of stress from their children is inevitable." (1814). As would follow, mothers are likely negatively affected by the pain their children endure from being victimized by their peers. Spillover of the stress from children's experiences to maternal adjustment is evident in one participant's account as reported by Midamba and Moreno:

Well we had an issue at our house where our child was text messaged a lot of negative connotations about herself and other people and the end result was she, our daughter's been trying to work through some pretty significant mental health issues, and it, um, caused her to be very sad, it regressed her depression, um, to the point a couple of times where she had expressed ideas of suicide. And it was very devastating and as a parent you feel very helpless because you have no way to connect with these people, it's just like that. And if your kid will not tell you who it is, it's hard to have a one-on-one with the other parent because, obviously, they are unaware of what their child is doing. (109)

As seen in this mother's account, parents whose children are victimized, either by traditional means or cyberbullying, experience higher levels of stress related to their parental role (Garaigordobil and Machimbarrena). Mothers worry about how bullying affects their children (Rigby), and the majority of parents report feeling ill prepared to assist their victimized children (Hannah). This sentiment is well captured by a mother participating in Tiffanie Jones's study:

Because it [cyberbulling] is so anonymous. Because it can be done so easily, and often without any repercussions, because you know.... Who do they tell? I am extremely concerned because it is so easy to do, and children aren't forthcoming and honest and they don't feel comfortable enough telling you about what is going on. It's more than likely that it can get to a point of no return before you know anything about it, and that scares the bejesus out of me! (79)

Some mothers also report coruminating with their children's social obsessions and agonizing with their children about online social exclusions and humiliations (Rose; Warner). Moreover, mothers participating in focus groups conducted by Rachel Young and Melissa Tully shared that they would need to control their own emotional reaction to their child being hurt from cyberbullying in order to best support their child. As evident in the lived experiences of the mothers presented above, not only does cyberbullying negatively affect bullies and victims, but it also adversely affects their mothers.

Deterring Children from Engaging in Cyberbullying

Parents are often referred to as gatekeepers of their children's technology access outside of school, and researchers and educators have suggested that this places additional responsibility on parents for their children's online conduct (Bauman and Campbell). Although we strive to provide comprehensive coverage regarding the role mothers can play in deterring cyberbullying, these findings should be interpreted with caution for a number of reasons. As noted previously, mothers are only part of a constellation of influences that extend beyond the family that also includes peers, teachers, as well as larger societal forces that affect children's online and offline behaviour (Espelage and Swearer). Moreover, research on maternal influences on cyberbullying is largely correlational in nature, making it difficult to establish causal relationships. Furthermore, mothers and children might share both hereditary and culturally influenced characteristics that render aggressive conduct more likely. For instance, there are temperamental risk factors for aggression, such as impulsivity, that are in part genetically based (Carrera et al.). Additionally, some factors associated with bullying may also create hardships for mothers, such as the intersection of race and class (Whittier), which shape bullying behaviours, victim reactions, and mother's responses to the bullying. Research suggests an association between lower socioeconomic status and bullying perpetration (Jansen et al.); however, it is critical to highlight that the conditions of economic hardship also affect mothering in important ways (Mistry et al.). Noting these cautions, we highlight previous research to provide a comprehensive overview of the associations between mothering and cyberbullying presented in the literature and offer tentative recommendations for mothers based on these findings.

Some parents rely on technological tools to reduce their children's likelihood of engaging in cyberbullying and other forms of delinquent activity online. Cigdem Topcu-Uzer and Ibrahim Tanrıkulu provide a detailed description of these technological tools, including a wide range of apps developed to assist parents in both cyberbullying prevention and intervention. For instance, some apps can help monitor children's text messages and social networking activities. Some have speculated that adolescents may be much more tech savvy than their parents, but others have suggested that the digital divide is decreasing and that these technological tools may help in reducing the gap (Smith).

However, many researchers suggest that the roots of cyberbullying are not simply technological in nature, as all forms of bullying are primarily relational and have long been widespread in schools (Stein). Scholars have highlighted relational and psychological issues contributing to cyberbullying perpetration (Smith). The relational view of cyberbullying is consistent with the feminist and socioecological perspectives. The feminist model examines the dynamics between gender and power in shaping bullying (Stein; Whittier). Feminist scholars often utilize the socioecological model (Gartner and Sterzing), which focuses on environmental influences that are proximal (e.g., immediate environmental contexts, including family, school, and peers) as well as distal (e.g., larger societal influences) and on how these environmental factors contribute to bullying dynamics (Espelage and Swearer; Smith). In this chapter, we focus on family-level factors and maternal influences, in particular, and understand that these additional environmental influences, cultural factors, and intersectional identities affect both children, as victims or bullies, and their mothers.

Mothers influence their children by the degree to which they are responsive, offer structure, and appropriately support their children's autonomy (Holden). These dimensions intersect in ways that differentiate parenting styles that Diana Baumrind and Judith Smetana have labelled as authoritative, authoritarian, and permissive. Authoritative parenting is characterized by high levels of responsiveness and structure—that is, authoritative parents are warm and sensitive to the needs of their children, including age-appropriate needs for autonomy while articulating expectations for mature behaviour and using firm and consistent discipline when these expectations are not met. Authoritative parenting has been shown to play a protective role, whereas as authoritarian (i.e., low level of responsiveness and high level of structure) and permissive parenting (i.e., high level of responsiveness and low level of structure) have been associated with cyberbullying (Buelga et al.; Lopez-Castro and Priegue). Translating parenting styles to the online realm, authoritative parents expect their children to display good digital citizenship, develop rules to support their children's appropriate online conduct, and explain the rationale for those rules while maintaining a warm relationship with their children. Permissive parents have a warm relationship with their children but do not enforce rules to regulate their children's online behaviour. Conversely, authoritarian parents display low warmth and value obedience to their rules for technology with limited explanation of their rationale. Although permissive and authoritarian styles predict higher levels of cyberbullying than does the authoritative style, it can be even more informative to unpack those parenting styles. Thus, we turn our attention to cohesion and communication as well as parental mediation.

Mother-child relationships characterized by warmth, support, and open communication serve a protective function against cyberbullying (Ang). Research has consistently found that maternal closeness and warmth are negatively associated with cyberbullying perpetration (Buelga et al.; Lopez-Castro and Priegue). The importance of open discussion, including conversations about cyberbullying, is highlighted in the following accounts of adolescent research participants. A sixteen-year-old male participant said, "Parents should explain to their children that online harassment is not acceptable and they should be kind to one another online and even offline"; and a thirteen-year-old female emphasized that parents should "simply talk with their children and find out the reason and care of why they did it. Explain the whole situation and help find a suitable solution" (qtd. in Cassidy et al. 6-7). Similarly, a mother in Jones's study reported the following: "We have already had to have discussions about what's appropriate to talk about and what's not. I think it is more about teaching him how to treat people" (95). Thus, children and mothers recognize the protective nature of positive communication.

Conversely, a lack of open communication within the mother-child dyad increases the risk of cyberbullying perpetration (Buelga et al.; Lopez-Castro and Priegue). Communication difficulties within the mother-child dyad can be associated with perceived lack of maternal support, as reflected in the sentiment of a fourteen-year-old female who suggested that parents could decrease the likelihood of cyberbullying "by being caring, loving parents and not forget[ting] about their kids" (Cassidy et al. 7). Recently, researchers have suggested that parents may convey a lack of caring by seeming preoccupied by their own technology when they are interacting with their children. The term "technoference" refers to this type of disruption due to preoccupation with technology, and research suggests that it negatively affects communication. Children may feel ignored, and technoference is negatively associated with perceptions of parental warmth, which in turn predicts cyberbullying perpetration.

In addition to warmth and open communication, parental monitoring of a child's online world can deter cyberbullying perpetration. Parental monitoring—defined as "a set of correlated parenting behaviors involving attention to and tracking of the child's whereabouts, activities, and adaptations" (Dishion and McMahon 61)—has long been studied as a protective factor against delinquent behaviour. Parents who know more about their children's conduct, both offline and online, have children who engage in less antisocial conduct, including cyberbullying (Ang). Interestingly, both children and parents note the importance of monitoring online activities, as seen by a fourteen-year-old male, who recommends that parents "should pay attention to what their children do online and ... should also encourage good behavior" and a fifteen-year-old female, who advocates that parents be able "to access some of the ongoings of social networking of their children" and to have a "computer in the living room where parents could watch over" their children's activities (qtd. in Cassidy et al. 7). Mothers often recognized the need to monitor in a tech savvy fashion, as one noted: "I do have it set up where they can't delete the history, and they can't alter anything to hide what they have done from me" (qtd. in Jones 120). These are examples of "parental mediation," which is the term used to describe the monitoring of children's online activities.

Parental mediation takes different forms, including restrictive mediation and instructive mediation (Buelga et al.; Katz et al.; Wright). Restrictive mediation refers to imposing rules for online conduct, such as regulations for time spent online and the type of content to access. A fifteen-year-old female research participant provides an example of restrictive mediation by recommending that parents set consequences: "If their children cyberbully, the cellphone is taken away or their FB [Facebook] account deleted" (qtd. in Cassidy et al. 7). Instructive mediation, in contrast, refers to guiding children's use of the internet by discussing risk and children's online activities. Instructive mediation was illustrated by a mother who shared as follows: "Just about three weeks ago she set up her Facebook account and I told her, Don't be negative towards others. If you are not going to say anything positive don't say anything. Don't give information about yourself too much if someone is asking. If you don't know the person, come ask me" (qtd. in Jones 111). Both restrictive and instructive mediation are associated with lower levels of cyberbullying; however, for older adolescents who crave autonomy, instructive mediation may be more effective (Ang).

Scholars have offered numerous recommendations for deterring children from engaging in cyberbullying (Bauman and Campbell; Demaray and Brown; Robinson; Yoon et al.). At the most basic level, mothers as well as fathers should strive to foster positive relationships with their children, as this is associated with higher levels of communication and lower levels of cyberbullying. Furthermore, it is critical to have rules about online conduct and monitor children's online activities. Along these lines, parents should clearly communicate that cyberbullying is unacceptable and explain that the children are accountable for their own actions online and offline. Children who believe their parents view cyberbullying as a serious and punishable offense are less likely to engage in this behaviour (Hindjua and Patchin, "Social Influences"). Frequent discussion about the online world would include empathy-building conversations intended to acknowledge the presence of cyberbullying and to focus on how cyberbullying negatively and profoundly affects victims, modelling appropriate online conduct, and reinforcing prosocial online behaviours (Klein). Resources to guide these discussions can be found free of cost and online through nonprofit organizations and research partnerships, including Stomp Out Bullying, Cyberbullying Research Center, and PREVNet, as well in many books addressing cyberbullying from a parental perspective. These discussions can decrease the likelihood children will engage in cyberbullying. In the event that children do cyberbully, consulting with teachers and counsellors can help to ensure consistency between home and school settings, which can help create a united front against cyberbullying (Robinson). To thrive, both perpetrators and victims of cyberbullying will need to be guided by parents, educators, peers, witnesses, and bystanders who support and value good relationships with others, create a sense of belonging, and encourage the development of interpersonal skills and competencies with the purpose of creating emotional resilience (Stein; Warner).

Supporting Victims of Cyberbullying

Just as mothers can take steps to deter cyberbullying perpetration, they can also help to support their children should they become victims. As is the case for cyberbullying, high quality parent-child relationships have been associated with lower levels of cyberbullying victimization (Bradbury et al.; Larrañaga et al.). In the event that youth are cyberbullied, maternal support can attenuate the association between victimization and maladjustment (Perren).

As children begin to recognize their own and others' intersectional identities, the risk of cyberbullying increases for those who do not conform to societal norms, such as the longstanding binary view of gendered behaviour. Some gender-conforming children who hold perceived power will cyberbully their gender-nonconforming peers. Cyberbullying victimization is often viewed as a fact of life by children with less perceived power and is often at its worst for children with LGBTQ+ identities (Stein). Mothers can function as a critical form of support for these youth (Yoon et al.)

Different forms of parent-child communication have also been associated with cybervictimization (Larrañaga). Children who experience severe levels of cybervictimization reported lower levels of open communication with their parents. Conversely, severe cyber-victimization was associated with greater levels of offensive and avoidant communication within parent-child dyads. Families with open communication may be more likely to discuss all forms of risk that affect children, including technology-related risks, such as cyberbullying victimization.

Monitoring can serve a protective function against cyberbullying victimization as well as against perpetration (Buelga). Restrictive mediation as well as instructive mediation may reduce the risk that youth will experience cyberbullying online. Parents learn about their children's online activities through active monitoring as well as discussions in which children disclose information about their online world. Research is beginning to address a new form of parental mediation in which parents connect with (e.g., "friend") their children via SNS (Mesch). Through SNS connections, parents can stay aware of what their adolescents are sharing online as well as how others are treating them. Those who are friends with their parents on SNS are less likely to experience cyberbullying; however, additional research is necessary to determine the mechanism underlying this association.

Mothers are only able to support their victimized youth and help them cope if they are aware of the cyberbullying. However, parents do not always know their children have been victimized, as one mother suggests: "The parent isn't seeing the kid with the torn blazer and the bloody nose or anything" (Monks et al. 44). Compounding the challenge of learning about children's online environment is that less than 10 per cent of victims report experiencing cyberbullying to their parents (Tokunaga). Although parents want their children to come to them with cyberbullying concerns, youth prefer to seek support from friends (Waidan). Adolescents desire autonomy and may worry they would be perceived as less mature if they turn to a parent for assistance, as reflected in the report of one research participant: "I don't know if I would [tell my parents] because it's my problem" (qtd. in Young and Tully 867). In addition, youth may be reluctant to turn to parents, as they see them as technologically inferior, as one youth exclaimed: "Mom, you do not understand. Like, you do not even know how to use a phone" (qtd. in Midamaba and Moreno 112). Perhaps, the biggest deterrent to reporting cyberbullying is fear that parents will seize technology, and access to technology is so desperately craved (Tokunaga).

When mothers are aware of cyberbullying, they can assist their children in coping with this form of peer maltreatment. Unfortunately, little is known about how youth can optimally cope with cyberbullying (Perren), which makes it challenging and stressful for mothers to support children who are subject to cyberbullying. Confronting the bully is not a recommended strategy, as this action increases the risk of retaliation. Avoidant coping is likely one of the most common strategies, as many youth report that they ignore cyberbullying (Perren). In terms of efficacy, technological solutions, such as blocking the perpetrator, can successfully reduce contact with cyberbullies. Research-based recommendations have been offered for supporting youth who have experienced cyberbullying. As was the case for cyberbullying, resources to guide discussions with victims of cyberbullying are available. Encouraging open discussions about online conduct can enable parents to provide support when children experience victimization. Parents can encourage these conversations by letting children know that they will respond calmly if cyberbullying occurs rather than behaving in a way that exacerbates the situation or strips adolescents of their technology (Morgan). In these discussions, it is critical to convey that the victim is not at fault (Robinson) and to offer empathy and compassion for their distressing experience (Klein). Parents can assist youth by helping them identify resources at school as well as connecting with prosocial peers (Morgan; Robinson). From a legal standpoint, parents can work with victims to document evidence of cyberbullying to share with school officials and potentially law enforcement (Roberto et al.).

Conclusion

As seen throughout this chapter, cyberbullying adversely affects bullies, victims, and their mothers. Through feminist and socio-ecological views of bullying, a wide range of environmental influences and intersectional identities come into play (Espelage and Swearer; Stein). For cyberbullying, family factors may be more influential compared with traditional forms of bullying, given that cyberbullying behaviours often unfold at home. Mothers, usually the primary caregivers, may be particularly affected by their children's experiences of cyberbullying.

Future research is needed to better understand the role of mothers in children's online peer experiences and how mothers are affected by their children's difficulties with peers. As previously noted, a great deal of the research in this area has been correlational in nature and fails to capture the complex system of environmental influences that affect children and their mothers. Additional work is necessary to understand how these multiple forces influence how mothers and children discuss cyberbullying. Previous work is also limited by a lack of discussion of intersectionality. Some of the researchers cited do not address race, ethnicity, or other relevant cultural and environmental factors. Other researchers have noted that because participants were primarily white, it was not feasible to examine race or ethnicity (Jones; Midamba and Moreno; Monks et al.). Future work should consider how intersecting identities—including age, race/ethnicity, gender, sexuality, socioeconomic class, religion, and geographic location—influence both children's and mothers' experiences online. Perhaps, most urgently, research identifying how mothers may best contribute to cyberbullying prevention and intervention is needed. School and community programs focused on children's online conduct would benefit from examining how to best harness the power of mothers in the fight against cyberbullying.

Acknowledgment

This work was supported by a grant from the Eunice Kennedy Schriver National Institute of Child Health and Human Development: R15HD098561.

Works Cited

Anderson, Monica. "A Majority of Teens have Experienced Some Form of Cyberbullying." *Pew Research Center,* www.pewresearch. org internet/2018/09/27/a-majority-of-teens-have-experienced -some-form-of-cyberbullying/. Accessed 20 May 2022.

Ang, Rebecca P. "Adolescent Cyberbullying: A Review of Characteristics, Prevention and Intervention Strategies." *Aggression and Violent Behavior* vol. 25, 2015, pp. 35-42.

Banks, Ashley et al. "Experiences of Cyberbullying and Phone Use after Dark: Effects on Adolescent Health." Poster presented at the annual meeting of Southwestern Psychological Association, 2015.

Barlett, Christopher P., and Miranda Fennel. "Examining the Relation between Parental Ignorance and Youths' Cyberbullying Perpetration." *Psychology of Popular Media Culture,* vol. 7, 2018, pp. 547-60.

Bauman, Shari, and Marilyn Campbell. "Summary." *Reducing Cyberbullying in Schools,* edited by Campbell, Marilyn and Shari Bauman, Academic Press, 2018, pp. 273-82.

Baumrind, Diana, and Judith Smetana. "Patterns of Parental Authority and Adolescent Autonomy." *New Directions for Child and Adolescent Development,* vol. 108, pp. 61-69.

Bradbury, Stacey, L. Dubow, and Eric Domoff. "How Do Adolescents Learn Cyber-Victimization Coping Skills? An Examination of Parent and Peer Coping Socialization." *Journal of Youth and Adolescence,* vol. 47, no. 9, 2018, pp. 1866-879.

Buelga, Sofia, Belen Martínez-Ferrer, and Gonzalo Musitu. "Family Relationships and Cyberbullying." *Cyberbullying across the Globe: Gender, Family, and Mental Health,* edited by R. Navarro, S. Yubero, and E. Larrañaga, Springer, 2016, pp. 99-114.

Campbell, Marilyn, and Shari Bauman. "Cyberbullying: Definition, Consequences, and Prevalence." *Reducing Cyberbullying in Schools,* edited by Campbell, Marilyn and Shari Bauman, Academic Press, 2018, pp. 3-16.

Carrera, Maria, Renee DePalma, and Maria Lameiras. "Toward a More Comprehensive Understanding of Bullying in School Settings." *Educational Psychology Review,* vol. 23, 2011, pp. 479-99.

Cassidy, Wanda, Chantal Faucher, and Margaret Jackson. "What Parents Can Do to Prevent Cyberbullying: Students' and Educators' Perspectives." *Social Sciences,* vol. 7, no.12, 2018, pp. 1-12.

Cyberbullying Research Center. *Cyberbully,* 2021, cyberbullying.org/resources/parents. Accessed 20 May 2022.

Dehue, Francine et al. "Cyberbullying: Youngsters' Experiences and Parental Perception." *Cyberpsychology & Behavior,* vol. 11, no. 2, 2008, pp. 217-23.

Demaray, Michelle K., and Christina F. Brown. "Prevent Cyberbullying: Suggestions for Parents." *Communiqué,* vol. 38, no. 4, 2009, pp. 1-12.

Dishion, Thomas, and J. McMahon. "Parental Monitoring and the Prevention of Child and Adolescent Problem Behavior: A Conceptual and Empirical Formulation." *Clinical Child and Family Psychology Review,* vol. 1, no. 1, 1998, pp. 61-75.

Dredge, Rebecca, et al. "Cyberbullying in Social Networking Sites: An Adolescent Victim's Perspective." *Computers in Human Behavior,* vol. 36, 2014, pp. 13-20.

Espelage, Dorothy, and Susan Swearer. "A Social-Ecological Model for

Bullying Prevention and Intervention: Understanding the Impact of Adult Communities Children Live." *The Handbook of Bullying in Schools: An International Perspective*, edited by S. R. Jimerson, et al, Routledge, 2010, pp. 61-71.

Garaigordobil, Maite, and Juan Machimbarrena. "Stress, Competence, and Parental Educational Styles in Victims and Aggressors of Bullying and Cyberbullying." *Psicothema*, vol. 29, no. 3, 2017, pp. 335-40.

Gartner, Rachel E, and Paul Sterzing. "Social Ecological Correlates of Family-Level Interpersonal and Environmental Microaggressions toward Sexual and Gender Minority Adolescents." *Journal of Family Violence*, vol. 33, 2018, pp. 1-16.

Hannah, Margaret. "Cyberbullying Education for Parents: A Guide for Clinicians." *Journal of Social Sciences*, vol. 6, no. 4, 2010, pp. 532-36.

Hinduja, Sameer, and Justin Patchin. "Cyberbullying Fact Sheet: Identification, Prevention, and Response." *Cyberbullying Research Center*, cyberbullying.org/Cyberbullying-Identification-Prevention -Response-2020.pdf. Accessed 20 May 2022.

Hinduja, Sameer, and Justin Patchin. "Social Influences on Cyberbullying Behaviors Among Middle and High School Students." *Journal of Youth and Adolescence,* vol. 42, 2013, pp. 711-22.

Holden, George et al. "Families, parenting, and discipline." *Social Development*, edited by Marion Underwood and Lisa Rosen, Guilford, 2011, pp. 127-152.

Hutson, Elizabeth et al. "Systematic Review of Cyberbullying Interventions for Youth and Parents with Implications for Evidence Based Practice." *Worldviews on Evidence Based Nursing*, vol. 15, no.1, 2018, pp. 72-79.

Jackson, Debra, and Judy Mannix. "Giving Voice to the Burden of Blame: A Feminist Study of Mothers' Experiences of Mother Blaming. *International Journal of Nursing Practice*, vol. 10, 2004, pp. 150-58.

Jansen, Pauline W, et al. "Prevalence of Bullying and Victimization among Children in Early Elementary School: Do Family and

School Neighbourhood Socioeconomic Status Matter?" *BMC Public Health*, vol. 12, no. 1, 2012, p. 1-10.

Jones, Tiffanie. *Adult Perceptions of Cyberbullying and Implications for Parental Education*. ProQuest Dissertations, 2014.

Katz, Idit, et al. "When Parents Are Inconsistent: Parenting Style and Adolescents' Involvement in Cyberbullying." *Journal of Adolescence*, vol. 74, 2019, pp. 1-12.

Klein, Jessie. *The Bully Society: School Shootings and the Crisis of Bullying in America's School*. New York University Press, 2012.

Larrañaga, Elisa, et al. "Loneliness, Parent-Child Communication and Cyberbullying Victimization among Spanish Youths." *Computers in Human Behavior*, vol. 65, 2016, pp. 1-8.

López-Castro, Leticia, and Diana Priegue. "Influence of Family Variables on Cyberbullying Perpetration and Victimization: A Systematic Literature Review." *Social Sciences*, vol. 8, no. 3, 2019, pp. 1-25.

Luthar, Suniya S. "Mothering Mothers." *Research in Human Development*, vol. 12, no. 3-4 2015, pp. 295-303.

Luthar, Suniya S., and Lucia Ciciolla. "Who Mothers Mommy? Factors That Contribute to Mothers' Well-Being." *Developmental Psychology*, vol. 51, no.12, 2015, pp. 1812-823.

Mesch, Gustavo S. "Parent-Child Connections on Social Networking Sites and Cyberbullying." *Youth & Society*, vol. 50, no. 8, 2018, pp. 1145-162.

Midamba, Nikita, and Megan Moreno. "Differences in Parent and Adolescent Views on Cyberbullying." *Journal of Adolescent Health*, vol. 60, no. 2, 2017, pp. 106-15.

Mistry, Rashmita S, et al. "Economic Well-Being and Children's Social Adjustment: The Role of Family Process in an Ethnically Diverse Low-Income Sample." *Child Development*, vol. 73, no. 3, 2002, pp. 935-51.

Monks, Claire, et al. "The Emergence of Cyberbullying in Childhood: Parent and Teacher Perspectives." *Psicología Educativa*, vol. 22, no.1, 2016, pp. 39-48.

Morgan, Hani. "Malicious Use of Technology: What Schools, Parents, and Teachers Can Do to Prevent Cyberbullying." *Childhood*

Education, vol. 89, no. 3, 2013, pp. 146-51.

Nixon, Charisse. "Current Perspectives: The Impact of Cyberbullying on Adolescent Health." *Adolescent Health, Medicine and Therapeutics*, vol. 5, 2014, pp. 143-58.

Perren, Sonja et al. "Tackling Cyberbullying: Review of Empirical Evidence Regarding Successful Responses by Students, Parents, and Schools." *International Journal of Conflict and Violence*, vol. 6, no. 2, 2012, pp. 283-93.

"Promoting Relationships and Eliminating Violence Network." *Prevnet*, www.prevnet.ca/resources/cyber-tool. Accessed 20 May 2022.

Rigby, Ken. "Bullying in Schools and Its Relation to Parenting and Family Life." *Family Matters*, vol. 92, no. 93, 2013, pp. 61-67.

Roberto, Anthony et al. "The Short-Term Effects of a Cyberbullying Prevention Intervention for Parents of Middle School Students." *International Journal of Environmental Research and Public Health*, vol. 14, 2017, pp. 1-8.

Robinson, Kathy. "Bullies and Victims: Primer for Parents." *Communiqué*, vol. 41, 2012, p. 25.

Rose A.J. "Co-Rumination in the Friendships of Girls and Boys." *Child Development*, vol. 73, no. 6, 2002, pp. 1830-43.

Smith, Peter. "Cyberbullying: Definition, Consequences, and Prevalence." *Reducing Cyberbullying in Schools*, edited by Marilyn Campbell and Shari Bauman, Academic Press, 2018, pp. 257-68.

Stockdale, Laura, et al. "Parent and Child Technoference and Socioemotional Behavioral Outcomes: A Nationally Representative Study of 10- to 20-year-Old Adolescents." *Computers in Human Behavior*, vol. 88, 2018, pp. 219-26.

Stein, Nan. "Locating a Secret Problem: Sexual Violence in Elementary and Secondary Schools." *Gender Violence: Interdisciplinary Perspectives*, edited by Laura O'Toole, Jessica Schiffman, and Rosemary Sullivan, New York University Press, 2020, pp. 314-324.

"Stomp Out Bullying." *Stomp Out Bullying Stop the Hate Culture*, 2021, www.stompoutbullying.org/parents-page. Accessed 20 May 2022.

Tokunaga, Robert S. "Following You Home from School: A Critical Review and Synthesis of Research on Cyberbullying Victimization." *Computers in Human Behavior,* vol. 26, no. 3, 2010, pp. 277-87.

Topcu-Uzer, Cigdem, and Ibrahim Tanrıkulu. "Technological Solutions for Cyberbullying Summary." *Reducing Cyberbullying in Schools,* edited by Marilyn Campbell and Shari Bauman, Academic Press, 2018, pp. 33-48.

Underwood, Marion, and Lisa Rosen. "Gender and Bullying: Moving Beyond Mean Differences to Consider Conceptions of Bullying, Processes by which Bullying Unfolds, and Cyber Bullying." *Bullying in American Schools: An Update,* edited by Dorothy Espelage and Susan Swearer, Lawrence Erlbaum, 2011, pp. 13-22.

Yoon, Jina et al. "Role of Adults in Prevention and Intervention of Per Victimization." *Bullies, Victims, and Bystanders: Understanding Child and Adult Participant Vantage Points,* edited by Lisa H. Rosen, Shannon R. Scott, and Samuel Y. Kim, Palgrave Macmillan, 2020, pp. 179-212.

Wadian, Taylor W., et al. "Cyberbullying: Adolescents' Experiences, Responses, and Their Beliefs about Their Parents' Recommended Responses." *Journal of Educational and Developmental Psychology,* vol. 6, no. 2, 2016, pp. 47-52.

Warner, Judith. *And Then They Stopped Talking to Me: Making Sense of Middle School.* Crown, 2020.

Whittier, Nancy. "Where Are the Children?" *Gender Violence: Interdisciplinary Perspectives,* edited by Laura O'Toole, Jessica Schiffman, and Rosemary Sullivan, New York University Press, 2020, pp. 325-34.

Wright, Michelle. "Parental Mediation, Cyberbullying, and Cyber-trolling: The Role of Gender." *Computers in Human Behavior,* vol. 71, 2017, pp. 189-95.

Young, Rachel, and Melissa Tully. "'Nobody Wants the Parents Involved': Social Norms in Parent and Adolescent Responses to Cyberbullying." *Journal of Youth Studies,* vol. 22, no. 6, 2019, pp. 856-72.

Chapter 13

"No Forwards Please": Indian Mothers on School WhatsApp Groups

Sucharita Sarkar

The explosion of digital social media in twenty-first-century India has affected digitally enabled mothers in multiple and diverse ways. The most popular app used by Indian mothers is WhatsApp, as attested by a recent survey on the digital usage of Indian mothers (Gupta). Compared to other social network sites, such as Facebook or Instagram, WhatsApp has a distinctly different purpose and use among Indian mothers. Many urban Indian mothers form or join WhatsApp groups with mothers of other children studying in the same class as their own children at school. These groups are formed when the school term begins and continue for the duration of the school year. Such groups share information about daily schoolwork-related matters and allow mothers to supervise their children's education on a platform that affords unlimited, free, and instant multimedia messaging. WhatsApp groups "provide the sense of an open conversation, as if one was actually talking to a person" (Willemse and Bozalek 6), and this easy conversationality makes it a convenient tool for mothers to use.

WhatsApp Groups Reinforce Neoliberal Motherhood

This chapter analyzes WhatsApp communication practices among Indian mothers not only as a resource for practical, need-based connection, but also as a site where both agentic mothering and/or heteropatriarchal, neoliberal motherhood may be performed. In the Indian context, the persistence of traditional patriarchal value systems superimposed with the socioconomic changes wrought by neo-liberalism and globalization (which were ushered in when the Indian government opted for the New Economic Policy in 1991) have ensured that "the roles of mother and father continue to be constructed as primary care-giver and primary provider"; that "the triple burden of childcare, housework and paid labour falls almost entirely on women and mothers"; and that women's incomes are usually "designated as a 'side income' so that the balance of power between men and women remains undisturbed" (Aneja and Vaidya 136). Paradoxically, however, Indian mothers (including those I interviewed)—although they are aware of continuing gender inequities—often uncritically perceive neoliberalism as a liberating, modernizing influence that has increased their autonomy because it provides increasing opportunities for paid work outside the home and for more agency within the home as compared to their mothers' or grandmothers' generations. I critique this notion of neoliberal, internet-enabled motherhood as agentic by unpacking the underlying discriminations and coercions that control the actions of Indian mothers, specifically focusing on their action of engaging in school WhatsApp groups. Although maternal use of WhatsApp technology is an underresearched area, this chapter can broadly be contextualized against other feminist research on "everyday entanglements of digital media and women's work," which shows the "myriad ways mothers come to absorb the punishing tides of advanced neoliberalism at the level of eveyday life" (Wilson and Yochim 2).

The observations that I make in this chapter are based on interviews with mothers who are participants in my fourteen-year old daughter's school WhatsApp group as well as on autoethnographic reflections from my participation in these groups. As my daughter studies in a private school where English is the medium of instruction, the mothers I interviewed belong to socioeconomically privileged identity intersections. Hence, my study does not include mothers who belong to poorer social locations, although they also use WhatsApp for various personal, professional, and maternal purposes. Although English-medium education in India dates back to the centuries of British colonization, the accelerated aspirational capital of English is one of the "consequences of neoliberal reform": "That the mention of globalisation indexes a concern with English should not come as a surprise" (LaDousa 15-17). I have separately interviewed ten mothers from my daughter's school group of thirty-three to understand their engagements with school WhatsApp groups, and I have used only the initials of their names to ensure confidentiality. All these mothers (including myself) belong to middle/upper-middle class, heteropatriarchal families in the urban location of Mumbai, India. Four mothers work outside the home in full- or part-time jobs, whereas six are stay-at-home mothers. However, English language competencies and communication skills are not homogenous, and this unevenness is one of the areas of discomfort for some mothers in the group (this is discussed later in the chapter).

A look at the memberships of most school WhatsApp groups reveal the lopsided gender composition of these groups. It is rare to find fathers opting to join such groups (Attari). In my daughter's school WhatsApp group of over a hundred members, there is only one father (who is mostly silent in the group chat), and he has been added by the group administrator as a special request because his wife works in a job that entails frequent travelling outside Mumbai. The marked absence of fathers has prompted this comment from social media observer Karishma Attari: "Have schools used technology to target mothers specifically? In principle, either parent can download the app, or check on the website. Yet, curiously, in a decade of parenting, I have yet to see a father post a query on the WhatsApp chat group." This observation is aligned to the school WhatsApp group that I study in this chapter, which has only one father who has never interacted in the group to date. The marginal presence and nonparticipation of fathers in school WhatsApp groups indicate how mothers are socioculturally expected to be primary caregivers for their children. This caregiving role, which originates in (and is historically justified by) the biological functions of pregnancy and breastfeeding, extends beyond infancy to encompass maternal supervision of school-going children's education. Ideal neoliberal mothers are expected to perform intensive mothering to produce performance-driven children and manage optimally functioning families (Giles 10). Attari's comment on schools specifically targeting mothers indicates the coercive impetus of maternal participation of school WhatsApp groups. Whereas participation in other social media, like Instagram, is optional, mothers are compulsorily expected—and often explicitly instructed—to join school WhatsApp groups. All the mothers I interviewed said that they had not even considered the possibility of not joining these groups. Thus, although these groups are perceived to be freely chosen information streams by the intervieewes and by other mothers I interact with, the functioning of such groups actually demean maternal choice and enforce the continuance of gender inequities even in modern, internet-enabled educational systems and interfaces. Even though most of the interviewees claim that information sharing on WhatsApp groups benefits their agentic mothering, this chapter will analyze these claims and explore how their participation also reproduces neoliberal patriarchal mothering roles.

Only two of the interviewees—both working in full-time jobs outside the home—expressed that they wished their spouses had joined instead of them or, at least, along with them. Both mothers, however, admitted that they had not discussed this as a viable option with their spouses, and neither did they expect that their spouses would have agreed to be a member unless they themselves were unavailable. AI, who is a highly-paid chartered accountant in a financial institution, said: "I didn't want to bring this up with my husband because I felt he would think I am too lazy. Other mothers who have full-time jobs are doing this. Even I'm managing quite well now. And he does help out when he can with the kids, driving them to classes and going out to buy school supplies and stuff." BD, who works in a senior managerial position in a bank, said: "My husband and I have the similarly time-consuming jobs. But he would never agree to join this group as long as I am here. I think it's fine, really, because almost all the other members are mothers, and he would [have] been awkward interacting with them anyway." When I reminded her that one father is also a member, BD responded: "That's only because his wife is not there in Mumbai for so much time. I am sure he would not have done so if she was here, like us."

Despite their awareness of the asymmetric gendering of parenting responsibilities, AI and BD seem to have accepted their culturally mandated roles of primary caregiver of their school-going children. It needs to be emphasized here that increasingly in urban India, the rigid convention of women bearing the entire responsibility of childrearing work is gradually changing and becoming more flexible. However, feminist scholars note that flexible gender roles within the home are often needs based rather than rights based. In urban India, multigenerational or joint families—where grandmothers and other female relations shared carework—are being replaced by nuclear families. Hence, when the mother is working outside the nuclear household, the father is forced to take up some domestic and caregiving responsibilities because there is nobody else to do so: "Clearly, norm-breaking is allowed if it is understood to be contingent.... A working-class woman's husband might assist with cooking if she has to leave early for work, but not if she is at home, resting or taking her day off" (Geetha 72). The mothers I interviewed regard their work as members of school WhatsApp groups as a part of their socially mandated motherhood responsibilities, which could, or should, only be shared by the father in exceptional situations, for instance in the case of the mother who travels frequently. Apart from such socially allowed norm breaking, they did not consider any other kind of nonnormative mothering choices (such as asking their spouses to share the work of WhatsApp school group membership). AI's fear of being labelled a lazy mother is a symptomatic reaction to the culture of blaming and shaming bad mothers—a culture that is the corollary of the ideology of good motherhood which the mothers I interviewed seemed to be socialized into.

WhatsApp Groups as Maternal Support

To the interviewees, these groups were not sites of maternal coercion (like Attari feels) but of maternal support. To understand the significance of WhatsApp as an instrument of maternal support, it is perhaps insufficient to categorize the mothers I interviewed as docile mothers obediently performing the patriarchal ideology of good motherhood. For a more nuanced understanding of mothers' perception of their work in school WhatsApp groups, I deploy Sara Ruddick's concept of maternal thinking and practice. Ruddick states as followes: "Maternal practice begins in a response to the reality of a biological child in a particular social world. To be a 'mother' is to take upon oneself the responsibility of child care, making its work a regular and substantial part of one's working life" (17). The mothers I interviewed all agreed that sending, reading, responding to, and acting upon the messages in the school WhatsApp group had become "regular and substantial part" of their lives, and they emphasized that this new social media gave them more control and agency over their children's education, which was their responsibility to supervise. In practical terms, mothering work for the members of the group—all of whom have children who belong to the age group of between five and twenty—includes completing carework for family members (which includes cooking and provisioning), supervising their children's education (liaising with the school, picking up and dropping off children to school and coaching classes, supplying everything that the children need for school), and also doing domestic work at home (cleaning and housekeeping).

All the mothers have paid household help, and four have paid drivers to assist them. Eight of the mothers live in nuclear families, but their parents or parents-in-law come to stay with them for extended periods when they also help in the work at home. The other two mothers have their parents or parents-in-law living permanently with them, but in both cases, they are ill and need special caregiving. Despite the paid and parental and/or spousal help, the primary responsibility and the supervisory duty of this work is that of the mother. She needs to organize the material and nurturant aspects of the family and synchronize and manage her own and her family's often divergent time schedules. Even if she works outside the home, the work at home remains mostly the same, although she may have more paid help or may have her spouse sharing some domestic chores. The supervisory responsibility—and accompanying stress—is still retained by the mother. School WhatsApp groups is an important part of the support system that gives mothers more time and agency to manage their maternal work.

RP is a stay-at-home mother with two children. She told me that when her older son was in school, there were no WhatsApp school groups, unlike her younger daughter's case:

I am so glad that things have changed now. Earlier, with my son, I had to call up other mothers if he missed a day in school, or we had to go over to his friend's place to catch up with whatever was taught that day. But with my daughter, if she is ill or absent for a day, I don't have to worry too much. I just have to ask in the group, and someone posts all the school work done.

RP points out an important utilitarian benefit of school WhatsApp groups: Since mothers are expected to supervise their children's education, it is necessary for them to update themselves regularly about their children's classwork and homework assignments. In case of the child's absence from school, which is often due to illness, the mother needs not only to care for the sick child but also to track the work that they might have missed at school. RP provides a comparative perspective, which reveals the benefits of belonging to school WhatsApp groups in such stressful situations, as compared to pre-WhatsApp times. Connecting with other mothers via WhatsApp is much more convenient than calling or visiting and allows connected mothers to perform their maternal responsibilities with more ease and less anxiety. Ruddick theorizes that maternal work is constituted of three demands—"preservation, growth, and social acceptability"—and that "to be a mother is to be committed to meeting these demands by works of preservative love, nurturance, and training" (17). RP's testimony underlines how school WhatsApp groups facilitate maternal work performed at the critical interjunction of nurturance (i.e., caring for the ill child) and training (i.e., educating the child).

All of the mothers I spoke with admitted that the school WhatsApp group has significantly improved the ease and speed of their maternal work. Mothers who work outside the home repeatedly emphasized the usefulness of the app, especially in their daily struggle to manage professional and maternal work. Both AI and BD, who spend more than eight hours per day at their workplace, acknowledged how the school WhatsApp group helped them to be aware in real time about what is going on at school on any given day. As AI said: "Sometimes during the rainy season if the school closes early, I get to know immediately from the WhatsApp group. I call my maid to go to the school to pick up my daughter and son. Saves me a lot of worry when I am at work." BD also mentioned: "It helps me a lot that I get to know of any school homework or project before I get home from my office. This way, on my way home, I can buy any stationery or other material my children may need for school. I do not have to go out again. I just hate doing that when I am back home tired." For "working mothers" like AI and BD, the school WhatsApp group offers tangible, time-saving benefits that enable them to manage their time schedules and mothering work better and to reduce stress.[1]

Even mothers who are not employed in paid work appreciate the enhanced comfort and connectivity afforded by the school WhatsApp group. PB, a mother whose son participates in competitive sporting events that require him to miss school sometimes for long hours of sports training, said: "I wouldn't be able to manage without WhatsApp. I rush from school to my son's training from morning till late evening. When he is absent from school because of tournaments, I get all the help I need from the group so that he can keep up with his schoolwork." PB's situation—the soccer mom who spends considerable time every day driving her son from school to practice to home—is common in urban nuclear families. For such mothers, the school WhatsApp groups form an instant, reliable support system that enables them to perform their time-consuming and exhausting maternal responsibilities efficiently.

Another mother, PV, who works as contractual teacher in a college —and goes to her workplace three days a week—adds a further advantage:

> For group projects and group activities, WhatsApp is a godsend. We mothers can coordinate so much more easily through our group chats. Sometimes, one of us goes to the shops to buy items for projects or rent costumes for stage performances for the other members' children also. I have myself done this for other mothers on my free days. And they have helped me out when I am busy at work.

PV's statement indicates how online connections in school WhatsApp groups extend into offline cooperation when required. Other mothers also corroborate PV's claim. PA, who works long hours outside the home, said:

> I always check updates when I'm in office to find out if my son needs anything specific to take to school the next day. If it is not there at home, and if I know I will be coming back late, I post a message in the group asking some mom to help me out and get those things [required at school] for me. Someone always volunteers, and I just send money through my son the next day to pay them back. A few weeks back, the school wanted the kids to bring two oranges the next day for distributing during an orphanage visit. I had no oranges at home, and the shops close

down before I leave office. So, I asked in the group for help, and so many moms sent extra oranges next day for A [her son] to take!

Like PV, PA also extends the connections forged by the group into offline spaces to help her in juggling professional and maternal work. Schools often have strict rules about students coming prepared to school with materials for assignments and projects. If the child forgets or fails to do so, then they are reprimanded in class: In some cases, the parents (usually the mother) are contacted and reminded not to let such lapses recur. Repeated lapses often result in punishment for the child and also in shaming the mother for failing in her responsibilities. Before WhatsApp, mothers had to depend on the child to remember all the instructions received at school, and children's memory and attention in class would sometimes be unreliable. With school WhatsApp groups, mothers have a second line of information for school activities and do not have to depend upon their often-unreliable children. As PA admitted: "You know how fidgety A [her son] is in class! He hardly sits still and never fully writes down what the teacher says. I always check the group updates or ask other mothers what has been done, so that A doesn't give me a headache even if he forgets."

The testimonies of the mothers reveal the dependability of the school WhatsApp group as a source of maternal support. Mothers working outside the home can negotiate their busy schedules with less stress because of this dependable support network. Mothers who stay at home volunteer to provide not only information but also offline help if required. In cases of group activities, both stay-at-home mothers and working-outside-home mothers collaborate together according to their schedules and capacities to ensure their children's academic and extra-curricular progress. All the mothers I spoke to expressed a sense of trust and reliability in the support they received and offered in the group. This is reflected in the messages of thanks that are often shared in the group, especially after completion of group activities like annual sports or cultural programmes that involve the participation of the entire class. The mutuality and benevolent cooperation evidenced in the group chats and in the maternal testimonies appear to subvert and debunk the media-circulated mommy wars between stay-at-home mothers and working mothers.

Lorin Basden Arnold and BettyAnn Martin, in their edited

anthology on mothers and social media, suggests how the "vitriolic" rhetoric of "mommy wars" may "create a heightened perception of division for mothers" and lead them to having "additional feelings of uncertainty regarding their role as mothers and their place in the larger cultural system" (loc.148). PA, for instance, admitted: "I sometimes feel guilty to ask too many times for help in the group, but I am helpless. What else can I do?"

PV, in contrast, replaces any implicit guilt with an explicit appreciation of the mutual give and take. When I questioned her about guilt, she responded: "No, I don't feel guilty. Why should I? I do ask for help sometimes, but I also do what I can to help others. Why should we measure how much we are giving or getting help? That's so pointless. We are all mothers here together, aren't we?" Awareness of shared responsibilities and shared expectations and anxieties in a culture of mother-shaming and mother-blaming binds the mothers together in the group. False media-disseminated binaries between working and stay-at-home mothers are erased in the close, mutually-dependant, and interconnected space of the school WhatsApp group, at least in the functional domains of school activities, which are a significant marker of responsible performance of neoliberal motherhood.

WhatsApp Groups as Sites of Discrimination and Coercion

The maternal solidarity made visible in the group chats and attested to in the mothers' testimonials is not entirely unproblematic. Although there appears to be no fissures between such media-constructed categories as "stay-at-home mothers" and "working mothers," there are other intersectional tensions among the group's participants based on situational differences. One area of difference is the (lack of) fluency in English communication. SK, who has studied in vernacular-medium schools, said: "I do not comment on the group unless it is very urgent. I did not go to English-medium schools, so I feel self-conscious. It is okay when I talk to people, but writing makes me awkward. My daughters are much better than me in English. Thank God!" SK's awkwardness is caused by the perceived differences in social status created by the divide between vernacular-medium education (which she has) and an English-medium education (which the other mothers and SK's own daughters have). Living in a multilingual cosmopolitan location like Mumbai for over fifteen years has increased SK's confidence in her oral skills, but she is still not confident in her written English skills.[2] The sense of relief and pride SK feels in her daughters' English fluency indicate the aspirational status of English-medium education in India, which is associated with better job opportunities and upward social mobility. Scholars have pointed out that differences in language-medium schooling is an important factor in the complex matrix producing the emerging middle classes that are "anything but homogenous" (LaDousa 6). This is replicated in the microcosm of the school WhatsApp group, where disparate English skills break up the compositional homogeneity of the group. In the context of maternal communication within the group, uneven English fluency is often a barrier that inhibits some mothers from connecting with others and prevents them from benefitting optimally from the group's support network.

SK's shame in her self-declared inadequate English competencies and her pride in her daughters' English fluency can both be linked to the demands of contemporary neoliberal Indian society, which affixes aspirational value to English skills. Another demand of neoliberal Indian society is excelling in competitive environments. Although most schools in India nowadays follow practices that discourage overt academic competition among school children, at least in the lower grades, mothers often push their children to excel. The effects of this kind of maternal competitiveness is reflected in the school WhatsApp groups, where mothers with better-performing children are noticeably more active and confident that mothers whose children do not perform well. PL, a stay-at-home mother who has two school-going daughters, aged fourteen and five, and a bed-ridden mother-in-law she has to care for, said:

> To be honest, I sometimes feel ashamed to ask in the group about what has happened in school. You know, K [her older daughter] has become really difficult to handle nowadays and does not want to study at all. Her grades are poor, and I am so worried.... She is so careless that half the time she does not write down what the teachers say in class. But I feel if I ask about that in the group, the other mothers will find out that K is doing badly. They might feel that I am a bad mother. So I wait to see if someone else has posted

the same query. If I get the information I need, fine! Otherwise, I prefer to call up one mother, she is a close friend. But I never ask on the group myself.

When I asked PL about her husband's role in the household, she said that he was "very busy" at work and had to "travel frequently." However, he also insisted that PL was responsible for her daughters' academic performance: "He says that her other classmates are doing well. Why can't I make K's results better?" Blaming mothers for children's poor academic performance is a direct consequence of shifting the primary responsibility of raising children onto mothers. So-called good mothers are those whose children excel in academic, sporting, or cultural performances, whereas those whose children are mediocre or poor performers are judged to be bad mothers. The increased competitiveness in neoliberal India accelerates the culture of blaming and intensifies maternal guilt. Although PL's testimony indicates that her daughter, K, may be having undiagnosed "invisible disabilities," such as ADHD, mothers like PL internalize the "mother-valor/mother-blame binary" and judge themselves as failed or bad mothers (Blum 202). PL's self-blaming disables her from assessing whether her daughter requires expert counselling. PL is also so inhibited by shame that it prevents her for seeking support within the group, which could potentially have connected her to mothers encountering similar issues. Like SK, PL is also a passive, silent member, who only benefits from information that is shared by other mothers in the group, as she is too inhibited to participate actively or benefit optimally from the group.

This self-regulation and self-shaming, coupled with an anxious performance of one's role in the WhatsApp group, demonstrate that in advanced neoliberal societies, women's work has intensified to encompass "two unrelenting and entwined modes of affective labor"— that is, the "caring work associated with proper government of children" and also the "ongoing self reflexivity and affective regulation of one's own life as a mother" (Wilson and Yochim 39).

Whereas mothers like SK and PL are disadvantaged within the group by situational inequities, such as perceived language inadequacies or maternal failures, there are mothers who assume positions of power within the group's hierarchy. Each school WhatsApp group has some mothers who function as the group administrators. They permit other members to join the group and sometimes liaise with the school authorities about the content posted on the group, for instance instructions regarding upcoming school activities. I spoke to two such mothers who were "group admins," and they both had more fluent English skills than SK and better-performing children than PL. Another significant commonality that they shared was an expressed intention of disciplining as well as helping the members of the group, often in accordance with the school's instructions. SM, who is a mother of twins and is also a member of the PTA (Parent Teacher Association) which is in regular, direct, and close contact with the school authorities, said:

> We create these groups with the permission of the school. I and the other admins check what the parents are saying in the group. If they complain about something, we tell it to the school so that they can fix the problem. We also try to share any information we get from the school as quickly as we can so that mothers have more time to follow any instructions given at school. I am also a mother. I know how tough it is if we come to know about things at the last moment or when it is too late.

SM's benevolent intentions of helping the mothers is intermeshed with her compliant intentions of helping the school. She confirmed that she "does not name any mother" when she conveys the complaints to the school authorities. However, she admitted that she sometimes intervened in group conversations to discourage any direct criticism of the school or its faculty, although, as she said, "that doesn't happen very often." When I asked about the methods she uses to intervene, SM said that usually she responds with a positive message on the group that clears up the criticism made by the mother, and if that does not work, she directly messages or calls up the mother to resolve the issue. Her intermediate, scrutinizing role necessitates not just being obedient herself but also ensuring obedience in the group.

Scholars have noted how Indian mothers are policed in contemporary mediatized neoliberal society through "TV soaps and ... women's magazines and newspapers, and [how] middle class mothers' practices are constantly scrutinized, critiqued and examined" (Donner 132). Through the interventions of the school-appointed administrators, the school WhatsApp group becomes a media for surveillance of, as well as a platform for support for, mothers. AB, another mother of one son, who is also a group admininstrator, said:

> Sometimes mothers post irrelevant comments on the group, like funny cartoons or political forwards or good morning message. Having to read such messages which are of no use to you whenever your phone pings is so annoying! So we have a policy of not sharing WhatsApp forwards that we may receive in our other groups. I step in anytime any mother posts anything like that, and directly ask her to delete the message and not to do such things again. I feel like a traffic police sometimes!

The no-forwards-please practice that is enforced by AB in the group helps to delimit the content to what is relevant for mothers in their maternal work. Opinion pieces in the media have commented on mothers' frustration with irrelevant content posted in groups: "Scrolling through countless messages to get to the one single sentence that could be of importance, has to be in the modern age, the most colossal waste of time" (Khanna paras. 6-7). Censoring unnecessary content on the group chat saves the time of busy, time-pressured mothers, and this policy is unanimously regarded as beneficial by all the mothers I interviewed. However, the policing of all disobedient content sometimes flattens the distinctions between irrelevant forwards and relevant complaints or opinions, as both are discouraged by the group administrators. This also forecloses any potential of the group chat becoming a space for sharing maternal opinions beyond the performance of obedient responsible motherhood.

It is significant that all the mothers have naturalized the censorship of maternal communication in the school WhatsApp group as beneficial and necessary. Such naturalization of control over maternal subjects is aligned to the "governmentality approach," in which "neoliberalism is understood in terms of practice" (Giles 16). Unpacking the policing practices of SM and AB exposes how dissenting mothers are regulated by governing systems (here, the school authorities') and also how "mothers identify themselves within this individualized self-actualizing narrative" (here, they identify with and obey the ideology of responsible neoliberal motherhood) (Giles 16). The no-forwards-please policy is crucial in controlling maternal defiance within the group and in depoliticizing mothers so that they fit into the contours of ideal neoliberal motherhood. Such mothers "must be neoliberal self-optimizing economic agents in the 'public' realm and maternalist self-sacrificing mothers in the 'private' realm" (Giles 4).

The testimonies and the group interactions of the mothers I interviewed—and the absence of dissenting or political maternal voices in the group—reveal how they strive to, and are regulated to, become either or both of these motherhood constructs and how the school WhatsApp group is a complicit tool in this project. However, the mothers I interviewed are not representative of the diverse kinds of mothering practiced in India. For instance, there are other self-identified feminist mothers in similarly privileged urban Indian locations, who choose to overtly resist other neoliberal regimes (such as that of the fashion-beauty complex) and schools' endorsement and perpetuation of these regimes by confronting school authorities and resisting conformity (Phadke 257-58).

Conclusion: Digital Intimacy at a Cost

The intimate, relatively safe environment of school WhatsApp groups initially suggests that these can be potential spaces for what Ruddick calls "maternal conversations": "shared, undefensive maternal reflections [which] assume a collectivity of mothers, engaged together in the separate or joint project of raising children" (102). Arnold and Martin also comment on the multiple spaces for "motherhood conversation" that have opened up across social media platforms, which mothers can participate in, in compliant or resistant ways: "What is most unique about this new way of interacting is the sheer volume of opportunity mothers have for stepping into the stream of motherhood conversation and deciding whether to move with or against the prevailing current" (loc. 228). The mothers I interviewed considered the group a site to share information necessary to perform their maternal work, and they also considered themselves as connected through the project of raising children, both in individual and collective ways. The thriving communication on school WhatsApp groups reveal a complex mesh of support, advice, anxiety, and judgment that is both enabling and disciplinary, especially in the context of prevailing motherhood constructs (such as the intensive supermom or soccer mom) and debates (such as the stay-at-home-mother versus the working mother).

Ruddick states that empowering maternal conversations can only take place when mothers have better support systems and more flexible routines, but they are "difficult" or "rare" in a "misogynistic society that routinely misdescribes or silences the suppressed or developing voices of women, in a competitive society that adores motherhood but barely notices maternal thinking" (102). Some mothers in school WhatsApp groups imbibe and project this sense of competitiveness, which makes them more defensive and less responsive to maternal conversations. Most mothers use the time gained through the time-saving app to perform other motherhood responsibilities; only a few of them use that saved time for self-care or consciousness-raising communication. However, the communication in the group is censored to remain child focused, not mother centred. The expected, compulsory participation and the school-authority-enforced obedience in these groups outweigh the interactive, collaborative affordances of WhatsApp that can potentially encourage resistant maternal thinking.

Although I had interviewed the participants before the onset of the COVID-19 pandemic, as a participant myself, I could observe how the culture of obedience within the WhatsApp group has intensified during the pandemic, especially when schooling shifted completely online. During the ongoing pandemic in India, the group's conversation has remained isolated and focused on school-related and child-centred issues. The parents would intermittently express concern over the pandemic—especially about the effects of online schooling and social isolation on children—and enquire about the school's pandemic-affected plans. Some mothers stated that they had become more dependent on the group's communication during the extended lockdown period. However, the no-forwards-please policy disallowed any critical interrogation of governmental and institutional COVID-related actions (or inactions) or of the adverse effects of continued online schooling on children, which are circulated elsewhere, for example in unmonitored WhatsApp groups or in offline conversations.

Although it is too early to predict if or how the pandemic will significantly alter maternal use of WhatsApp communication, at this present juncture, the relentless pressures of a time-driven, result-oriented, and highly pressurized neoliberal society continue to restrict school WhatsApp groups to being functional tools for performing ideal neoliberal motherhood in more effective, even agentic, ways instead of allowing them to become liberating spaces for feminist maternal conversations.

Endnotes

1. I use quotation marks for the term "working mother" in this case because, although most of the mothers I interviewed used it, I consider the term "working mother" problematic, as it diminishes and invalidates the work done by stay-at-home mothers.

2. In offline communication among mothers, for instance when picking up children from school, the language spoken is a mixture of English, Hindi, and sometimes other familiar Indian languages. So, nonfluent speakers of English would be more comfortable in face-to-face situations as compared to group chats on WhatsApp, where the communication is almost exclusively in English.

Works Cited

Aneja, Anu and Shubhangi Vaidya. *Embodying Motherhood: Perspectives from Contemporary India*. Sage and Yoda Press, 2016.

Arnold, Lorin Basden, and BettyAnn Martin. "Introduction." *Taking the Village Online: Mothers, Motherhood, and Social Media*, edited by Lorin Basdin Arnold and BettyAnn Martin, Demeter Press, 2016, loc. 93-268. Kindle e-book.

Attari, Karishma. "Indian Schools Are Using WhatsApp to Enslave Mothers and Crush Children's Independence." *Scroll*, 24 Apr. 2017, scroll.in/magazine/834036/indian-schools-are-using-whatsapp-to-enslave-mothers-and-crush-childrens-independence. Accessed 21 May 2022.

Blum, Linda. "Mother-Blame in the Prozac Nation: Raising Kids with Invisible Disabilities." *Gender and Society*, vol. 21, no. 2, 2007, pp. 202-26.

Donner, Henrike. *Domestic Goddesses: Maternity, Globalization and Middle-class Identity in Contemporary India*. Ashgate Publishing, 2008.

Geetha, V. *Patriarchy*. Stree, 2015.

Giles, Melinda Vandenbild. "Introduction: An Alternative Mother-

Centred Economic Paradigm." *Mothering in the Age of Neoliberalism*, edited by Melinda Vandenbild Giles, Demeter Press, 2014, pp. 1-30.

Gupta, Parul. "Is Instagram Your Preferred App Too? An Exclusive Report on What Moms Like." *Kids Stop Press*, 15 May 2020, kidsstoppress.com/is-instagram-your-preferred-app-too-an-exclusive-report-on-what-moms-like/. Accessed 21 May 2022.

Khanna, Priyanka. "Modern Parents and the Overactive WhatsApp Group: A Discussion." *Vogue India*, 29 May 2019, www.vogue.in/culture-and-living/content/modern-parents-and-the-overactive-whatsapp-group-a-discussion. Accessed 21 May 2022.

LaDousa, Chaise. *Hindi Is Our Ground, English Is Our Sky: Education, Language, and Social Class in Contemporary India*. Berghahn Books, 2014.

Phadke, Shilpa. "How to Do Feminist Mothering in Urban India? Some Reflections on the Politics of Beauty and Body Shapes." *Aesthetic Labour: Rethinking Beauty Politics in Neoliberalism*, edited by Rosalind Gill, Christina Scharff, and Ana Sofia Elias, Palgrave Macmillan, 2017, pp. 247-61.

Ruddick, Sara. *Maternal Thinking: Towards a Politics of Peace*. Beacon Press, 1995.

Willemse, Juliana J. and Viviane Bozalek. "Exploration of the Affordances of Mobile Devices in Integrating Theory and Clinical Practice in an Undergraduate Nursing Programme." *Curationis*, vol. 38, no. 2, 2015, pp. 1-12.

Wilson, Julie A. and Emily Chivers Yochim. *Mothering through Precarity: Women's Work and Digital Media*. Duke Univeristy Press, 2017. Kindle e-book.

Chapter 14

Parenting in the Shadow of Corporate Surveillance: Reflections on Children's Privacy after the Widespread Pandemic-Induced Adoption of Education Technology

Jane Bailey and Vanessa Ford

Introduction

Heightened use of digital technologies during COVID-19 exacerbated the complexity of children's entanglements with technology and adult caregivers'[1] related responsibilities, with particularly negative effects on women's caring burden (Power) and for "trap[ping] already disadvantaged people into precarity" (Madianou 3). Increased screen time was simultaneously lauded as a solution to some of the negative psychological effects of pandemic-generated social isolation and condemned as a threat to young people's wellbeing (Campbell). And even though adults have often liked to chastise young people for spending too much time online, as stay-at-home orders proliferated globally so too did technology-facilitated education, which further blurred any remaining distinction between online and offline and embedded nontransparent surveillance even deeper into the lives of young people and their families.

Although some critical scholarship has examined how this shift online has affected adults (Power; Madianou), less attention (at least initially) was given to its effect on privacy. This might be partially explained by the fact that education technology ("edtech") has increasingly intruded into the private space of the home and into children's learning environments (Regan and Bailey 56-58), but social isolation and quarantine policies arising from the pandemic accelerated that intrusion on an unprecedented scale. Press coverage—and prevailing social attitudes—of edtech as a solution to the problems created by COVID-19 often overshadowed its attendant problems. When problems were addressed, considerable early coverage focused on the important issue of inequality of access.[2] Initially less was said about edtech's effects on the privacy of children and their families (especially those from marginalized communities already disproportionately negatively affected by state and corporate surveillance) or about the potential long-term consequences of the deepened mass integration of the market-based logics of the technology industry on our understandings of caregiving in familial contexts.

This chapter focuses on these gaps, with the ultimate goal of thinking about the potential implications of mass adoption of edtech during the pandemic for understandings of family responsibilities for caring for children (and their privacy) in the future. Part I explores prepandemic research on children's privacy. It begins with an overview of the complex relationship between the privacy rights of children and families and highlights potential tensions between adult caregivers' protection of children's privacy rights against intrusion by external sources and young people's developmental need for privacy from their adult caregivers. The section then discusses examples of international, national, and provincial protections for children's privacy rights in Canada, notes the impact of technology on adult caregiver responsibilities for protecting children's privacy, and discusses corporate incursions on children's and families' privacy in a digitally networked environment. Part II builds on Part I's discussion of corporate incursions by first focusing specifically on the corporate threat to children's (and families') privacy rights arising from edtech. After providing a brief snapshot of some of the early research relating to the the mass migration to online and distance education in wake of the pandemic in Canada, Part II highlights examples of two different sorts of coverage of this migration—one emphasizing more individualized accounts of responsibility for addressing related privacy impacts and the other focusing on the need for state-based regulation of corporate practices. It ends by calling for collective action and public dialogue to mitigate against the risk that technology hastily adopted in response to a global health crisis will be unquestioningly accepted as a new normal, notwithstanding its implications for children's and families' privacy. The conclusion focuses on mechanisms for supporting children's privacy rights against the opportunistic commoditization of children, their families, and learning environments in the postpandemic future. It urges responses that look beyond the neoliberal model, which would further exacerbate the burden on adult caregivers and children to protect their privacy themselves, and towards regulations that would prohibit such commoditization by corporations.

Part I: Children's Privacy in a Digitally Networked Environment

Children[3] have internationally and nationally guaranteed privacy rights, but whether those rights are protected on the ground is another story. The place of children's privacy rights within the context of the family, for example, has long been a contested matter both in scholarship (Shmueli and Blecher-Prigat 759-95; Steeves and Jones 187-191) and in life. Children's privacy rights are often treated as extensions or aspects of familial privacy rather than as independent rights (Shmueli and Blecher-Prigat 759-95). This dynamic in part reflects the complex relationships between adult caregivers and children as well as between families and the state. These relationships are further constrained by historic and ongoing disrespect for the privacy and self-determination of families who are marginalized by the complex intersections of systems of power, such as heteronormativity,[4] colonialism (Blackstock), racism (Phillips and Pon), and classism (Maki).

However, there can also be an uneasy relationship between adult caregiver surveillance and children's privacy. Even within the family, at certain developmental stages, children are completely dependent on their adult caregivers to protect them and their rights (Shmueli and Blecher-Prigat 759-95). Such protection is often achieved through intense and ongoing adult caregiver monitoring of children—a sort of surveillance of care (Rooney and Taylor 2-4)—which can simultaneously be focused on preventing the state and other outsiders from intruding on children's privacy and autonomy.[5] This type of care can be a matter of urgent importance for systemically marginalized families who are disproportionately targeted by both state and corporate surveillance.

As children mature into adolescents, teenagers, and young adults, their healthy development requires reduced adult caregiver surveillance.[6] Achieving the right balance has always been a complicated task and one in which digital technologies have for some time been intimately implicated (Siibak 104-06).

Certainly, decades of government policy have been aimed less at protecting children's privacy and more at getting and keeping young Canadians online in order to gain a competitive advantage in a technologized global marketplace (Bailey 4). Schools have been a primary locus for carrying out that agenda. As a result, young Canadians were early adopters of the internet and now, consequently, many live a largely seamlessly integrated online-offline existence (Steeves, "Young Canadians" 2-3). Even though policymakers often misinterpret young people's intense engagement with digital communications technologies as a lack of concern about their privacy (Steeves, "Privacy, Sociality, and the Failure" 246), in fact young Canadians continue to value their privacy. It is just increasingly difficult for them to protect and enjoy it in the face of the in/actions of policymakers and the surveillance practices of corporations, whose technologies are integrated into children's social, familial, and educational environments. Too often the actions of corporations are obfuscated by a singular focus on the individual responsibilities of children, families, and teachers (Steeves, "Taking Online Rights Seriously").

Legal Guarantees of Children's Privacy Rights in Canada

Canada is a signatory to the United Nations' *Convention on the Rights of the Child* ("UNCRC"),[7] of which Article 16 guarantees children's right to privacy (Covell et al.). In Canada, although federal (*Personal Information Protection and Electronic Documents Act* [PIPEDA]) and provincial (e.g., Ontario's *Freedom of Information and Protection of Privacy Act*) privacy statutes regulate the collection, use, and disclosure of personal information in various contexts, there is no specific blanket statutory protection for children's privacy. However, provincial and territorial statutes in Canada that limit the collection, use, and disclosure of personal information about students in the education sector (e.g. Ontario's *Municipal Freedom of Information and Protection of Privacy Act* [MFIPPA] and *Education Act* [EA] and British Columbia's *School Act*) offer a measure of protection to children in that context.

Private sector protections provided for under PIPEDA treat the privacy (of both children and adults) largely as a matter of data control, which is premised on obtaining the consent of individuals, often by clicking "I agree" to difficult-to-understand online privacy policies (Steeves, "It's Not Child's Play" 182). Because in many situations, including with respect to privacy, children are not considered legally capable of consenting, parents and legal guardians are authorized to make decisions on their behalf.[8] A caregiver-as-gatekeeper approach that vests authority in parents beyond an age at which young people have reached a state of maturity that enables them to competently make their own decisions affords little-to-no recognition of children's right to autonomy and its relationship to privacy (Shmueli and Blecher-Prigat 761) or children's right to have a say in matters that affect them (Steeves, "Taking Online Rights Seriously"). It can also make it difficult to distinguish children's privacy from family privacy in the domestic context (e.g. Ontario's *Child, Youth and Family Services Act* groups children's rights with familial rights)—an outcome inconsistent with children's distinct internationally recognized right to privacy and with young people's clearly expressed desire for privacy in relation to both familial and nonfamilial intrusions (Steeves, "Privacy, Sociality, and the Failure" 249). In any event, regardless of whether adult caregivers are positioned as gatekeepers assigned to protect children's best interests or young people themselves are recognized as bearing that right/responsibility, in the digital context, the individual making the decision is often pitted against far more powerful corporations with a vested interest in maximizing extraction of data, a point to which we will return below.

In the context of provincial privacy legislation applicable to the education context, whether or not consent from adult caregivers or children is necessary in relation to personal information can be situation specific. For example, in Ontario, under the MFIPPA, in certain circumstances school boards are authorized by law to directly collect the personal information of students without their consent or that of their caregivers, where as indirect collection of personal information from other sources may in some situations be authorized via student or caregiver consent (IPC 7). Furthermore, the age at which adult caregivers are positioned as gatekeepers may vary. In Ontario, for example, under the MFIPPA, an individual with legal custody of a student does not have the ability to provide consent on behalf of the student after they are sixteen, whereas under the *Education Act*, a parent or guardian may consent on behalf of a student until they are eighteen (IPC 14).

The Impact of Technology on Adult Caregiver Obligations

Digital communications technologies complicate adult caregivers' exercise of their responsibilities for children's privacy for a variety of reasons. We focus here on three of them. First, adults may misinterpret children's self-disclosure of information and images online (especially on social media platforms) as an indication that they do not care about their privacy (Steeves, "Privacy, Sociality, and the Failure" 248). However, it is essential to recognize that corporations trading on the data disclosed online structure communications in ways that incent such disclosure. This leaves children (or their caregiver gatekeepers) with little choice but to "agree" to disclosure of information as the price of admission to participate in a medium that is increasingly interconnected with all aspects of their lives (Dusseault 19-20). Research repeatedly shows Canadian children's concern for their privacy, the strategies they adopt to protect it, and their frustrations with the structurally imposed limitations on their ability to do so (Steeves et al., "Young Canadians in a Wireless World" 20).

Second, extensive coverage of online threats to children, such as predation and cyberbullying, have been coupled with allegations of parental ignorance and/or negligence that put pressure on adult caregivers to monitor their children (Shuvelitz). Corporations have capitalized on caregiver fears by creating and marketing surveillance technologies to families and educators—the use of which often ironically maximizes corporate access to children's data (Steeves and Marx 197), which has created a multimillion-dollar industry in the US and Canada (Shuvelitz). Unfortunately, as noted by the Office of the

Privacy Comissioner of Canada (OPC), caregiver surveillance and monitoring in this context have been demonstrated to undermine trust between child and caregiver, as children who are routinely monitored are more secretive with their parents (OPC, "Surveillance Technologies and Children").

Third, adult caregivers may themselves nonconsensually disclose information about their children online as part of "sharenting" culture (McLeod Rogers and Green 33)—a phenomenon which itself needs to be understood in the context of corporatized images of perfect motherhood (Steinberg 839-884; Green and Holloway 22-26).

The Role of Corporations

While it is important to note that decisions by adult caregivers can and do affect their children's privacy, conceptualizing children's privacy as primarily an individual or family matter risks obfuscating the troubling corporate practices that structure the digitally networked environment in which much of the world is immersed. Much like in the environmental context where corporations (especially) prefer to pin responsibility on individuals (Levermann), an unproductive focus on what individuals should and should not do also often leads to ignoring the foundational and pervasive role played by technology corporations in shaping user options and experiences (Lupton and Williamson 780-94; Berson and Berson 135-47) in ways that limit the ability of adult caregivers and children to protect children's privacy.

Growing corporate "datafication" of children "via mobile media, wearable devices, social media platforms, and educational software" (Green and Holloway 22) has increasingly restricted children's agency (Naughton) as their online lived experiences become fodder for marketing and surveillance (Green and Holloway 22). This threat to children's privacy, agency, and autonomy directly results from surveillance capitalism—described in part by Shoshana Zuboff as "a new economic order that claims human experience as free raw material for hidden commercial practices of extraction, prediction, and sales. ... A rogue mutation of capitalism marked by concentrations of wealth, knowledge, and power unprecedented in human history" (ix).

In this data-in-exchange-for-services model of digital networks that all of us, including children, currently inhabit, the challenges for protecting children's privacy have simultaneously become both increasingly vital and increasingly difficult.[9] Although research indicates that many children and their families realize corporations collect their data and reject the commercial model that drives their online activities, retreating from the online world ultimately limits their self-expression and participation (Steeves et al., "Young Canadians in a Wireless World 9). And even though children have strategies for protecting their privacy, neither children nor their adult caregivers can easily read or understand corporate-written privacy policies governing online spaces. In addition, current legal approaches to consent do not always account for children's developmental needs, and surveillance capitalism has normalized a culture of surveillance as a "necessary evil to help pay for the 'online playgrounds' on the Internet" (Lawford 53). These corporate surveillance practices affect not only children's privacy rights but also their rights to equality and free expression. The data extracted from children are used to create marketing materials that often reinforce narrow representations of youth, gender, race, and sexuality and disincentivize children's participation for fear of judgment, discrimination, and harassment, making them passive consumers and limiting expression essential to development (Steeves, "Taking Online Rights Seriously" 2). Further-more, these data are used to profile and categorize children, sometimes in discriminatory ways. This can affect their life chances based on stereotypes around factors, such as gender, race, sexuality, and their intersections (Bailey et al.)—thereby reinforcing and magnifying pre-existing discrimination against children and families from marginalized communities.

Part II: Intensification of Corporate Threats to Children's Privacy and the Case of Edtech

The corporate threat to children's privacy in all aspects of their daily lives (and those of their families) is particularly acute in the context of education—a threat that was both highlighted and magnified by the mass migration to online and distance education in the wake of COVID-19.

Edtech Pre-COVID-19: A Snapshot

Although adult caregivers have long faced the challenge of protecting and supporting children against growing corporatization and commodification of education (Gidney 22-26), edtech and its expanded use in the pandemic era have exacerbated that challenge. Edtech includes classroom technologies—such as digital whiteboards, videoconferencing, and platforms—that measure and monitor students' activities (Regan and Bailey 58). It is used to track students' use of social media, to monitor their keystrokes and constantly track their activity, to award "virtual points" for children's behaviour that are shared with parents on smartphones, (Steeves et al. "Digital Surveillance" 446), and to monitor their eye movements (Hooijdonk). The use of edtech has exponentially increased surveillance of children in educational environments through, for example, evaluating their performance, determining their future likelihood of success, and purportedly protecting them from dangers, such as cyberbullying and online predators (Steeves et al. "Digital Surveillance" 448). Whereas parents and educators may use edtech for these kinds of reasons, for the edtech industry that produces them, the data collection, tracking, and profiling made possible by their use constitute business opportunities (Williamson).

As with other industries seeking to profit from surveillance capitalism, a key potential outcome of the edtech industry is to "turn student data into a marketable product" (Boninger et al 3). Unfortunately, educators are increasingly being encouraged to adopt edtech in an effort to train twenty-first-century learners, yet they often are not aware of its implications for children's privacy and equality, nor do they always receive meaningful guidance from school boards, ministries of education, or privacy commissioners in this regard (Regan and Bailey 59). The mass global migration to tech-facilitated education in response to COVID-19 exacerbated risks to the privacy and equality rights of children and their families, but it might have also generated greater public awareness of these issues.

Edtech and COVID-19: Early Patterns and Responses

The closure of schools in jurisdictions around the world due to the pandemic escalated reliance on technology in education, an impact documented in early research in the US (Venzke) and in Canada (Canadian Teachers Federation [CTF]). A 2020 CTF survey reported that Canadian teachers used a variety of digital communications technologies to connect with students during shutdowns, including email, texting, instant messaging, social media, telephone calls, and video calls/virtual meetups (CTF 15). The platforms used most frequently to communicate included Google Platforms (28.2 per cent), Microsoft Teams (19 per cent), Seesaw (12.4 per cent), Zoom (8.3 per cent), and YouTube (1.6 per cent) (CTF 39). More than two-thirds of respondents (67 per cent) reported having concerns about the impact of digital technologies used during the pandemic; concerns about excessive screen time/online safety (77.7 per cent) were the most frequently cited (CTF 41). One-third of teachers surveyed also expressed concern about equity and access both during the pandemic and as foreseeable future challenges (CTF 41, 45), and over 25 per cent cited privatization and digitization of education as one of their top two concerns about education post COVID-19 (CTF 50).

Other publicly available information from early in the pandemic also demonstrated Canadian educators using a variety of education-specific and noneducation-specific technologies. Education-specific technologies included Microsoft Teams (in BC, Alberta, Ontario, and Quebec schools), G Suite for Education (in many Ontario school boards, in the Winnipeg School Division, and in the English Montreal School Board), Brightspace (in the Toronto District School Board), and Go-Guardian (in the Winnipeg School Division) (Paglinawan). Non-education specific technologies in use included Zoom (available, for example, under a province-wide agreement negotiated by BC's Ministry of Education), although the English Montreal School Board reportedly stopped using Zoom due to security and privacy concerns (Paglinawan). Postsecondary institutions—such as the University of Ottawa (Panico), Concordia, and Wilfrid Laurier University—had authorized use of exam software some uses of which required young people to film themselves while writing online exams (Matte).

In the initial stages of the pandemic, the privacy and security risks associated with edtech were eclipsed in media coverage by the immediate and pressing concern of inequality of access and later security issues, such as Zoombombing.[10] Gradually, however, concerns began to surface about the privacy impacts of the technologies used (Venzke; Bailey et al.; Durrani and Alphonso). Media coverage began to include concerns about exposure of the family home during videoconferences (Paglinawan), about technology compliance with domestic privacy legislation (Caron), and about tracking of children in the virtual classroom and beyond (Han).

A frequent focus of the early coverage was on what individuals can and should do—including recommendations for teachers, parents, and children themselves (see for example Caron; Common Sense Media; Huang et al.) as well as advice for school boards and education ministries to negotiate privacy-respecting contracts with technology companies and to develop lists of approved technologies to support teachers in making privacy-protective choices (see for, example, Bailey et al.).

Eventually, however, the discourse began to incorporate perspectives that shifted beyond individualized accounts. In July 2020, for example, privacy and data commissioners from several international jurisdictions, including Canada, recognized the impact that widespread use of videoconferencing services in areas such as education could have on privacy rights and issued a joint statement on global privacy expectations of videoteleconferencing companies (OPC, "Joint Statement"). Later, in its 2020 annual report, the OPC again emphasized the privacy concerns arising with the proliferation of edtech, noting that it can "result in commercial organizations having access to information related to learning difficulties or other behavioural data of students" (OPC "2019–2020 Annual Report"). In that report, the OPC emphasized the need for "explicit laws to set permissible uses" rather than "relying on the good will of companies to act responsibly" (OPC "2019–2020 Annual Report"). A 2022 Human Rights Watch report similarly called for improved protections for children's privacy following an international investigation of edtech that indicated widespread tracking of young people (Han). Commentaries such as these help to shift emphasis away from classic neoliberal approaches that would focus on what children and families should do to protect their privacy and towards recognizing the role that more explicit corporate regulation can play and whether a shift beyond individual consent-based data control models is needed. Such a shift could be animated by larger systemic considerations about whether, to paraphrase Zuboff, the human experience of children's education should be permitted to become raw material for commercial endeavours or subject to unprecedented tracking and monitoring.

Although more systemic, collective action had been needed in relation to edtech for some time, mass adoption of edtech prompted by COVID-19 escalated its urgency, especially because its hurried adoption as a solution during the pandemic could, like other surveillance technologies adopted in response to COVID-19 (Dupont), become an easily accepted part of a new normal without much needed public dialogue, interrogation, and regulation. Such acceptance could have profound effects on children and adult caregivers in a number of areas, including protecting children's rights to privacy and equality.

Conclusion

It has long been a challenge for adult caregivers to protect and support their children's human rights to privacy and equality, both in relation to their own practices and the external practices of those outside of their families. This has been especially true for families and children disproportionately targeted for surveillance as both a result and reflection of systems of oppression such as racism, colonialism, homophobia, transphobia, and their intersections. The influx of data-hungry technologies within education that exacerbate this challenge expanded exponentially during the COVID-19 pandemic (Durrani and Alphonso). Experiences with edtech during the pandemic could permanently affect our understandings of caregiving responsibilities by, for example, deepening or at least reinforcing the gendered burden of caregiving (Power). Adoption of a classic neoliberal approach to the situation could further responsibilize adult caregivers by relying on them to police the use of edtech by requesting disclosure of privacy and security policies of the technologies in use, demanding that school boards and ministries verify these technologies' compliance with domestic legislation, requesting investigations by privacy commissioners[11] and human rights commissions, demanding a voice in deciding which technologies are used and how they are used, and ensuring that children play a central role in those decision-making processes. However, we could also focus on the responsibility of school boards and ministries to negotiate privacy-respecting agreements with edtech providers and to carefully investigate technologies before recommending or mandating their use by individual educators. And individual educators can choose not to adopt surveillance edtech even when it is approved in their institutions, not to use platform features to record their students' interactions and interjections during class, and to allow students to choose whether their video is on or off during class.

Overall though, we believe that it is essential to think beyond the responsibility of the individual child, caregiver, family, teacher, and even school board and provincial responsibility to investigate and contract for legislative compliance. We share the OPC's view that explicit regulatory measures are needed in relation to corporate practices (see also Han). Such an approach can help to refocus attention on corporate behaviour and practices and to engage deeply with the foundational problem of the commoditization and memorialization of children's learning and family homes through technology as well as edtech's potential to reinforce and deepen existing patterns of discrimination against members of marginalized communities. Approaching the issue as one of corporate regulation helps to relieve pressure on individual adult caregivers to engage in the virtually impossible task of policing corporate privacy practices; instead, it rightfully places that burden on the state. If the path of corporate regulation is to be followed through legislative reform, it will be essential to insure that adult caregivers and children from a broad range of social locations and their lived experiences with technology are centred in these initiatives.

Endnotes

1. In this chapter, we use the term "adult caregiver" wherever possible to describe adults responsible for raising children in order to avoid the exclusionary effect of the term "parent." We use the term "parent" occasionally when we are discussing legal rights and responsibilities, since that is the term used in relevant legislation, although we are conscious of the fact that heterocentric assumptions in law too often result in failure to recognize the multiple ways in which families are formed beyond the confines of heterosexist orthodoxies (Cameron; Kelly).

2. In Canada, for example, the shift to online learning has clearly demonstrated the disproportionately negative effect of the digital divide on families living in northern communities (Rosenberg and Lappalainen).

3. In this chapter, we use the term "children" to refer to those under eighteen years of age, in accordance with the definition of "child" in the United Nations *Convention on the Rights of the Child*, Article 1, which is applicable to Canada. Occasionally, policymakers identify a subset of "children" as "young people," typically focusing on those aged thirteen to eighteen (See, for example, Office of the Privacy Commissioner of Canada, "Collecting from Kids?"). When we refer to "young people" in this chapter, we are referring to that subset of children.

4. Included among these examples must be considerations relating to sperm-donor anonymity in women-led families to ensure against insertion of an "unwanted third party" into these families by law (Cameron 246).

5. In other cases, such as in domestic violence situations, adult caregiver surveillance of children violates rather than safeguards these rights.

6. Different kinds of considerations may apply with respect to children whose physical and/or mental abilities require detailed ongoing care from adult caregivers (Shmueli and Blecher-Prigat 779, 791).

7. Article 16 states: "No child shall be subjected to arbitrary or unlawful interference with his or her privacy, family, home or correspondence, nor to unlawful attacks on his or her honour and reputation."

8. The exact age at which a person will be considered legally capable of consenting in relation to their personal information under privacy legislation varies from jurisdiction to jurisdiction and from statute to statute. In 2018, the OPC articulated the position that for the purposes of PIPEDA, "in all but exceptional circumstances," parental consent was necessary for collection, use, and disclosure of the personal information of anyone below age thirteen (OPC, "Guidelines").

9. Concerns about the digital environment's impacts on human rights, particularly those of children, have led to numerous policy initiatives in Canada and in other parts of the world (O'Neill).

10. "Zoombombing" is a term used to describe "a type of cyber-harassment in which an individual or a group of unwanted and

uninvited users interrupt online meetings over the Zoom video conference app. This disruption occurs when intruders gate-crash gatherings—sometimes for malicious purposes, such as sharing pornographic or hate images or shouting offensive language—without the host's permission" (Rouse).

11. In Canada, for example, a parental complaint triggered investigations by the federal and Ontario privacy commissioners into the security practices of CoreFour Inc. with respect to its Kindergarten to Grade 12 learning management and analytics system, Edsby (Tymochenko).

Works Cited

Bailey, Jane. "Canadian Legal Approaches to 'Cyberbullying' and Cyberviolence: An Overview." *Ottawa Faculty of Law Working Paper*, 2016, papers.ssrn.com/sol3/papers.cfm?abstract_id=284 1413. Accessed 22 May 2022.

Bailey, Jane, et al. "Children's Privacy Is a Risk with Rapid Shifts to Online Schooling under Coronavirus." *The Conversation*, 21 April 2020, theconversation.com/childrens-privacy-is-at-risk-with-rapid-shifts-to-online-schooling-under-coronavirus-135787. Accessed 22 May 2022.

Berson, Illene R., and Michael J. Berson. "Children and Their Digital Dossiers: Lessons in Privacy Rights in the Digital Age." *International Journal of Social Education,* vol 21, no. 1, 2006, pp. 135-47.

Blackstock, Cindy. "Residential Schools: Did They Really Close or Just Morph into Child Welfare?" *Indigenous LJ*, vol. 6, no.1, 2007, pp. 71-78.

Boninger, Faith, Alex Molnar, and Kevin Murray. *Asleep at the Switch: Schoolhouse Commercialism, Student Privacy and the Failure of Policymaking.* Report on Schoolhouse Commercializing Trends, nepc.colorado.edu.proxy.bib.uottawa.ca/files/publications/RB%20 Trends%202017_2.pdf. Accessed 26 May 2022.

Campbell, Emily. "Quebec Teens Getting Less Exercise, More Screen Time during Pandemic: Study." *CTV News,* 2 Aug. 2020, montreal. ctvnews.ca/quebec-teens-getting-less-exercise-more-screen-time-during-pandemic-study-1.5049341. Accessed 22 May 2022.

Cameron, Angela. "A Chip Off the Old (Ice) Block?: Women-Led Families, Sperm Donors, and Family Law." *Within the Confines: Women and the Law in Canada*, edited by Jennifer Kelly, Canadian Scholars Press, 2014, pp. 246-70.

Canadian Teachers Federation (CTF). "Canadian Teachers Responding to Coronavirus (COVID-19)—Pandemic Research Study." *CTF*, 2020, vox.ctf-fce.ca/wp-content/uploads/2020/07/National-Summary-Report-OVERVIEW-Pandemic-Research-Study-Jul-22.pdf. Accessed 22 May 2022.

Caron, Christina. "How to Protect Your Family's Privacy During Remote Learning: Building a Safe Digital Environment Is Essential to Making Remote Learning Work, Experts Say." *The New York Times*, 21 Aug. 2020, www.nytimes.com/2020/08/20/parenting/online-school-privacy.html. Accessed 22 May 2022.

Common Sense Media. "Protect Your Students' Data and Privacy." *Common Sense*, 2020, www.commonsense.org/education/teaching-strategies/protect-your-students-data-and-privacy. Accessed 22 May 2022.

Convention on the Rights of the Child. 20 November 1989, 1577 UNTS 3 (entered into force 2 Sept. 1990).

Covell, Katherine, et al. *The Challenge of Children's Rights for Canada.* Wilfrid Laurier University Press, 2018.

Dupont, Benoit. "Covid-19: les derives possibles de surveillance des données personelles." *The Conversation*, 29 May 2020, theconversation.com/covid-19-les-derives-possibles-de-surveillance-des-donnees-personnelles-139443. Accessed 22 May 2022.

Durrani, Temur and Caroline Alphonso. "Technology used by educators in abrupt switch to online school shared kids' personal information, investigation shows." *The Globe and Mail*, 24 May 2022, www.theglobeandmail.com/canada/article-online-school-kids-privacy-data/. Accessed 25 May 2022.

Dusseault, Pierre-Luc. "Privacy and Social Media in the Age of Big Data. Report of the Standing Committee on Access to Information, Privacy and Ethics." *House of Commons Canada*, April 2013, www.ourcommons.ca/Content/Committee/411/ETHI/Reports/RP6094136/ethirp05/ethirp05-e.pdf. Accessed 22 May 2022.

Education Act. RSO 1990, c E2.

Freedom of Information and Protection of Privacy Act. RSO 1990, c. F.31.

Gidney, Catherine. *Captive Audience: How Corporations Invaded Our Schools.* Between the Lines, 2019.

Green, Leila, and Donell Holloway. "Introduction: Problematising the Treatment of Children's Data." *Media International Australia Incorporating Culture & Policy*, vol. 170, no. 1, 2019, pp. 22-26.

Han, Hye Jung. "How Dare They Peep Into My Private Life?: Children's Rights Violations by Governments that Endorsed Online Learning During the COVID-19 Pandemic." *Human Rights Watch*, 24 May 2022, www.hrw.org/report/2022/05/25/how-dare-they-peep-my-private-life/childrens-rights-violations-governments. Accessed 25 May 2022.

Hooijdonk, Richard van. "The Magic of Biometric Eye-Tracking in Education and Rehabilitation." *Emerging Edtech,* 23 June 2016, www.emergingedtech.com/2016/06/the-magic-of-biometric-eye-tracking-in-education/. Accessed 22 May 2022.

Huang, R.H., et al. "Personal Data and Privacy Protection in Online Learning: Guidance for Students, Teachers and Parents. Beijing: Smart Learning Institute of Beijing Normal University." *UNESCO,* 2020, iite.unesco.org/wp-content/uploads/2020/06/Personal-Data-and-Privacy-Protection-in-Online-Learning-Guidance-for-Students-Teachers-and-Parents-V1.0.pdf. Accessed 22 May 2022.

Information and Privacy Commissioner of Ontario (IPC). "A Guide to Privacy and Access to Information in Ontario Schools". *Information and Privacy Commissioner of Ontario,* 2019, www.ipc.on.ca/wp-content/uploads/2019/01/guide-to-privacy-access-in-ont-schools.pdf. Accessed 22 May 2022.

Kelly, Fiona. *Transforming Law's Family: The Legal Recognition of Planned Lesbian Motherhood.* University of British Columbia Press, 2012.

Lawford, John. "All in the Data Family: Children's Privacy Online. Ottawa: Public Interest Advocacy Centre." *Public Interest Advocacy Centre,* 2008, www.piac.ca/wp-content/uploads/2014/11/children_final_small_fixed.pdf. Accessed 15 September 2020.

Levermann, Anders. "Individuals Can't Solve the Climate Crisis: Governments Need to Step Up." *The Guardian,* 10 July 2019, www.

theguardian.com/commentisfree/2019/jul/10/individuals-climate-crisis-government-planet-priority. Accessed 22 May 2022.

Lupton, Deborah, and Ben Williamson. "The Datafied Child: The Dataveillance of Children and Implications for Their Rights." *New Media & Society*, vol. 19, no. 5, 2017, pp. 780-94.

Madianou, Mirca. "A Second-Order Disaster? Digital Technologies during the COVID-19 Epidemic." *Social Media & Society*, vol. 1, 2020, pp. 1-5.

Maki, Krys. "Neoliberal Deviants and Surveillance: Welfare Recipients under the Watchful Eye of Ontario Works." *Surveillance & Society*, vol. 9, no. 1/2, 2011, pp. 47-63.

Matte, Ryan. "U of O will allow faculties to use controversial Respondus Lockdown software to curb academic fraud". *Fulcrum*, 1 July 2020, thefulcrum.ca/sciencetech/u-of-o-will-allow-profess ors-to-use-controversial-respondus-lockdown-browser-to-curb-academic-fraud/#:~:text=As%20of%20now%20Concordia%20 University,them%20from%20committing%20academic%20fraud. Accessed 22 May 2022.

McLeod Rogers, Jaqueline, and Fiona Joy Green. "Mommy Blogging and Deliberative Dialogical Ethics: Being in the Ethical Moment." *Journal of the Motherhood Initiative Research and Community Involvement*, vol. 6, no. 1, 2015, pp. 31-49.

Municipal Freedom of Information and Protection of Privacy Act. RSO 1990, c M 56.

Naughton, John. "'The Goal Is to Automate Us': Welcome to the Age of Surveillance Capitalism." *The Guardian*, 20 Jan. 2019, www. theguardian.com/technology/2019/jan/20/shoshana-zuboff-age-of-surveillance-capitalism-google-facebook. Accessed 22 May 2022.

Office of the Privacy Commissioner of Canada (OPC). "Collecting from Kids? Ten Tips for Services Aimed at Children and Youth." *Office of the Privacy Commissioner of Canada*, Dec. 2015, www.priv. gc.ca/en/privacy-topics/business-privacy/bus_kids/02_05_d_62_ tips/. Accessed 22 May 2022.

Office of the Privacy Commissioner of Canada (OPC). "Guidelines for Obtaining Meaningful Consent." *Office of the Privacy Commissioner of Canada*, May 2018, www.priv.gc.ca/en/privacy-topics/ collecting-personal-information/consent/gl_omc_201805/#_ consent. Accessed 22 May 2022.

Office of the Privacy Commissioner of Canada (OPC). "Joint Statement on Global Privacy Expectations of Video Teleconferencing Companies." *Office of the Privacy Commissioner of Canada*, 21 July 2020, www.priv.gc.ca/en/opc-news/news-and-announcements /2020/let_vc_200721/. Accessed 22 May 2022.

Office of the Privacy Commissioner of Canada (OPC). "Surveillance Technologies and Children." *Government of Canada*, Oct. 2012, www.priv.gc.ca/en/opc-actions-and-decisions/research/explore-privacy-research/2012/opc_201210/. Accessed 22 May 2022.

Office of the Privacy Commissioner of Canada (OPC). "2019–2020 Annual Report to Parliament on the Privacy Act and Personal Information Protection and Electronic Documents Act." *Office of the Privacy Commissioner of Canada*, 8 Oct. 2020, www.priv.gc.ca/ en/opc-actions-and-decisions/ar_index/201920/ar_201920/ #heading-0-0-2. Accessed 22 May 2022.

O'Neill, Brian. "Policies for the Digital Environment: Online Safety and Empowerment in a Global Context" *The Routledge International Handbook of Children, Adolescents, and Media*, (2d) edited by Dafna Lemish Routledge, 2022, 450-458.

Ontario's Child, Youth and Family Services Act. 2017, SO 2017, c 14, Sched 1.

Paglinawan, Denise. "Schools Urged to Ensure Students' Security and Privacy When Conducting Classes Online." *CBC News*, 5 July 2020, www.cbc.ca/news/technology/schools-virtual-learning-privacy-1.5615999. Accessed 22 May 2022.

Panico, Giacomo. "UofO Students Wary of 'Extreme' Anti-Cheating Software." *CBC News*, 2 July 2020, www.cbc.ca/news/canada/ ottawa/exam-surveillance-software-university-ottawa-1.5633134. Accessed 22 May 2022.

Personal Information Protection and Electronic Documents Act, SC 2000, c 5.

Phillips, Doret, and Gordon Pon. "Anti-Black Racism, Bio-Power and Governmentality: Deconstructing the Suffering of Black Families

Involved with Child Welfare." *Journal of Law and Social Policy*, vol. 28, 2018, pp. 81-100.

Power, Kate. "The COVID-19 Pandemic Has Increased the Care Burden of Women and Families." *Sustainability: Science, Practice and Policy*, vol. 16 no. 1, 2020, pp. 67-73.

Regan, Priscilla, and Jane Bailey. "Big Data, Privacy and Education Applications." *Education and Law Journal*, vol. 29, no. 1, 2020, pp. 55-78.

Rooney, Tonya, and Emmeline Taylor. *Surveillance Futures: Social and Ethical Implications of New Technologies for Children and Young People*. Routledge, 2017.

Rosenberg, Catherine, and Andrew Lappalainen. "Tech Giants Need to Step Up to Help Close Canada's Digital Divide." *The Conversation*, 18 Feb. 2021, theconversation.com/tech-giants-need-to-step-up-to-help-close-canadas-digital-divide-154142. Accessed 22 May 2022.

Rouse, Margaret. "Zoombombing." *What Is*, searchsecurity. techtarget.com/definition/Zoombombing. Accessed 15 22 May 2022.

School Act, RSBC 1996, C 412.

Shmueli, Benjamin, and Ayelet Blecher-Prigat. "Privacy for Children." *Columbia Human Rights Law Review*, vol. 42, no. 3, 2011, pp. 759-95.

Siibak, Andra. "Chapter 6. Digital Parenting and the Datafied Child." *Educating 21st Century Children*, edited by Tracey Burns and Francesca Gottschalk, OECD iLibrary, 2019, pp. 104-20.

Steeves, Valerie. "It's Not Child's Play: The Online Invasion of Children's Privacy." *University of Ottawa Law & Technology Journal*, vol. 3, no.1, 2006, p. 169-188.

Steeves, Valerie. "Privacy, Sociality, and the Failure of Regulation: Lessons Learned from Young Canadians' Online Experiences" *Social Dimensions of Privacy: Interdisciplinary Perspectives*, edited by Beate Roessler and Dorota Mokrosinska Cambridge University Press, 2015, p. 244-60.

Steeves, Valerie. "Taking Online Rights Seriously: Ensuring Children's Active Participation in Networked Spaces). An NGO Report Submitted with Respect to the 5th/6th Review of Children's Rights in Canada (Convention on the Rights of the Child)." *The eQuality Project*, 1 Mar. 2020, http://www.equalityproject.ca/wp-content/uploads/2020/03/eQuality-Project-Report-on-CRC-Canada-State-Report.pdf. Accessed 22 May 2022.

Steeves, Valerie. "Young Canadians in a Wired World, Phase III: Life Online." *Media Smarts,* 2014, mediasmarts.ca/sites/default/files/pdfs/publication-report/full/YCWWIII_Life_Online_FullReport.pdf. Accessed 22 May 2022.

Steeves, Valerie, and Gary T Marx. "From the Beginning: Children as Subjects and Agents of Surveillance." *Surveillance & Society,* vol. 7, no. 3-4, 2010, pp. 192-230.

Steeves, Valerie, and Owain Jones. "Editorial: Surveillance, Children and Childhood." Surveillance & Society, vol. 7, no. 3-4, 2020, pp. 187-191.

Steeves, Valerie, et al. "Young Canadians in a Wireless World, Phase IV: Talking to Youth and Parents about Online Resiliency." *Media Smarts,* 2020, mediasmarts.ca/sites/mediasmarts/files/publication-report/full/report_ycwwiv_talking_youth_parents_online_resiliency.pdf. Accessed 22 May 2022.

Steeves, Valerie, et al. "Digital Surveillance in the Networked Classroom." *The Palgrave International Handbook of School Discipline, Surveillance, and Social Control,* edited by Jo Deakin, Emmeline Taylor, and Aaron Kupchik, Palgrave Macmillan, 2018, pp. 445-66.

Steinberg, Stacey B. "Sharenting: Children's Privacy in the Age of Social Media." *Emory Law Journal,* vol. 66, no. 4, 2017, pp. 839-84.

Tymochenko, Nadya. "Investigation of CoreFour Inc. (Edsby) by Privacy Commissioner of Canada" *Miller Thomson,* 3 June 2021. www.millerthomson.com/en/publications/communiques-and-updates/education-law-newsletter/june-3-2021-education/investigation-of-corefour-inc-edsby-by-privacy-commissioner-of-canada/?utm_source=Mondaq&utm_medium=syndication&utm_campaign=LinkedIn-integration. Accessed 26 May 2022.

United Nations. *Convention on the Rights of the Child,* 20 November 1989, 1577 UNTS 3 (entered into force 2 September 1990).

Venzke, Cody. "For Remote Learning, Privacy Challenges Go Beyond

Zoombombing." *Center for Democracy & Technology*, 2020, cdt.org/ insights/for-remote-learning-privacy-challenges-go-beyond-zoombombing/. Accessed 22 May 2022.

Williamson, Ben. "Meta-edtech." *Learning, Media and Technology*, vol. 46, no. 1, 2021, pp. 1-5.

Zuboff, Shoshana. *The Age of Surveillance Capitalism: The Fight for a Human Future at the New Frontier of Power.* PublicAffairs, 2019.

Notes on Contributors

Amalia Ackerman graduated from Lewis & Clark College with a Bachelor of Arts in rhetoric and media studies and will pursue postgraduate study on the transformative power of communication for doctor-patient relationships and health outcomes. She plans to create effective interventions that can improve healthcare delivery both in the US and abroad.

Carolin Aronis, PhD, is an assistant professor in the Department of Ethnic Studies at Colorado State University. She is a communication and media studies scholar studying gender, race, antisemitism, and Jewish experiences through the intersection of critical media studies, rhetoric, and technologies. Her work focuses on the phenomenology of communication within challenging/impossible settings and on the rhetorical and technological systems of hate and exclusion. Her research on the exclusionary reconstruction of Jewish motherhood, public mediated intimacy, the politics of liminal architecture, and current antisemitism has appeared in journals *Discourse & Communication, Cultural Studies, Journal of Communication, Israel Studies, Explorations in Media Ecology*, and *ETC: A Review of General Semantics* as well as in the edited collections *Urban Communication Reader IV: Cities as Communicative Change Agents* (Peter Lang) and *Tel-Aviv, the First Century: Visions, Designs, Actualities* (Indiana University Press).

Jane Bailey is a full professor of law at the University of Ottawa where she teaches cyberfeminism, technoprudence, and contracts. Her research focuses on the intersections of law, technology and equality. Jane coleads The eQuality Project, a seven-year SSHRC funded partnership focusing on the impact of online commercial profiling on young Canadians' identities and relationships. In 2021, she coedited *The Emerald International Handbook of Technology-Facilitated Violence and Abuse*, an open access publication.

Victoria Bailey is currently completing a PhD in creative writing and has a master's in women's studies. She is coeditor with Dr. Fiona Joy Green and Dr. Andrea O'Reilly of the upcoming Demeter Press collection *Coming Into Being: Mothers on Finding and Realizing Feminism*. Her poetry has been included in a wide range of feminist-focused publications including other Demeter Press anthologies. She is also a feminist mother of three.

Shelley Buerger, PhD, is an early career researcher and teacher in Australia whose scholarship centres around cultural depictions of mothering and motherhood, with a particular focus on the ethical considerations of blogging and digital subjectivity.

Matthew Flisfeder is an associate professor of rhetoric and communications at the University of Winnipeg, where he teaches courses on communication theory, critical studies of social media, and critical theories of discourse and ideology. He is the author and editor of four books, including *Algorithmic Desire: Toward a New Structuralist Theory of Social Media* (2021).

Robyn Flisfeder teaches in the Department of Rhetoric, Writing, and Communications at the University of Winnipeg. She received her MA in sociology at Queen's University and her BEd at the Ontario Institute for Studies in Education of the University of Toronto.

Vanessa Ford, JD, is a University of Ottawa alumni and former research assistant with The eQuality Project, where (among many other things) she supported development of educational programs exploring the internet's societal and cultural impacts on youth.

Janis L. Goldie (PhD University of Calgary) is dean, academic programs at the Alberta University of the Arts. She publishes on issues of digital media and privacy, pedagogy, as well as on representations of war and popular culture artifacts. Her recent coedited books include *New Perspectives on the War Film* (2019, Palgrave) and *"The Handmaid's Tale": Teaching Dystopia, Feminism, and Resistance Across Disciplines and Borders* (2019, Rowman and Littlefield).

Daena J. Goldsmith is professor of rhetoric and media studies at Lewis & Clark College. Her research examines how communication (face-to-face and online) enacts identities, sustains relationships, and builds communities, particularly when families live with illness or disability. She is currently writing *Polyphonic Resistance: Blogging Motherhood and Autism,* a book about how blogs by mothers of autistic children challenge dominant narratives of intensive mothering and provide alternative ways of understanding autism.

Fiona Joy Green is a cisgender, temporarily able-bodied, straight feminist mother who believes in the power of revolutionary feminist parenting. She is a White Settler and holds the position of professor in the Department of Women's and Gender Studies at the University of Winnipeg, located within Treaty No. 1 Territory, the traditional lands and waters of the Anishinaabe, Ininew, Oji-Cree, Dene, and Dakota, and the homeland of the Métis Nation. Dr. Green is the author of *Practicing Feminist Mothering* (ARP) and coeditor of five Demeter Press collections that address evolving feminist parenting practices and maternal pedagogies. Her current interests include exploring parenting and families in relation to the everchanging digital world in her role as coauthor of the blog *Family Blog Lines: Tal[k]ing Care* (familybloglines. com/blog/).

Florence Pasche Guignard is assistant professor in religious studies at the Faculty of Theology and Religious Studies at the Université Laval (Quebec City). Her research explores issues at the intersection of religion and ritual, digital and material cultures, embodiment, and gender. She brings her interdisciplinary scholarship in conversation with anthropology, ritual studies, media studies, gender studies and women's studies. More information is on her website: fpg.bio.

Astrid Joutseno's PhD dissertation, *Life Writing from Birth to Death: How M/others Know,* approaches mothering on mommy blogs as a digital material phenomenon. Joutseno graduated from University of Helsinki in October 2021. Joutseno is a songwriter by the name of Astrid Swan. She won the prestigious Teosto Award for songwriting in 2018. In 2019, she published the Finnish -anguage memoir *Viimeinen kirjani,* addressing life with incurable cancer. Her latest solo album *D/other* (2021) explores the relationality between mothers and children. Joutseno's current research interests are grief of the dying, life writing, and Finnish women songwriters. She is affiliated with Turku University's SELMA, *Centre for the Study of Storytelling, Experientiality and Memory.*

Elaine Kahn is the author of *Been Hoping We Might Meet Again: The Letters of Pierre Elliott Trudeau and Marshall McLuhan.* Dr. Kahn, an immigrant to the US from Canada, earned both her master and doctoral degrees in global affairs from Rutgers University. As a journalist, she often worked on issues of multiculturalism and other kinds of borders. Elaine sits on the editorial board of the online journal *New Explorations: Studies in Cultural and Communication.*

Suzanne Kamata is an associate professor at Naruto University of Education in Japan. She earned an MFA from the University of British Columbia. She is the author or editor of fourteen published books, including the memoir *Squeaky Wheels: Travels with my Daughter by Train, Plane, Metro, Tuk-tuk and Wheelchair* (Wyatt-Mackenzie 2019) and the novel *The Baseball Widow* (Wyatt-Mackenzie, 2021). Her academic essays appear most recently in *Intercultural Families and Schooling in Japan: Experiences, Issues, and Challenges* (Candlin & Mynard, 2020) and *The Journal of Gender Awareness in Language Teaching.*

Andrew McGillivray is an assistant professor in the Department of Rhetoric and Communications at the University of Winnipeg. He is the author of *Influences of Pre-Christian Mythology and Christianity on Old Norse Poetry* (2018).

Angela McGillivray is a department assistant for women's and gender studies, classics, philosophy, and disability studies at the University of Winnipeg, where she completed an MA in cultural studies.

Jaqueline McLeod Rogers, PhD, is a mom of two young adult daughters and professor and chair of the Department of Rhetoric, Writing, and Communications at the University of Winnipeg. Her doctorate thesis studied fiction by women (published as *Aspects of the Female Novel*), and she has remained committed to exploring women's experiences and writing. Her collaborative blog work studying mothers, families, and digital pressure and exposure—familybloglines. com/—eventuated in this coedited collection. Recently, she has been examining communications, urban space, and local place and has just published *McLuhan's Techno-Sensorium City: Coming to our Senses in a*

Programmed Environment (Lexington). Marshall McLuhan used to tell us we would soon live in houses without walls: Are we there yet?

Lisa H. Rosen, PhD, is an associate professor and director of the undergraduate psychology program at Texas Woman's University. Her research focuses on identifying factors that place students at increased risk for peer victimization, examining the relations between peer victimization and adjustment, and exploring ways that parents and teachers can best support victimized youth. More recently, she has examined how the pandemic has affected working mothers. Her work on children's peer relationships is supported by the Eunice Kennedy Shriver National Institute of Child Health & Human Development, R15HD098561.

Linda J. Rubin, PhD, is a professor of psychology and licensed psychologist at Texas Woman's University. Her research, clinical, and teaching interests target traumatic stress and violence against women. She has offered empirically based intervention to college students who experience domestic and dating violence, sexual assault, rape, and stalking. She contributes to a research program focused on peer victimization in the forms of bullying and cyberbullying and has provided clinical services to combat veterans who suffer with posttraumatic stress disorder.

Sucharita Sarkar is associate professor, DTSS College of Commerce, Mumbai, India. Her recent work includes the international collaborative project, *New Directions for International Scholarship on Motherhood in Religious Studies* (beyondmg.study/); articles in *Current Sociology, Qualitative Inquiry,* and *Open Theology,* and chapters in *Representing Abortion* (Routledge, 2021), *Food, Faith and Gender in South Asia* (Bloomsbury, 2020), *The Politics of Belonging in Contemporary India* (Routledge, 2020), and *Thickening Fat* (Routledge, 2020). Her research is detailed at mu.academia.edu/SucharitaSarkar.

Cover Artist Statement

Lilia Kamata

"I had not drawn my family very often, so I took that chance and was able to draw them. I strongly wanted to include not only my family, but also my cats, and even the shape of my house in the drawing. It was a lot of fun. I am really happy as an artist."

Deepest appreciation to
Demeter's monthly Donors

DEMETER

Daughters
Rebecca Bromwich
Summer Cunningham
Tatjana Takseva
Debbie Byrd
Fiona Green
Tanya Cassidy
Vicki Noble
Naomi McPherson
Myrel Chernick

Sisters
Amber Kinser
Nicole Willey
Christine Peets